The Energy Efficient Home

A COMPLETE GUIDE

The Energy Efficient Home

A COMPLETE GUIDE

PATRICK WATERFIELD

THE CROWOOD PRESS

First published in 2006 by
The Crowood Press Ltd
Ramsbury, Marlborough
Wiltshire SN8 2HR

www.crowood.com

This impression 2007

British Library Cataloguing-in-Publication Data
A catalogue record for this book is available from the British Library.

ISBN 978 1 86126 779 5

Cover images
Front cover, clockwise from top left: examples of different styles of low energy lamps (courtesy of the Energy Saving Trust); house built using Kingspan TEK structural insulated panel system; PV shingles (courtesy of www.solarcentury.com); laying mineral fibre insulation in a roofspace (courtesy of the Energy Saving Trust).

Back cover, left to right: installing Warmcel recycled newsprint insulation into a timber stud wall (courtesy of Excel Industries Ltd); EU Energy Rating label as seen on domestic appliances (courtesy of the Energy Saving Trust); Solartwin flat plate solar water heaters.

Typeset by Jean Cussons Typesetting, Diss, Norfolk

Printed and bound in Singapore by Craft Print International

Contents

Dedication

To self-builders and DIY-ers everywhere – especially those who *really* want to grasp the nettle of energy efficiency – you will need more dedication than just this one!

To Gillian Corry, of Corry Homebuilding Ltd, Saintfield, Northern Ireland, who gave me the initial inspiration to write this book.

To my wife Louise and our children Zoë and Leo – for not being there when I didn't need them.

Acknowledgements

Thanks are due to the organizations that provided images used here. The captions to the images give the name/type of the product/system/service and the name of the company that supplies/manufactures/operates it. Full contact details for each organization are given in the 'Useful Contacts' section at the back.

The depiction of and reference to specific products/systems/services should not be taken as endorsement of them and no responsibility can be accepted for the subsequent use of such.

Acknowledgements are also made where relevant to other sources from which images have been adapted. The details of such publications are given at the back.

Introduction

BACKGROUND ISSUES

So – you have taken the plunge and decided to build your own house or carry out renovations to your existing property. You will be aware already that there are many things that need to be taken into account – the legal requirements, technical factors, economic considerations, as well as the less tangible, aesthetic matters – all of which will determine the scope of your project. Much thought will be given, quite rightly, to how the finished design will look, how robust it will be and how much it will cost. Often, however, the energy aspects of a design are not thought through properly. This may be because the necessary information is not to hand – that is where this book comes in.

Or perhaps you are happy with your house the way it is but would like to carry out minor improvements to make it more energy efficient? Maybe you are simply looking to adopt a 'greener' lifestyle? Whatever your focus and proposed level of involvement, you should find something of interest in this book.

We are all aware these days of the impact of fossil fuel consumption upon the environment. The relationship between global warming and increased environmental emissions is now broadly accepted, even if we do not know exactly what changes are taking place, nor how quickly. Although this uncertainty exists, it still makes sense to use energy efficiently to avoid the wastage of finite natural resources.

The first and most obvious way in which we think of energy is in terms of that used to heat, light, power and ventilate our homes throughout their lifetime. Lower energy consumption not only benefits the environment through reduced emissions but it also saves us money. The second less obvious issue concerns the energy taken to produce materials and products (known as 'embodied energy'), which can be offset partly by recycling. This book focuses mainly on the energy used (or saved) by the building in use, but also makes reference to the wider environmental issues.

Let me also dispel a commonly held belief: energy efficiency need not mean 'doing without'. The most important thing is that you end up with a house that meets your key requirements. Of course, I would like to think that energy efficiency is one of your requirements, but you do not need to change your lifestyle in order to achieve it. For those who want to make a lifestyle change, the possibilities are, of course, much greater. Personally, I do not see why we should expect to be able to walk around our houses in light clothing at all times of the year, but some people do. Also, everyone has his or her own definition of 'comfort temperature'. There is no point in being energy efficient if you are cold and miserable any more than there is in allowing high solar gains if you cannot stand the heat in the room. Energy efficiency is not simply about saving as much energy as possible but about meeting your performance requirements for minimum energy usage and cost.

As with any building project, there will be several competing factors that need to be reconciled with each other to arrive at an optimum design. However, if you can achieve your design objectives within your desired budget and also reduce the running costs and environmental impact over the life of the building then that is surely a win-win situation.

Environmental Concerns
Regarding Energy Consumption

A word or two first on the reasons for the current concern regarding the environmental impact of energy consumption.

Global Warming

The 'greenhouse effect' is so called because the earth's atmosphere has the same effect upon temperatures on its surface as glass does in a greenhouse. Glass allows heat from the sun to pass through it more easily than it allows heat to be lost back the other way. This is because glass is more transparent to short-wave solar radiation than it is to the long-wave thermal radiation emitted from warmed surfaces within the greenhouse (*see* the illustration below). The greenhouse thus heats up and provides a warmer environment for plants. In a similar way, gases such as carbon dioxide in the earth's atmosphere have the property of being more transparent to solar radiation than to heat emitted by the earth's surface, thus trapping heat within the atmosphere. The greenhouse effect, it should be noted, is essential for all life on earth, we would not be here without it. What has been concerning scientists and, more lately, politicians is the 'accelerated greenhouse effect'. Increasing levels of 'greenhouse gases', principally carbon dioxide (CO_2), in the atmosphere are resulting in rising global temperatures. There are several sources of atmospheric CO_2, but the greatest man-made one is the burning of fossil fuels.

Now, you may think that a little global warming would not go amiss in the United Kingdom and Ireland – we could save a packet on those foreign holidays. Unfortunately, as with most things to do with nature, it is not that simple. One of the main concerns with global warming is the effect upon the polar ice caps, which are already melting at an increasing rate. Large volumes of cold water flowing down from the North Pole could have the effect of pushing the Gulf Stream south. The Gulf Stream is a major contributor to our moderate climate; without it we might have a climate similar to that at the same latitude in North America – which happens to be Hudson Bay – not terribly tropical.

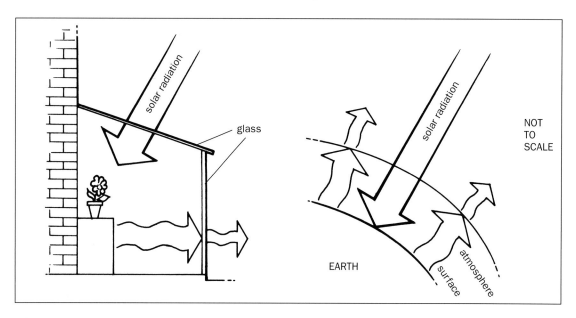

The greenhouse effect and why it is so-called. Glass is more transparent to short-wave, solar radiation entering the greenhouse than to long-wave, thermal radiation trying to leave it, resulting in the greenhouse warming up. Certain atmospheric gases, principally carbon dioxide (CO_2), have a similar effect upon the earth's atmosphere and surface.

8

The Depletion of Finite Fossil Fuels

As long ago as 1922, Frederick Soddy, who worked with Ernest Rutherford of atom-splitting fame, recognized the impending problems linked to increasing rates of fossil fuel consumption. Soddy coined the terms 'capital energy' and 'revenue energy'. Capital energy, or fossil fuels, he likened to a fixed lump sum of money in the bank which, if continually used, would gradually dwindle away to nothing. Revenue energy, or renewables, on the other hand, are continually replenished and will last indefinitely.

Most people faced with the choice of, on the one hand, continually depleting a limited amount of capital and, on the other, of keeping the capital while earning an income would prefer the latter, thus leaving something for their children. It seems an easy choice to make where money is concerned – why not energy and the environment?

Other Environmental Emissions

Apart from carbon dioxide, other key environmental emissions resulting from the burning of fossil fuels include particulates (tiny soot particles) and also the oxides of sulphur and nitrogen. Particulates contribute to poor air quality, especially in inner cities, while the oxides of sulphur (formed by burning coal and oil and derivatives) and those of nitrogen (a result of inefficient combustion) cause acid rain.

Cost Drivers

Another factor concerning finite resources is their effect on fuel prices. The resources (of oil and natural gas, for instance) which are the cheapest to extract are always exploited first – a basic rule of economics. Suppliers will need to raise prices to account for the increased costs of extracting ever-depleting and harder-to-reach supplies of fossil fuels. Added to this, energy cost reductions due to privatization in Britain have reached their limit. British Gas was on record in 2004 as saying that the era of cheap energy is over, the only way is up. Meanwhile, the taxation of fuels will increase to encourage energy efficiency, in line with international commitments to reduce environmental emissions.

Thus, however economically attractive energy efficiency measures may be today, they will become more and more so year after year and certainly during your lifetime and that of your house. This is a key reason to practise energy efficiency now. Even measures which do not appear economically attractive now may become common practice in just a few years. However, while certain measures (such as solar water heating) can be retrofitted relatively easily, others (such as building components) are more costly and/or difficult to replace. Consider this when deciding whether or not to adopt a particular energy-efficiency measure in your build.

THE SCOPE AND CONTENT OF THE BOOK

This book is very much a personal account derived from my own experience as an energy consultant, working on other people's building projects (and occasionally on my own). A wide range of issues is covered, from site factors and methods of construction, to specific components and technologies and how they influence the energy efficiency of the design, through to the legal framework and the wider environmental issues. Reference is made also to lifestyle factors, which can be important in determining how energy efficient your home is in practice.

Consequently, the book does not go into great detail in any one area. The idea is to make you think of energy efficiency in your build and to give an insight into the options you might wish to consider. In most cases you will need to seek specialist advice, for example, from architects, engineers, product manufacturers and suppliers, and other sources of information such as books, magazines and the web (*see* 'Useful Contacts' section) in order to incorporate these options into your build.

You will notice some repetition between the sections of the book. This is intentional since it is not designed to be read sequentially from beginning to end, but to be dipped into as and when a particular issue needs to be addressed. But to avoid excessive repetition, frequent reference is made to other sections throughout. While covering a wide range of issues, the book does not set out to be all-encompassing nor to cover every energy technique and technology available on the market today. Between the writing and publication the picture will change since there are new energy-efficiency technologies and products coming on to the market all the time, in response to legislative developments and increased public environmental awareness.

The book is aimed primarily at the self-build/DIY refurbishment/extension market – which in itself covers a wide range of activities, technical knowledge and levels of involvement – although it should also be of interest to others with a concern for energy and the environment. Self-build can cover anything from actually putting brick upon brick or timber to timber yourself, to commissioning someone else to project-manage a build on your site – and anything in-between. As it covers such a wide range of issues, it is unlikely that all parts of the book will be relevant to everyone. However, I hope that you will find enough to interest you and to spur you on to greater energy efficiency.

There is an ever-increasing number of publications and organizations aimed at self-builders these days, reflecting the growing interest in self-building. Lists of many of these are contained in the 'Useful Contacts' section. There may be a self-build organization or cooperative in your area – such groups can be a useful source of information and an opportunity to share experiences with like-minded people. But if no such organization exists, why not start one? The Hockerton Housing Group in Nottingham and the Ashley Vale Action Group in Bristol (*see* the 'Useful Contacts', section 16–18) are examples of community self-build projects with an energy and environmental focus. Even if you are not intending to be involved in the build, except in the concept (and, of course, in the financing), at least you should be aware of the energy-related issues that will influence the internal environment and running costs of the finished product – after all, you are going to have to live in it.

The focus is on the United Kingdom and Ireland, with reference to the regulations and vernacular building styles in these islands. Did you know that there are more self-builders in Ireland (north and south) than in the whole of Great Britain? So come on England, Scotland and Wales – it is time to play catch-up!

THE LAYOUT OF THE BOOK

The book is divided into chapters addressing issues as they occur along the process of a build. Thus we start with the site itself and plan form (how the house is to be laid out) and move on to the methods of construction, building fabric and components, glazing, insulation and so on. Conservatories and loft conversions, two of the most common areas of DIY/self-build are addressed separately. We then look at the services, that is, heating, hot water, lighting and ventilation, including renewable energy technologies, an area of increasing interest, and then move on to appliances and lifestyle factors – or what happens when the build is finished and you are actually living in it – which apply equally well to existing homes. We finish with the wider environmental issues, such as water economy and embodied energy, as well as the regulatory requirements. Finally, at the end of the book are a glossary and a list of useful contacts and further information.

PLANNING YOUR BUILD

This book focuses on the energy-related aspects of housing design and refurbishment, for the self-builder or the DIY-er. It does not, therefore, attempt to cover all the issues that you might encounter in the design and construction of your project. There are other books, periodicals, magazines and websites (*see* the 'Useful Contacts', section 16–19) which do this, covering important issues such as project planning and management, budget setting and control and planning applications. However, good forward planning is the key to achieving a good energy-efficient building, as it is to achieving success in all aspects of the design.

The Design Process

It is almost always worth engaging an architect, even for the smallest loft conversion or conservatory/sun room. A qualified architect (a member of the RIBA, the RIAS, the RSUA or the RIAI) will not only have the experience to put your thoughts into practice, he or she will also be able to visualize your ideas and express them in drawings in a way that will satisfy planners and Building Control.

We have all heard of cases where the architect-client relationship has become strained or has broken down. That is not a reason not to engage an architect;

there are doubtless many more cases where the relationship has worked well and the client's visions have been successfully translated into a building, but that does not make interesting gossip, television or magazine articles. What is most important, especially in a self-build project, is that you select an architect who has had experience of working with self-builders. You will not be embarking on a self-build project without some clear ideas of what you want and an intention to be involved in the design process if not the actual construction. A starting point might be a local self-build organization or architectural body. Alternatively, you might hear of someone by word of mouth. But whatever means you use to locate potential architects, always ask to see examples of their work. Everyone has his or her own particular sense of aesthetics, and designers often adopt a trademark style. Thus you should satisfy yourself that the architect's style is in keeping with your own concept.

Budget-Setting and Control

This is one of the areas where projects can most easily come unstuck. All too often, unless realistic budgets are set and adhered to, there comes a time in the design or the construction process when cuts are looked for, and the energy-efficiency elements are usually the first casualties. A good architect should be able to work within an approximate pounds per square foot (or metre) figure which gives you the space you want within your budget. Specific technologies such as renewables can then be factored in as additional costs within the whole project.

It is not likely that the building you end up with will be exactly that represented by the architect's final drawings. There will probably be some changes – it is one of the advantages of self-build that you can more easily accommodate modifications along the way. However, and especially if you are working with outside contractors, be aware that such changes may become disproportionately expensive, the more so the further you go down the design and construction processes. It is much better to put the time into the early design and project-planning stages to avoid having to make such changes later.

If you are carrying out extensive refurbishment measures to an existing property, say insulation and boiler/heating system replacement, make sure the latter is sized on the basis of the thermally improved fabric. Also, include all energy-efficiency measures in the standard specification rather than as 'extras' since otherwise you may find that contractors try to charge more for them.

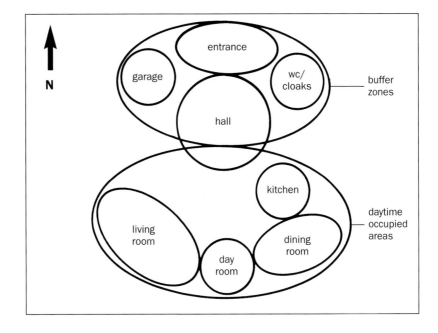

Blobs on a page: the earliest stage of the design process showing the preferred location of zones from a solar viewpoint. The same exercise can be repeated for other factors such as functionality, views, privacy and noise.

The Earliest Design Stage

At the very earliest stage of the design, even before you have engaged an architect, you can carry out a simple exercise of placing 'blobs' on a page (*see* the illustration on page 11). Mark down where you want the various 'zones' of the house from a solar/energy point of view (*see* the section 'Passive Solar Design' in Chapter 1). Then carry out the same exercise from a functional viewpoint in terms of the interrelationship between areas. Then perhaps do the same thing again with access in mind. Do it as many times as you like from all the different viewpoints you can think of: views, privacy, noise, for instance, and see where issues conflict and where they complement each other. In this way you can address each issue, avoiding time-consuming and possibly costly changes further down the line. The order in which you carry out the exercise and the priority you assign to each issue will be up to you. However, if you adopt this kind of approach, at least you will be able to say that you took on board all the aspects at an early stage and arrived at an optimum balance.

CHAPTER 1

Site and Built Form

MICROCLIMATE

The term 'microclimate', as it sounds, refers to such climatic factors as solar gains, and wind speed and direction immediately around a building. With an existing building, as well as with a new one, several measures may be taken to reduce the negative aspects of our climate and to enhance the positive ones. The orientation of your house is a key one in creating a microclimate around the building. Think of your house responding to the climate in much the same way as a plant, opening up to the sun while avoiding excessive heat, seeking shelter from cold winds and being open to favourable winds, being able to 'close up' at night (in practice, this might mean shutters or even simply good, thick, well-lined curtains). This practice is embodied in vernacular styles of architecture all around the world and which vary according to climate. Many of such simple principles are also embodied in the ancient Chinese practice of *feng shui*. The recommendation may be phrased some-

thing like 'place your house in the belly of a sleeping dragon', but the actual meaning is 'seek a sheltered spot'.

Shelter

This is one of the primary functions of a house – to provide that basic need for shelter from the elements. Fortunately, in a European maritime location such as Britain and Ireland have, the summer prevailing wind is from the south-west, with harsher, winter winds coming from the north and the east. This means that a south-facing house can not only embrace solar gains but also turn its back on the unwanted cold winds. Reducing the impact of wind, particularly cold winds, can reduce the heat loss from your house, especially in exposed sites. The movement of air along the outside walls of a building reduces the surface temperature of the walls and increases heat flow from the inside. This is even more true if the wall is wet. In an exposed site, planting or earthworks

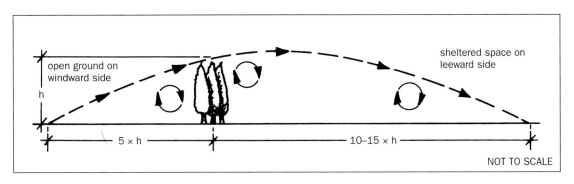

Optimum size and position of a shelter belt (for instance, coniferous trees) relative to a proposed or existing dwelling.

can significantly improve the heat retention of the dwelling, as well as protecting it from the possibility of water ingress from driving rain. Look for land forms and vegetation that provide shelter and shade where needed. If none such exist, consider how they might be introduced.

Coniferous species should be used for shelter since these will retain their foliage in the winter when the cold winds are at their fiercest. You might think that the best form of planting would be that with the densest foliage. In fact, experience has shown that foliage of medium density, or trees planted not too close together, is actually more effective, absorbing the wind rather than deflecting it, which can cause eddies and vortices. The correct sizing of the shelter belt or planting (when fully mature) will also provide a sheltered area on the leeward side, which can again be beneficial in exposed sites (*see* the illustration on page 13). A shelter belt of H (height) positioned with at least 5 × H of open space on the windward side, can provide up to 10–15 × H of sheltered space on the leeward side.

Evergreen hedges, rows of coniferous trees or even high fencing can be used to good effect to attract, deflect or accelerate winds in the vicinity of the building (*see* the illustration below). Generally, you should be wary of channelling winds towards your

building. However, for a very sheltered site you might wish to enhance favourable south-westerly winds for summer ventilative cooling. This aspect is also addressed in the section on natural ventilation in Chapter 8.

Even if it is not possible to shelter the house from cold winds, you can use the form of the building itself to provide a sheltered outside area. The longer the leading edge of the roof on the windward side, the greater the extent of the sheltered area on the leeward side (*see* the illustration on top of page 15).

Shading

There may be times when shading is an advantage, for example, in more southerly latitudes in the summertime or perhaps to prevent a conservatory from overheating in midsummer. Deciduous trees to the south (not too close to the house) can provide some shade to the house and/or garden areas in summer while allowing the sun's rays to pass through in winter (*see* the illustration on bottom of page 15), when solar gains are most useful. Unless such planting already exists, however, it will take many years to become effective. Other means of shading, by the building itself (for instance, roof overhangs) or specific shading devices, are addressed in the section on passive solar design.

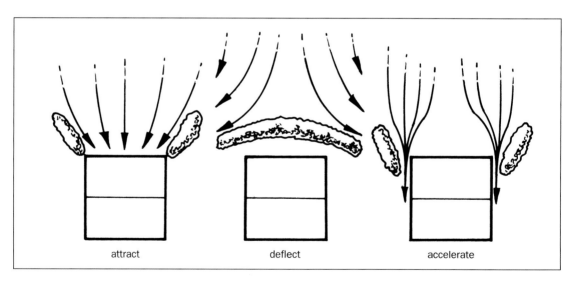

attract   deflect   accelerate

This plan view shows how evergreen hedges, rows of coniferous trees or high fencing can be used to good effect to attract, deflect or even accelerate winds in the vicinity of the building.

The longer the leading edge of a roof on the windward side, the greater the extent of the sheltered area on the leeward side.

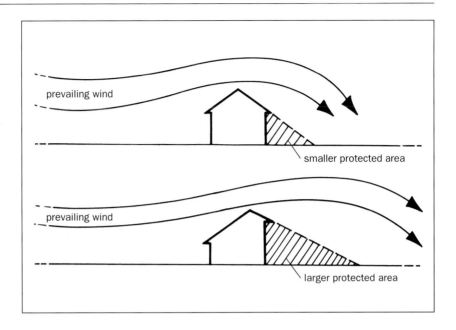

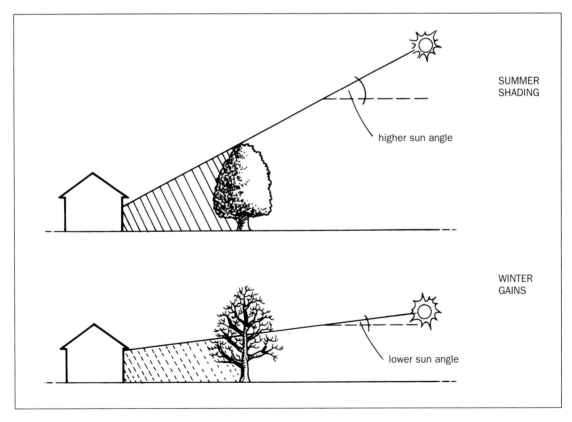

Deciduous trees to the south can provide shading in summer while allowing useful solar gains in winter.

The Sun-Trap

We have all experienced the phenomenon of the 'sun-trap', whether in our own home, that of friends or on visits to the gardens of stately homes, for example. A sun-trap is a south-facing area which traps the heat of the sun and protects from the wind. The shelter may come from natural features such as surrounding higher ground or planting (hedges, rows of trees) or from man-made structures such as walls. The effect can be heightened by the provision of masonry elements in the form of walls and paving which soak up the sun's heat and reradiate it back later in the day. With the appropriate orientation and sheltering, the house, or indeed the whole site, can become a sun-trap.

Miscellaneous Factors Concerning Planting

Much has been said in recent years on the subject of fast-growing conifers, planted in order to provide shelter quickly (or, more often, privacy). These can then become a nuisance for owners and neighbours alike, by either blocking the sun and views or re-quiring frequent maintenance. Feuds and even law-suits have resulted. Consider instead slow-growing, lower-lying shrubs – and live at peace with your neighbours. As far as possible, indigenous species should be used as these will be better suited to the climate, soil conditions and exposure levels. Indigen-ous species will also provide a habitat for insect and animal life, which will enhance your garden. If possible, leave at least one corner of your garden semi-wild – the natural habitats of many delightful creatures such as butterflies and birds are being lost through the development and over-cultivation of gardens.

On another planting subject, use slow-growing grass when sowing new lawns. While it will take longer for the lawn to become established, you will save energy – your own as well as that of your lawn-mower – in not having to cut the grass as often.

PASSIVE SOLAR DESIGN

There are two basic approaches to energy efficient design, as characterized by interaction with the out-side environment. These are the 'selective' approach and the 'exclusive' approach. The first makes use of natural solar heating, natural ventilation and day-lighting to offset the energy otherwise used in providing a comfortable internal environment – in other words, 'passive solar design'. The term indicates that use is made of the sun 'passively', by virtue of the design of the building, without 'active' systems such as solar collectors. Passive solar design may involve increasing the area of your south façade and of the external surfaces of the building as a whole, since single-storey structures are more easily accessed by natural means.

With the exclusive approach the emphasis is on reducing the external surface area for a given volume (that is, achieving a compact form) and using high levels of insulation and advanced glazing systems, for instance – in other words 'super-insulation'. Passive solar design is the subject of this section, while super-insulation is addressed in Chapter 3.

The two approaches are not entirely mutually exclusive and can be combined in a single building. Elements of passive solar design can be incorporated in the south façade of a super-insulated building, while the super-insulated approach would be a feature of the north side of a passive solar house. However, it may be easier to regard them as separate methods in order to examine the pros and cons of each.

Orientation and Solar Gain

A word here in case this book should ever get as far as the Southern Hemisphere – for 'south' read 'north' and vice versa. I remember a visiting academic from Australia who kept referring to passive solar houses being 'north-facing' – which was right where he came from, but very confusing for us.

Orientation, the direction your house faces, is something you will be able to influence only if you are building from scratch. Even then you will be limited by constraints such as planning permission, access and the position of adjacent dwellings. There may also be other considerations such as privacy and views which you wish to take into account. Such competing factors need to be reconciled to arrive at an optimum design.

Ideally, to make best use of heat and light from the sun your house should face south; this does not mean that the front entrance must be to the south, rather,

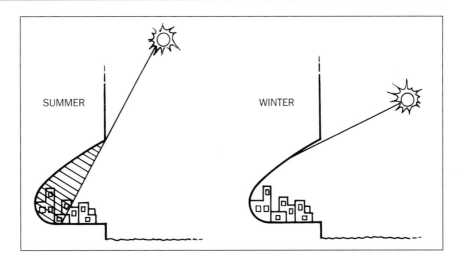

The early Navaho native Americans sited their dwellings in large, south-facing caves, to provide shade in summer and solar gains in winter.

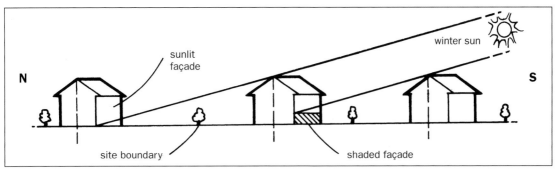

Dwellings too close together can overshadow one another (RHS). Locate your house to the north of your plot to maximize potential solar gains (LHS) while taking care not to deny solar gains to your neighbour to the north.

the house should address available solar gains in terms of its layout and the area and position of glazing. So you would have higher levels of glazing on the south façade and your main daytime-occupied areas on the south side of the house. Nor does the house have to face south direct – 25 degrees or so on either side will not make that much difference.

The early Navaho native Americans knew the value of passive solar design. They sited their settlements in large caves at the foot of south-facing cliffs, beside a river. The river gave them water, sustenance and a route for transportation. In addition to shelter and security, the cave gave them shade from the hot high summer sun while allowing the lower winter sun angles to penetrate to the rear of the caves (*see* top illustration above).

The ideal site is one gently sloping to the south, where there are less likely to be obstructions to solar gains in the form of other buildings, trees and the ground itself. In a smallish plot you should try to maximize the amount of south-facing garden by placing your house to the north end of the site (while taking care not to deny solar access to your neighbours to the north). This will reduce the likelihood of your being overshadowed by other buildings to the south and will also give you plenty of south-facing garden for the cultivation of plants and general amenity value (*see* the bottom illustration above). This works especially well if access is from the south since you will then have greater separation from the road, which will be better for acoustic and privacy reasons.

I remember once, just after completing my master's course on energy in buildings, hitch-hiking in Cornwall and getting a lift from a local farmer. When I explained to him what I had been doing (passive solar design, mostly) he immediately understood and told me the story of how he had approached the design of his own house. It was situated on his own land and he had had ample opportunity to observe, over the seasons, the orientation and the height of the sun, exactly where it rose and set at different times of the year, the position of any obstructions, and also the wind direction through the seasons and especially where the coldest winds came from. He used this information, which he never wrote down but kept in his head, to position and lay out his house for optimum solar gains and protection from harsh winds. Fortunately, you do not need to spend years observing your own site, nor enrol on a master's course, as the following section shows.

Sun-Path Diagrams

With the use of a sun-path diagram you can see where the sun will rise and set at different times of the year and its altitude angle (height in the sky) at any time of day. The sun-path diagram differs according to latitude and it is important to get the right one in order to be accurate in your calculations. Times shown are equivalent to GMT, that is, not taking into account daylight-saving adjustments.

The illustration below shows a sun-path diagram for latitude 52 degrees North. Imagine your house positioned in the centre – on an actual chart you could draw a thumbnail plan sketch of it there. Ideally, for a planned new build, face south or as near

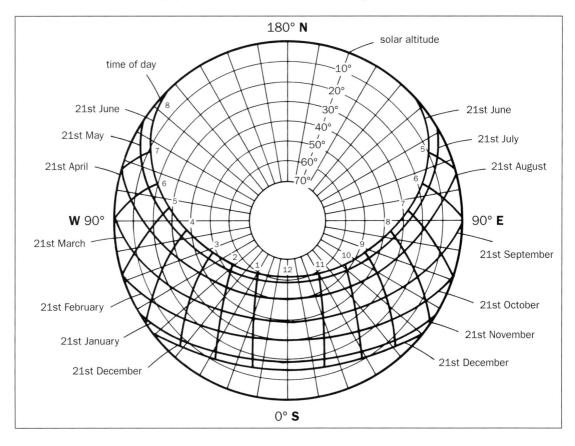

A sun path diagram for latitude 52 degrees North, showing solar altitude angle and orientation at different times of the day and year.

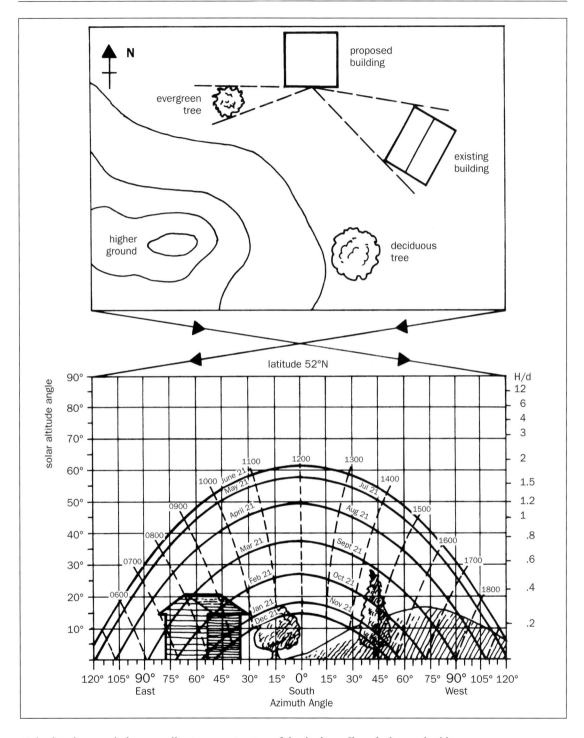

Cylindrical sun path diagram allowing examination of the shading effect of adjacent buildings, nearby trees and high ground. (Adapted from Achard and Gicquel, see 'Useful Contacts', section 2)

as possible. If constrained to be off-south, or in the case of an existing house, position the house on the diagram according to the actual orientation.

Then take a time of year, say 21 June, the summer solstice. At latitude 52 degrees N and reference longitude of the Greenwich meridian, the sun will rise in the north-east at approximately 3.30am GMT (or 4.30am BST). At solar noon it will be due south and reach a maximum altitude angle of just over 60 degrees, before setting at around 8.30am in the north-west. At the spring and the autumn equinox, 21 March and 21 September, the sun-path is the same, rising due east at 6am, reaching a maximum altitude angle at solar noon of around 38 degrees and setting due west at 6pm. At the winter solstice, 21–22 December, the sun does not rise until about 8.30am, tracking across from the south-east to the south-west and setting at around 3.30pm, reaching a maximum altitude angle at solar noon of only around 15 degrees. There are free programs which can be downloaded from the web for plotting sun-path diagrams – just type 'sun-path diagram' into your search engine. I found one at www.usc.edu/dept/architecture/mbs/tools/ecsdnld.html but there are sure to be others.

Note that you will need to adjust the times to represent longitude either side of the reference longitude. Add 4 mins for every 1° East and subtract 4 mins for every 1° West. Knowing where the sun will be and when, you can then plot the sun angles at different times of the day and year on to sketch plans and elevations to observe the actual solar access in different parts of the house. Rooms can be located on the plan and windows sized and positioned according to the desired solar access at a given time of the day and year. Roof overhangs can be sized accurately to keep out higher summer sun angles if desired. An alternative type of sun-path diagram is shown in the illustration on page 19. This is known as a cylindrical projection and allows you to examine more easily the effect of existing buildings, large trees and steep rises in contours, for example, such as might present obstructions to solar gains. The time of day and the duration of any obstruction at a given time of the year can be assessed, as shown. Again, you should be able to find down-loadable programs to provide this type of sun-path diagram.

This does not need to be a detailed or lengthy process, but it can be worthwhile to make sure that you select the optimum position on site, orientation and plan form layout for your house with respect to solar gains, while taking into account other constraints mentioned already.

Solar Resource

Just in case you should question the point of designing for solar access in this part of the world, especially in the more northerly parts of the British Isles, you may be surprised to know that southern parts of Scotland have similar average daily solar radiation levels to the midlands of England, while Northern Ireland has similar levels to the south-east of England (*see* the illustration on page 21).

The Midlands and the southerly regions of Ireland, meanwhile, are on a par with the south-west of England. Of course, higher latitudes tend to have lower average external temperatures – Tiree, on the west coast of Scotland, is one of the sunniest parts of the United Kingdom, but is also prone to being windy and therefore cold. However, if anything, that improves the viability of passive solar design – a more favourable balance of supply and demand.

Plan Form

Generally speaking, you should try to put your main daytime occupied areas on the south façade. Ideally, the kitchen is best located on the south-east side; there it will get the morning sun but be less prone to overheating (an obvious risk in kitchens) in the afternoon, when temperatures both inside and outside are more likely to have risen. The living room, on the other hand, may benefit from solar gains later in the day and could be located to the south-west side.

To the north you can place 'buffer zones' such as corridors, storage areas and garages – in fact, any area that does not need significant daylight or does not need to be heated to the same comfort temperatures as occupied areas. In a two-storey house a typical ground-floor layout might look something like this (*see* the illustration on page 22).

Bedrooms do not tend to be occupied during the daytime and therefore do not need to be south-facing, although they may benefit from morning sun and, generally, a bright, sunny aspect. Bathrooms can

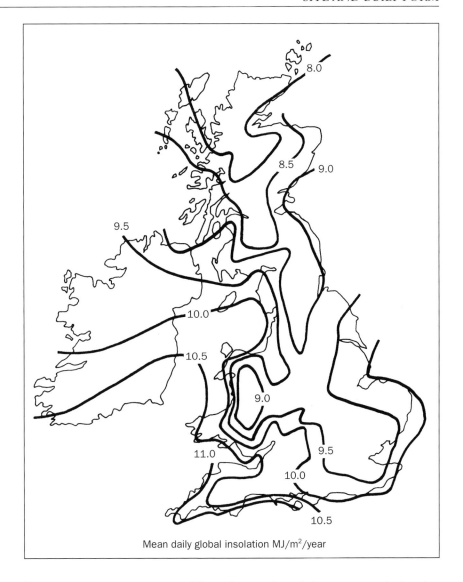

Map of the United Kingdom and Ireland showing approximate annual average levels of solar radiation. (Adapted from McNicholl and Lewis, see 'Useful Contacts', section 2)

Mean daily global insolation MJ/m²/year

also be located to the south-east, to receive morning sun and help to combat the dampness that can be associated with them (although ventilation, dealt with in Chapter 8, is an equally if not more important issue). In a two-storey house, the first floor layout might look something like the illustration on top of page 23.

For a single-storey dwelling, you will have more competition for the south façade. However, since bedrooms are not primarily occupied in the daytime, a layout such as this might be adopted (*see* illustration at bottom of page 23).

These plans are intended to represent the location of zones from a solar/thermal viewpoint only and should not be taken as blueprints for a house design. There will be other factors to be taken into account, including the functional interrelationship between rooms, space-allocation, visual amenity and the impact on the external appearance of façades.

Design for Future Changes
There will be a cost and energy advantage in taking into account possible future changes in use. For example, a bedroom could be made into a study. If

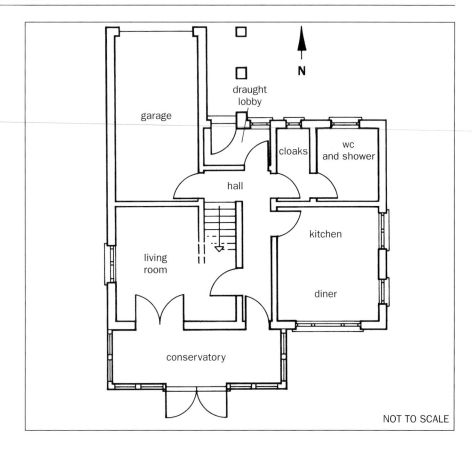

Notional ground-floor layout for a two-storey house from a passive solar viewpoint.

there were a bathroom en suite that would not work so well unless access could be made from another bedroom instead. If you think you might want an additional bathroom in the future, this could be located in a suitably sized multi-purpose room. Ideally, this would be located adjacent (horizontally or vertically) to the existing bathroom, to facilitate the supply of hot and cold water and minimize disruption. At times these factors may conflict with passive solar and other functional requirements, but should be taken into account nevertheless, as part of a total life-time low-energy approach.

The Upside-Down House

If your site slopes to the north or is very tight and you cannot avoid overshadowing by existing buildings, all is not lost – but you will need to be more inventive in accessing those solar gains. You should still locate your building as far to the north of the site as possible, to reduce overshadowing, while at the same time taking care not to deny solar access to your neighbours to the north (*see* left-hand side of illustration in centre of page 17).

Convention has it that daytime-occupied areas are on the ground floor and bedrooms on the upper floor(s). However, this may not be ideal from a solar gain viewpoint, especially in a tight urban site (*see* right-hand side of illustration in centre of page 17). A solution may be to turn the house upside-down, so that the main daytime-occupied areas are raised up and more able to receive solar gains. This can be particularly effective on a tight site sloping steeply to the south, so that the ground floor at the north façade becomes the first floor at the south façade (*see* the illustration at top of page 24). If the main access is also from the north, people's expectations on entering the building about the kinds of room you should have, can be met, while you are still getting the sun when and where you want it most.

Notional first-floor layout for a two-storey house from a passive solar viewpoint.

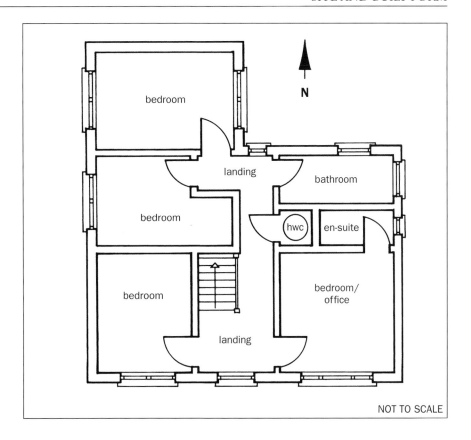

Notional floor layout for a single-storey house from a passive solar viewpoint.

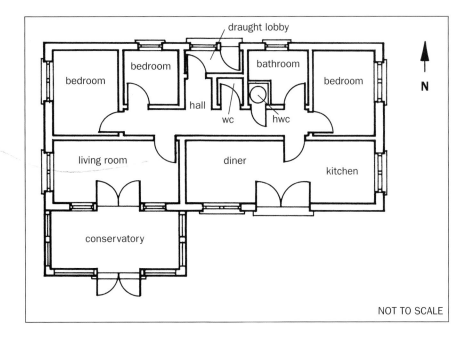

South-Facing Glazing

South-facing, vertical glazing has the property of being, to an extent, self-regulating with regard to solar gains. The illustration at the bottom of this page, shows that, in the summer, when the sun angle is higher, much of the solar radiation is reflected off the glazing, whereas in winter, with lower sun angles, more of the radiation is transmitted through the glazing. The higher sun angle also means that the area of window 'seen' by direct radiation (called the 'solar aperture') is lower in real terms in summer than in winter. Furthermore, south-facing glazing, even single glazing (which I do not recommend, by the way) is neutral over the year in terms of the balance of energy gained (from the sun) and lost (from the house). South-facing double glazing (or better) can

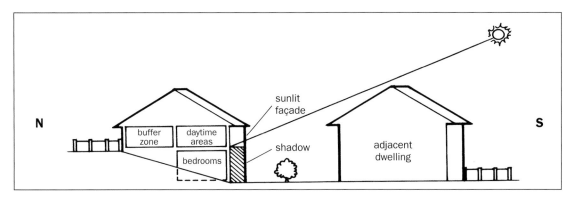

The 'upside-down' house – a solution to a tight site, allowing solar gains to daytime-occupied spaces.

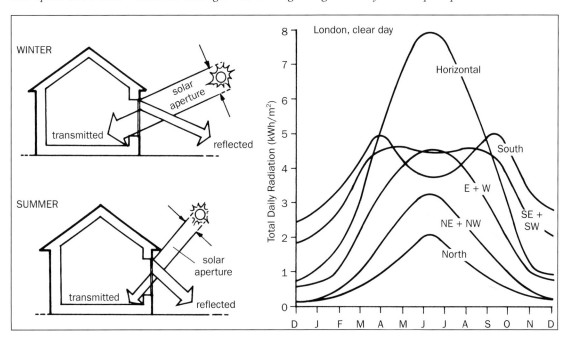

South-facing glazing is self-regulating to a degree, reflecting away more solar radiation from the high summertime sun and allowing more of the lower wintertime sun to pass through. (Adapted from Achard and Gicquel, see 'Useful Contacts', section 2)

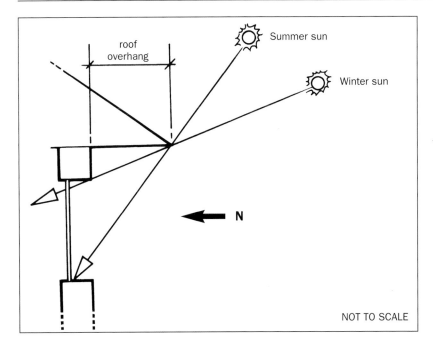

roof overhang

Summer sun

Winter sun

N

NOT TO SCALE

Shading can be incorporated into the design of roof overhangs and window reveals, sized according to sun angles from the sun path diagram.

be a significant net contributor to heating in the building over the year. However, care must be taken not to allow excessive solar gains, leading to over-heating.

Solar Shading – Fixed or Movable?

There may be times when you want to screen out solar gains from your house. This can be done by deciduous trees, as mentioned previously; however, if none such exist where you want them, you will be waiting many years for the shading to become effective. There will be times, therefore, when you need the shading to be positioned in or on the building. This is best done in theory with external, movable shading, which allows you to screen out solar gains before they penetrate the glazing and which also can be adjusted depending on the weather conditions, time of day, time of year and so on.

However, external shading is exposed to the elements and movable systems are more prone to breakdown, especially if automated (in which energy is required for motors). Further, they may not fit in with your architectural aesthetic, in which case fixed shading may be more suitable. This can be incorporated into roof overhangs and depths of window

reveals (*see* the illustration above) using angles from the sun-path diagram to determine the optimum dimensions. The disadvantage of fixed shading is, of course, that it is fixed – it cannot be repositioned at different times of the day or year. The next illustration on page 26 shows how this can be a disadvantage, especially in the spring time, when there may be modest solar gains available while the outside temperature is still low. Fixed shading, sized to screen out the higher summer sun angles, may block too much of the useful springtime solar gains.

Shutters, Blinds and Solar Control Films
A good set of shutters (something the Victorians knew) can serve well as shading devices, as well as providing security and night-time insulation (if well-fitting). Blinds can be used, of course, although they tend to be something of an afterthought. Careful consideration of the geometry of the building, as mentioned above, may reduce the need for blinds. While horizontal blinds work well on south façades, vertical louvres are more effective on east and west façades, when the sun is at a lower angle (*see* the illustration on page 27).

If blinds complement your desired look, glazing systems are available which incorporate the blinds

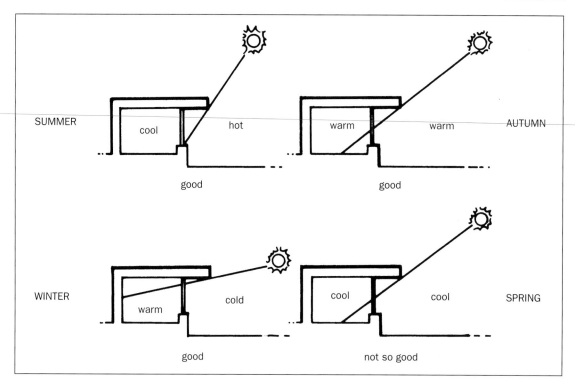

Fixed shading can work well at most times of the year except spring, when there is still a heating demand, but the sun, at a mid-height in the sky, may be screened out, thus denying solar gains. (Adapted from Achard and Gicquel, see 'Useful Contacts', section 2)

between glazing layers. While more commonly seen in offices, for example, to provide privacy with glazed internal walls, these might be worth considering. Their advantages include space-saving and protection from dust build-up, although if the mechanism were to fail it could prove costly.

Other variations on the blind theme are prismatic blinds and parabolic blinds (*see* the illustration at the bottom of page 27). Prismatic blinds feature triangular-section ridges which redirect the angle of solar radiation, as in a prism. Parabolic blinds have louvres with a parabolic profile, which can allow daylight to enter a room but keep out direct gains no matter what the angle of solar radiation. Some types have louvres perforated towards the inner edge, to allow views of the outside while still screening out the solar gains.

In the case of a conservatory, a configuration can be adopted by using movable, internal shading (*see* the illustration on page 28). Although requiring manual intervention and/or maintenance, especially if automated, this form of shading can be effective in providing summer/daytime shading as well as winter/night-time insulation, as shown.

Finally, especially in an existing building, films can be applied to glazing to reduce the amount of solar gains entering the building. Several types of solar-control glass are also available, although at a considerable over-cost compared to standard glass. These, of course, represent fixed shading. Different types of film and glass have different properties in terms of daylight and heat transmission and it is important to select the type which gives the right balance. Again, while more often seen in commercial locations, these might be worth considering, especially if excess solar gains are a serious issue, for example, on the upper floors of multi-storey buildings.

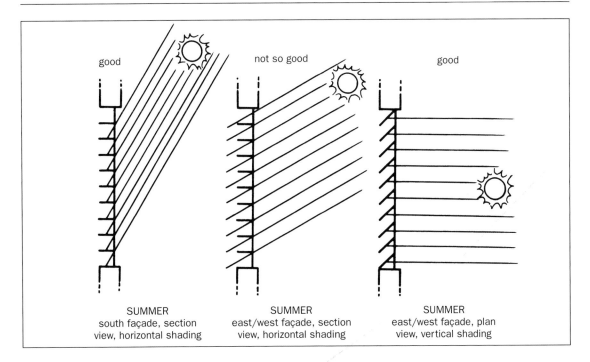

good   not so good   good

SUMMER
south façade, section
view, horizontal shading

SUMMER
east/west façade, section
view, horizontal shading

SUMMER
east/west façade, plan
view, vertical shading

Horizontal shading can work well on a south façade but is less effective on east and west façades, where vertical shading can be better.

Prismatic and parabolic blinds can allow daylighting gains while preventing direct solar heating gains and glare by 'bending' sunlight from any altitude angle – the blind angle can also be varied. (Adapted from McNichol and Lewis, see 'Useful Contacts', section 2)

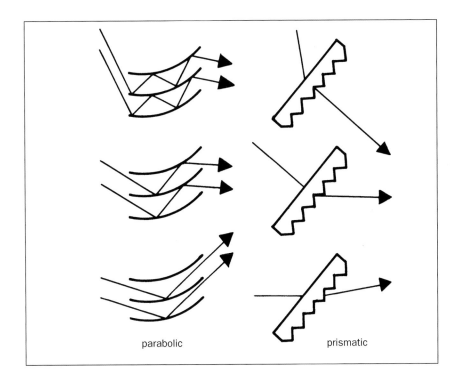

parabolic   prismatic

A movable blind, for example, in a conservatory, can serve as shading and also assist ventilation via the stack effect in summer/daytime (LHS) as well as providing thermal insulation in winter/night-time (RHS).

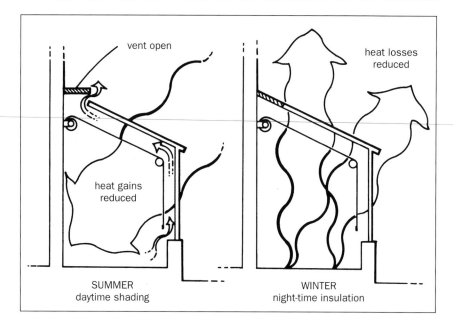

SUMMER
daytime shading

WINTER
night-time insulation

Thermal Mass

Thermal mass is a term applied to materials which can absorb and hold significant amounts of heat and is a key element of passive solar design. It can also be used to good effect in energy-efficient design in general. Any material with a high heat capacity can be used as thermal mass.

Materials Used for Thermal Mass	
concrete	slow release
brick	slow release
stone	slow release
water	faster release, but problem of containment

The darker the surface, the more solar energy is absorbed and thus the more energy potentially stored in the thermal mass. Thermal mass is especially useful for moderating indoor temperature swings. In a passive solar design, thermal mass can store solar energy during the day for release later in the evening. For example, the floor of a conservatory might consist of a masonry covering, say tiles, laid on to a continuous cement bed, on top of a concrete slab or screed. This would allow the excess solar gains to be absorbed by the tiles and, if in sufficient quantities, conducted down to the concrete (the continuous bed is important here), helping to reduce excess temperatures during the day. Later in the evening, when temperatures were reduced, physical laws governing the flow of heat from a hotter body to a cooler one would result in heat being released from the floor back into the conservatory. Thermal mass works best in this context if exposed to direct solar gains.

The term sometimes leads people to assume that you need huge thicknesses of masonry. However, in most cases, the thickness of thermal mass which will actually be effective is no more than 60–120mm (about 2½ to 5in). By the time heat has been absorbed by the mass to this depth, the temperature in the room is likely to have dropped and heat will start to be re-radiated back from the mass.

There are more complex configurations of thermal mass known as rock-stores, where heat is stored in crushed rock beneath the floor and can be extracted under action of a fan. However, this type of approach is generally only viable in lower latitudes where there is a large difference between daytime and night-time temperatures.

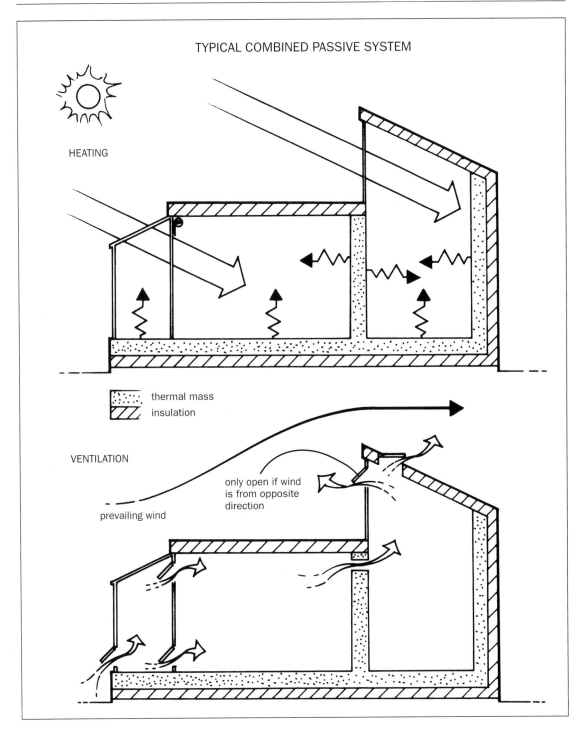

TYPICAL COMBINED PASSIVE SYSTEM

HEATING

thermal mass
insulation

VENTILATION

only open if wind
is from opposite
direction

prevailing wind

Schematic of a combined passive system, showing heating and ventilation modes. (Adapted from Achard and Gicquel, see 'Useful Contacts', section 2)

It is certainly possible to have too much thermal mass, especially with an intermittently occupied dwelling or space within a dwelling. You may have experienced the discomfort of a holiday home or out-of-season B&B, where it takes practically all weekend for the place to warm up. This is because you have to put a lot of heat into the building fabric (thermal mass) before it reaches an equilibrium temperature with the internal air – this is especially true of old, solid-walled houses.

It is equally possible to have too little thermal mass. There is actually a greater possibility of summer overheating with a lightweight fabric. It might make sense, therefore, with, say a timber-frame construction, to build a masonry fire surround and chimney in the centre of the house to accommodate a wood-burning stove, for example. The stove would not present a continuous ventilation heat-loss route and would utilize a sustainable fuel, while the fire surround and chimney would provide some thermal mass to retain heat from the stove when in use, as well as absorbing excess heat gains in summer. Positioning the chimney in the centre of the building would ensure that useful heat was retained. The stove doors could also be opened in summer (without a fire being lit) to aid ventilation and heat removal if needed.

A word of caution if you are proposing to make use of thermal mass: make sure that you do not end up by isolating it with floor coverings, for instance. This advice extends to underfloor heating systems (see Chapter 6), 'wet' types of which utilize the thermal mass of the floor slab or screed. An inherently slow-response system, underfloor heating works best with masonry tile flooring or timber laid direct on to a concrete screed. A carpet, especially a thick one, would further slow down the system and prevent heat from being radiated into the room.

Daylighting and Natural Ventilation

Daylighting and natural ventilation are key aspects of passive solar design and just as important as the utilization of solar heat gains and the retention of heat in the building. However, rather than being included along with other passive solar issues, they are addressed in the sections on lighting and ventilation, respectively, in Chapters 7 and 8.

Combined Passive System

Schematic configurations for a combined passive system are shown in the illustration on page 29. In heating mode, use is made of thermal mass, with a well-insulated envelope, to retain heat in the building. A south-facing conservatory (unheated, of course – see the section on 'Conservatories' in Chapter 5) can act as a buffer space. The temperature of the conservatory will almost always be higher than that of the outside air, allowing a greater than normal area of glazing to the adjacent area of the house, without penalty of heat loss. Note that the presence of the conservatory itself will reduce the amount of daylight entering the adjacent space, although this should be more than compensated for by the larger area of glazing permitted. Blinds (or curtains or shutters) between the conservatory and the main body of the house will allow excess solar gains to be controlled during the day and also reduce heat loss at night. Clerestory (high-level) windows can allow solar heating and daylight to penetrate the north zones of the house, as shown.

In ventilation mode, the conservatory can also preheat ventilation air, enhanced by the placing of vents in the external conservatory wall and the wall separating off the main body of the house. The appropriate location of openings in internal walls and around the clerestory windows, as shown, can also allow cross-ventilation through the building.

CHAPTER 2

Insulation and U-Values

THERMAL PERFORMANCE: U-VALUES

Definition of U-Value

The thermal performance of a building element (wall, window, roof, floor) is expressed in terms of a 'U-value'. An overall U-value can also be given for the whole building. The proper name for U-value is 'thermal transmittance', which is an expression of the rate at which heat is transmitted through an element, therefore indicating the level of insulation. Elements of a highly-insulated house will transmit heat through to the outside at a lower rate and will have lower U-values, again, the same applying to the building as a whole.

U-values are expressed in watts (representing energy) per square metre of element and degree temperature difference between inside and outside, in symbols, W/m^2K, where K (Kelvin) is equivalent to °C in terms of temperature difference. So, for a wall of a given area and U-value, and known inside and outside temperatures, the steady state heat loss in watts can be calculated. In general, however, U-values are used to indicate the energy efficiency of the building fabric and to allow comparisons to be made between different methods of construction or building materials.

For those who may have experience of building in North America, you will recall that they use the R-value (thermal resistance) which is simply the reciprocal of the U-value. This has arguably the advantage of higher values for more insulation (Americans like bigger to mean better). However, in the UK and Ireland, lower is better: a wall U-value of $0.35W/m^2K$ is the base-case value currently assumed

in UK-wide Building Regulations for a dwelling. In practice, you are likely to have to do better than this to comply with the Regulations, possibly around $0.3W/m^2K$ (*see* Chapter 11).

However, we also use the R-value in U-value calculations. In practical terms, the U-value of an element is calculated by first calculating the R-value, the sum of the individual resistances (r) of all the material layers in the element. The individual resistances are calculated from the thickness (l) of the material, divided by its thermal conductance (k-value) – a physical property which varies from one material to another but is constant for a given material. The full calculation procedure is thus:

$$r = l/k$$
$$R = (r_1 + r_2 + r_3 + \ldots \text{etc.})$$
$$U = (1/R)$$

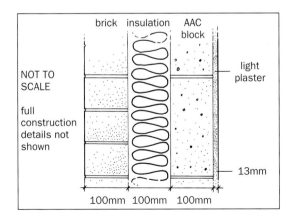

Construction for sample U-value calculation, showing dimensions and materials.

Sample U-Value Calculation

Take, as an example, a masonry cavity wall of the following construction (*see* the illustration on page 31): 100mm brick, 100mm cavity fully filled with EPS insulation, 100mm AAC Block, 13mm lightweight plaster internal surface.

An additional value of r = 0.18m²K/W is used to represent the surface resistances of the internal and the external surface (the same value may be used to represent an air cavity, although such is not represented in the example below).

Layer	Thickness l (m)	Conductance k (W/mK)	R = l/k (m²K/W)
brick	0.100	0.840	0.119
insulation	0.100	0.035	2.86
AAC block	0.100	0.200	0.500
light plaster	0.013	0.160	0.0813
surfaces			r = 0.18
Total		R = 3.74m²K/W; U = 1/R = 0.267W/m²K	

This construction would comply with an elemental U-value for walls of 0.27W/m²K. However, if the insulation used had a thermal conductance of 0.04W/mK instead of 0.035W/mK, then the overall U-value would be higher, actually 0.296W/m²K. The construction would no longer comply with an elemental U-value of 0.27W/m²K. Accuracy in assuming physical properties and dimensions of layers is all-important, as is adherence to design-stage assumptions in actual construction otherwise your building will not be as thermally efficient as you intended. What is more, if you are sailing close to the legal minimum requirement (*see* section on 'Building Regulations' in Chapter 11), a good Building Control Officer will notice.

BRE U-Value Calculator

To calculate the U-value of a wall, for example, by longhand (as above) requires knowledge of the thermal conductivity (k-value, W/mK) and the thickness of each material in the wall – for example, plaster, block, insulation, air gap and brick – to calculate the individual resistances of the materials and thence the total resistance and U-value.

It is much simpler to use a computer program which will not only carry out all the calculations in the blink of an eye but will provide a database of different types of material with their k-values hard-wired – all you have to do is specify the thickness of each material in order.

One such program, available for a little over £20 only, is the BRE U-value calculator. BRE (*see* 'Useful Contacts', section 1) is the Building Research Establishment, a former government research organization now privatized, which has been the UK's leading centre for building-related research and development for a number of decades. The calculator is available from the BRE bookshop. The program not only carries out calculations quickly but allows for the easy comparison of different material options and thicknesses.

Response Time and Thermal Mass

Two subjects related to thermal transmittance are thermal mass and response time (*see* also the section on passive solar design in Chapter 1). The response time of a heating system simply describes the time taken between introducing heat into a cold room and comfort temperatures being reached. To demonstrate this point, consider three heating systems: a warm air system, a wet system with radiators and a wet system with underfloor heating. The warm air system will have the quickest response time, of the order of a few minutes since it heats the very air which is fed into the room. A radiator system will take about 30min to 1hr (depending on various factors, including the thermal properties of the building), while the underfloor system would take several hours.

The thermal properties of the building fabric will also have an impact on the response time. An old, solid-walled house will take much longer to heat up than a modern, well-insulated one since the fabric of the building (thermal mass) will absorb heat until it reaches a temperature equal to that of the air inside the building. A timber-framed or prefabricated house (or one internally dry-lined with insulation) will have the quickest fabric response time as it has the lowest exposed thermal mass. As well as the main building elements, other surface finishes will have an impact on the thermal mass/response time, for example, a thick carpet will isolate the available thermal mass of the floor and reduce the response time.

The response time is important if you are considering a house or a part of a house which is intermittently occupied. You do not want to have to preheat the building fabric for long periods in order to provide comfort temperatures for only a short time. The heat you have put into the fabric will then be lost gradually while the building is unoccupied. On the other hand, for a continuously occupied dwelling, the thermal mass can be useful in balancing out extremes of temperature. Thermal mass can also be useful in absorbing excessive solar gains during the day and storing heat for the evening (*see* the sections on passive solar design and conservatories in Chapters 1 and 5, respectively).

INSULATION

Why Use Insulation?

Thirty years ago most new housing in Britain and Ireland had practically no thermal insulation. Over the intervening years, the Building Regulations minimum legal requirements on building thermal performance have been introduced and tightened up progressively, with the aim of reducing energy consumption and environmental emissions. This means that today, for a new house or an extension to an existing one, you *must* incorporate insulation – it is not conceivable that a new design would comply without it. In certain cases, and increasingly in the future, you may also be required to upgrade the thermal properties of an existing house which is being extended or refurbished (check with your local Building Control office about this). Fortunately,

---

Types of Insulation

Several types of insulation are available, some of which can be used in a variety of ways while others are more appropriate for certain applications. The basic types are set out in the table below:

Material	Main use	Relative cost	Thermal properties	Other advantages	Disadvantages
expanded polystyrene (EPS)	cavity wall insulation (CWI), pitched roofs, roofs, floors	low	good	easy to handle/cut, rigid	
extruded polystyrene	CWI, pitched roofs, floors	medium	very good	easy to handle/cut, good where rigidity needed	
mineral fibre/ mineral wool	timber frame walls, plane roofs	low	good	good where flexibility needed	can be unpleasant to handle
polyurethane/ polyisocyanurate	CWI, pitched roofs, floors	high	very good	good where rigidity needed	can be less environmentally friendly
cellulose fibre/natural wool/cork	timber-frame walls, plane roofs	high	good	environmentally friendly	

EPS and mineral wool/fibre insulation have similar thermal properties and are relatively cheap to buy. Polyurethane and polyisocyanurate have better thermal properties but are more expensive. Cellulose fibre, cork and natural wool products are among the most environmentally friendly. For this reason they have been included together in the table, although they are quite different in terms of their nature and their applications.

insulation not only saves energy and the environment but also money, which makes it most cost-effective to use.

How Does Insulation Work?

Insulation comes in many types and forms, but the one thing they all have in common is that they trap air. It is not simply the foam (or whatever) material that provides the insulation but the still pockets of air trapped in it. Air has a low thermal conductance and, when still, gives rise to no convective heat losses. Radiation will still occur, but only across each individual pocket. Certain insulation types now incorporate reflective layers (also known as low-emissivity layers) that aim to reduce radiative heat loss and can also provide a resistance to moisture. Insulation measures should always be carried out before boiler replacement or heating system upgrades. In this way, the heating system can be sized according to the reduced heat loss resulting from the insulation.

Expanded Polystyrene (EPS)

EPS board is available in several thicknesses and is used mostly for floors, pitched roofs and cavity wall insulation, where rigidity is required. The best types are tongued-and-grooved (T+G) for improved jointing between boards. Proprietary products include full cavity insulation and a product with a 'concertina' action which can be squeezed in between rafters (*see below* on roof insulation). A recent development of EPS now available is the so-called 'grey' type. This has a graphite coating which acts as a low-emissivity barrier across each closed cell, improving the thermal performance over standard EPS (k = 0.031–0.033W/mK, compared with 0.035W/mK).

Extruded Polystyrene

Often referred to by the DOW company trade-marked name 'Styrofoam', this product is formed via a continuous extrusion process. Though having greater thermal performance and moisture resistance than EPS, the use of halogenated blowing agents has reduced its overall environmental credentials.

Mineral Wool/Mineral Fibre

These terms describe a range of materials including glass fibre and mineral or rock wool (produced from diatomaceous rock). These materials come in rigid batts, or flexible 'quilts' which can be cut and draped around contours. Again, the material is available in a range of thicknesses. Mineral fibres and mineral wools are unpleasant to handle as they produce irritating fibres; care is needed when handling these materials and gloves and a mask are required – preferably a boiler-suit too. A type of glass wool insulation is available in rolls wrapped in a very thin, perforated, plastic sheeting, thus making it much easier to handle. The material itself, which is white rather than the normal yellow, is also different from conventional glass-fibre insulation, the fibres being omni-directional. This makes it less abrasive and less friable (less likely to be broken into small fibres) in case contact with skin should be made.

Polyurethane/Polyisocyanurate

These are higher-performance insulants although they also tend to be more costly. In the past, they were associated with being less environmentally friendly, but now that all chlorofluorocarbons (CFCs) and hydrochlorofluorocarbons (HCFCs) have been banned, the distinction is no longer so valid, although hydrofluorocarbons (HFCs) may still be in use. They can be especially useful when the attempt is being made to achieve a given U-value in an element of restricted width (for instance, on the pitch of a roof or, in certain cases, in floors). This type of insulation is often provided with a reflective foil backing, providing a low-emissivity layer and moisture resistance.

Cellulose Fibre

Cellulose fibre insulation produced from recycled newsprint gives an environmentally friendly alternative to conventional insulation materials. It can be blown dry into a roof space to provide insulation in the plane of the ceiling (*see* the illustration on page 35), or sprayed wet into a timber stud to provide wall insulation (*see* the illustration on page 36). Contrary to what you might suspect, as a result of various treatments, the material is very resistant to insects, vermin and also fire.

Natural Wool

A relative newcomer to the construction field

'Warmcell' cellulose fibre (recycled newsprint) insulation from Excel Industries Ltd, being blown dry into a roofspace.

(although well established in other fields) is sheep's wool. If it is good enough to see a sheep through Welsh hillside winters, then it must be worth a try in your roof space. Unlike mineral fibre materials, this insulation is not an irritant to the skin or the respiratory passages and does not require handling gloves, mask and overalls (*see* the illustration on page 37).

Cork
Cork is a good natural insulant and a renewable resource. The move from cork to synthetic materials and screw-tops in wine-bottling may mean that new markets are sought for cork, making it more competitively priced as an insulation material.

Environmental Credentials

There are two criteria used to represent the environmental impact of an insulation material; these are the ozone depletion potential (ODP) and the global warming potential (GWP). In both cases, the reference is to blowing-agents used in the manufacture of the insulation, and therefore refers only to foamed types. CFCs and HCFCs, which have high ODP and GWP, are now banned from new materials, although stocks of certain materials or products may still contain these substances. Pentane scores zero on both indices, while carbon dioxide has zero ODP but a GWP of 1 (on a relative scale); HFCs have zero ODP, but a GWP of 300. Manufacturers and suppliers of foamed insulation materials should always be able to confirm the blowing agents used in their products.

How Much Insulation Should I Use? Is the Building Regulations Minimum Enough?

In the past I have answered this question by saying: 'Do not limit yourself to the Building Regulations minimum – put in as much as you can – you will not regret it.' Insulation is relatively cheap and is easily installed during construction. Retrofitting is practically impossible where floors are concerned and not easy with walls.

'Warmcell' cellulose fibre (recycled newsprint) insulation from Excel Industries Ltd, being sprayed wet into a timber stud wall.

Historically, the Building Regulations minimum has been very much the legal minimum and not in any way the energy-efficiency or economic optimum. Nevertheless, as the construction industry is largely cost-driven, the lowest-cost option is generally adopted, especially by volume builders. Therefore, the Regulations minima are rarely bettered. Because of this, and in response to the national carbon dioxide emissions reduction target, the new UK-wide Building Regulations thermal standards are actually quite stringent. In the Republic of Ireland the minimum elemental U-values have been reduced

'Thermafleece' sheep's wool insulation from Second Nature United Kingdom Ltd, laid in quilts in a roofspace. Note that the material does not require handling gloves, mask or overalls, as would mineral wool/fibre materials.

within the past couple of years to levels similar to those proposed in the United Kingdom. Therefore one can say now, 'meet the legal minimum and you will be doing well'. However, it is always possible to do better.

But, you may say, what about the law of diminishing returns, whereby you get progressively fewer and fewer energy savings from successive layers of insulation? Right enough: starting with nothing at all, 150mm of roof insulation will make a big difference, while a further 150mm will cost the same as the first but will not save as much energy and thus will not be as cost effective. There are two responses to this question. First, energy will go on getting more expensive during the lifetime of your building.

Therefore, the economic viability of insulation installed now will only improve with time. Insulation generally pays back within about five years. However, if a measure pays back in ten years at today's energy prices, it will end up paying back in a shorter time as energy prices increase. The other answer is that, with insulation in dwellings, there comes a point where there is a step change. You reach a level of insulation so good that you do not need conventional heating systems, the house can maintain comfort temperatures at most times with just the internal gains from occupants, lighting and so on. As a rough rule of thumb, this point is reached when overall fabric U-values are below about $0.2\text{W/m}^2\text{K}$. If you can save altogether on the capital cost of a heating system as well as the running costs, that improves the economics of the extra insulation considerably. You may need a small amount of heating input at times during the mid-heating season – although good design for wintertime passive solar gains will reduce such need (see the section on super-insulated houses in Chapter 3).

WALL INSULATION

The Introduction of the Cavity in Masonry Construction

Cavities were introduced into masonry construction in order to prevent a problem often experienced with solid walls – that of moisture seeping through the masonry from outside and presenting on the internal walls. This is not only unsightly and unhealthy, especially if mould growth results, but also increases heat loss. The idea of the cavity was that any rain penetrating the outer leaf would be shed down its inner face and would not be able to track across to the inner leaf, which would remain dry. Even the wall ties, incorporated for structural rigidity, had twists in the centre at which droplets could form and drip down into the centre of the cavity.

The air in the cavity itself improved the thermal properties (reduced the U-value) of the wall. However, the next step was to improve the effectiveness of the air insulating layer by encapsulating it in an insulation material, thus preventing air movement (still air is a better insulator than moving air). The cavity was not fully filled with insulation since this was seen to contradict the reason for the cavity being introduced in the first place, the concern was that water would track across the insulation and once again present on the internal surfaces. And so cavities were partially-filled. A standard cavity (80mm in Britain until the 1980s and 100mm thereafter) would have been filled with, say, 40–60mm of insulation, depending on the properties of the insulation, the thermal requirements of the day and the energy efficiency awareness of the builder. Insulation-retaining clips were introduced, slotted over the wall ties. The purpose of the clips was to stop insulation from slipping out of place and thus introducing a route for heat loss. The relatively cold surface of the internal wall behind which the misplaced insulation

was located could become a point for interstitial condensation, again increasing the risk of mould growth.

Full Cavity Insulation

Newbuild

Following the logic of the above sequence of developments, the idea of fully filling the cavity would not have been considered by most people, and that is still often the case today. However, as the Building Regulations minimum thermal requirements become tighter and people become more energy- and environmentally aware, there will be a greater tendency to fill cavities fully or to move to a wider cavity altogether – or both.

Full cavity insulation materials and systems have been developed which are resistant to moisture tracking across to the inner leaf and generally can be used where recommended by manufacturers, subject to levels of exposure and driving-rain index. Where a good layer of external render is used, this should provide an effective weatherproof barrier and allow the full filling of cavities with confidence (*see* also the section on 'Masonry Cavity Construction' in Chapter 3, especially 'A Word About Render', on page 52).

One particularly well-designed system (*see* the illustration on page 39) uses tongued and grooved EPS boards with an intermittent projection on the outer face. This preserves a minimal cavity to the inner face of the outer leaf down which rain may thus be shed. The tight-fitting, tongue-and-groove joints angled downwards away from the inner leaf also prevent moisture transfer. An additional benefit of this kind of system is that the plastic insulation-retaining clips used with partial cavity insulation need no longer be fitted to the wall ties. Once builders become familiar with the system they warm to it – I heard of one who said, 'it's just like using Lego bricks.'

Careful detailing is needed at the corners, incorporating a vertical damp-proof course (DPC) internally and externally (manufacturers and suppliers will be able to give advice on this). Mortar droppings need to be prevented from fouling the exposed edges of the boards as they are installed so that the tongue-and-groove joints are clear. A board very slightly narrower than the cavity width may be placed on the top of the

'ECOwarm Fulfil' tongue-and-groove full cavity insulation from Springvale EPS Ltd – note the intermittent profile maintaining a minimal rain-shedding cavity and moisture barrier while providing high levels of insulation within a normal 100mm cavity.

insulation as the masonry courses are laid above it to catch any mortar droppings. Also, joints on the inner face of the outer leaf need to be cleaned of surplus mortar – this is good practice anyway.

In case you are still concerned about the dampness penetration issue with this product, the following account of the British Board of Agrément testing, carried out at the BRE, should reassure you. Normally, the testing procedure would involve constructing, in the laboratory, outer and inner leaves, with the insulation in between, to represent an actual installation. Water is then sprayed on to the outer leaf to represent rainfall and any moisture penetration to the internal surface of the inner leaf is carefully monitored. In this case, however, the testers did not even bother constructing an outer leaf but sprayed water direct on to the surface of the EPS board. After a week, not a spot of moisture was found on the inner surface.

Blown fibre or bonded bead systems (*see* 'Retrofit Cavity Wall Insulation', on page 40) can also be applied to newbuild and obviously provide full-cavity insulation. This has become quite popular in recent years as it means you can put the walls up more quickly, without having to think about the insulation at the same time. Installing the insulation by blowing it in is also a much quicker process than placing rigid boards in the cavity and fixing the plastic retaining clips (although not, of course, required for full-fill boards). However, to my mind, in a newbuild situation, it makes better sense to put the insulation in as you go, then you can be sure that it is right.

Retrofit Cavity Wall Insulation (CWI)

If you have a masonry cavity dwelling built before it was normal practice to include insulation in the cavity (say, 1930s to1970s) then cavity wall insulation (CWI) will be the most obvious way of improving the thermal performance of the walls. The alternatives, dry-lining or external cladding, are more expensive, disruptive and complicated operations. There has been a substantial specialist industry built up over the years in retrofitting cavity wall insulation to such dwellings. Had there been problems (such as moisture penetration to the inner leaf) one would assume that we would have heard of them and that the industry would have suffered. Since neither is the case, we may assume that, in the vast majority of cases, there are no such problems.

In a UK survey of private home owners who had had CWI installed, 94 per cent were prepared to install it in their next home. The findings also included an up to 25 per cent reduction on fuel bills. Additional benefits were that boilers could be switched on later and houses were more comfortable. Regarding the rain-penetration risk, another survey compared failure rates between houses with filled cavities and those with cavities unfilled. For the filled cavities, failure was defined as problems occurring post-fill which had not occurred previously. The rate for filled cavities was 0.257 per cent, compared to the unfilled cavities at 0.224.

Rendered outer leaves should not present a problem regarding moisture penetration, provided that a good-quality render is used. As regards outer-leaf facing brickwork, there does appear to be a significant increase in its moisture resistance over a period of a few years following construction. The precise reason for this does not seem to be known, although suggested mechanisms include the leaching of salts from mortar and masonry and also the plugging of gaps via particulate pollution (not to be used as a case for continuing environmental emissions). Whatever the reason, this means that retrofitting CWI to existing brick houses is not likely to present a problem, especially in non-exposed locations.

There are two types of insulation material commonly used in retrofit CWI: chopped mineral fibre and EPS beads. The latter are now of 'bonded' type, which addresses the problem of settling and of loss of insulation when, for example, replacing windows or otherwise going through the wall. Since the beads touch only in certain places, there are voids for water to run down in between, rather than track across. The worst you might encounter with chopped fibre is a slight settling of material, especially beneath cills and wall-plates, causing minor gaps. Otherwise you should really not think twice about filling empty cavities since it will improve comfort levels, reduce response time and pay back in fuel saved generally within five years.

Urea formaldehyde foam can also be retrofitted into cavities although it is not recommended for exposed locations. Installation should be carried out according to the relevant British Standards (BS5617: 1985 and 5618:1985).

Note that in certain cases, with early cavity construction, you can find a reduced cavity width which may be unsuitable for filling. Such constructions are rare, although a reputable cavity wall insulation company should be able to spot them before starting unnecessary work. Look for a British Board of Agrément or an Irish Agrément Board certificate for chopped fibre or bead insulation. A CIGA (Cavity Insulation Guarantee Agency) guarantee will also give you peace of mind that the work has been carried out to a high standard.

Dry-Lining with Internal Insulation

In cases where there is no cavity to fill there are two options – either internal 'dry-lining' incorporating insulation, or the applying of an external insulation and render system. Dry-lining can involve fixing wooden battens to the internal surface and plasterboarding over. Insulation can then be incorporated to the depth of the battens. Alternatively, the same effect can be achieved by using a plasterboard/insulation laminate fixed to the wall with plaster 'dabs'. In either case, issues arise at openings where cills, for example, will need to be extended to cover the additional depth of the dry-lining. There may also be internal architectural features (especially in older, solid-walled houses) such as architraves, cornicing and mouldings which you do not want to compromise. For these reasons, in addition to the level of disruption caused, internal insulation may not be an attractive option in practice, unless very extensive works are being carried out. Another disadvantage is the slight reduction in room size, which may be significant for very small rooms. Advantages, however, include faster warm-up times due to the thermally lightweight internal surfaces and the fact that the process is relatively DIY-friendly.

External Wall Insulation

If cavities do not exist and internal insulation has been ruled out, external insulation is the only other option. It is also the most expensive and is a specialist operation requiring an experienced contractor. Again, issues arise at openings, with outer cills usually requiring extension. Rainwater goods will also require to be repositioned. External insulation is most commonly used in the extensive refurbishment of blocks of flats, for example, and is not generally considered for most single dwellings.

Timber-Frame Construction

The discussion so far has centred on masonry cavity construction. However, in the interests of even-handedness I should mention that timber-frame construction avoids a number of the problems encountered with masonry construction (*see* also the section on 'Timber Frame Construction' in Chapter 3). Insulation is incorporated within the depth of the structural timber studs. Thus a 100mm stud will allow the same amount of insulation as would a standard masonry cavity, fully-filled. Actually, with timber frame, no cavity is necessary, provided that an appropriate vapour-proof membrane is incorporated into the construction. In practice, for aesthetic reasons more than anything else, a brick skin tends to be built outside the timber frame. This provides a cavity that can be partially filled, thus increasing the insulation further.

ROOF INSULATION

'On the Plane'

Roof insulation has been most commonly placed on the floor of the roof space, in between the ceiling joists; this is sometimes described as 'on the plane' (of the ceiling). Insulation is easily accommodated here since it does not need to be retained and can be laid

to any depth required. Mineral fibre insulation is the type most commonly used as it complements both these conditions. However, there are other types suitable for insulation on the plane, such as cellulose fibre and natural wool. Roof insulation is also the most cost-effective type of fabric insulation; as we know, heat rises and it is most important to block off its main route of escape – upwards.

When insulation was first placed in the roof space, it was laid to a depth of about 50mm (2in). Gradually the recommended, Building Regulations minimal thickness has increased, to 100mm (mineral fibre equivalent), then 150mm and then 200mm; today, the EST standard for retrofits is a top-up to 270mm. However, at about 300mm the law of diminishing returns really starts to bite and it is unlikely that we shall see significant further increases beyond this level.

When the recommended depth of insulation reached the top of the ceiling joist (usually 150mm or maybe 100 in some older houses), it became good practice to cross-lay subsequent thicknesses (*see* the illustration on page 42). This has two clear advantages over simply laying a thicker layer of insulation between the joists. First, any gaps resulting from the lower layer not quite filling the space between the joists will be accounted for, and second, the relative thermal bridge of the ceiling joists themselves is addressed.

It is essential to ensure that any insulation on the plane of the ceiling at the eaves does not block ventilators located in the soffit. Ventilation is one means of inhibiting condensation, which could potentially damage roof timbers. There are proprietary ventilation trays which can be used for this purpose; these maintain an air gap above the insulation, allowing ventilation air to enter the roof space.

One obvious consequence of extending the insulation above the top of the joists is that it becomes difficult to use the roof space for storage, and it becomes hard to pick your way across the tops of the joists. For housing built to the new UK-wide thermal standards, you will certainly find it difficult to use the roof space for storage. With an existing house, if you want to use your roof space for storage, you should board over the joists with T+G chipboard in any case, for safety reasons. However, if you do this, the

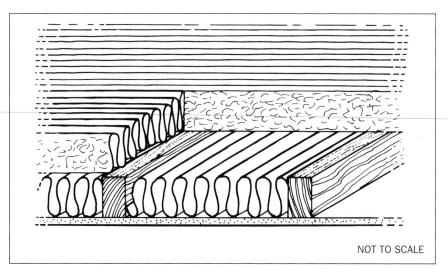

NOT TO SCALE

Loft insulation in the plane of the ceiling should be laid in two layers, the first to the depth of the joists and the rest cross-laid, to account for the relative cold bridge of the timber and any gaps in the first layer.

amount of insulation you can accommodate will be limited to the depth of the joists. In a newbuild situation, this may not satisfy the minimal thermal standards and you will need to incorporate some insulation between or beneath the rafters (*see below*). Alternatively, you might possibly be able to cross-batten the joists incorporating more insulation and board over, although this starts to get tricky.

More likely, I think, is that in new houses the roof space will cease to become a storage space. Either it will simply function as insulation to the rest of the house or, and possibly more likely, it will be included within the insulated envelope since it will otherwise be seen as wasted space. This raises other issues, as addressed below. In either case, extra dedicated storage may need to be provided elsewhere in the house.

'On the Pitch'

Insulation 'on the pitch', or between the sloping roof timbers (rafters), means that the roof space itself is part of the insulated volume of the building and is therefore included in heat-loss calculations. Where you wish to maximize internal space this can be a clear option and is sometimes referred to as 'room in the roof' construction. Equally, you may not wish to occupy the roof initially, but to leave the option open for the future. For an existing house, where the loft is being converted for living space and therefore comes

under Building Regulations requirements, this is addressed in Chapter 5. The following therefore refers to newbuild only.

One key difference between insulating on the pitch as opposed to on the plane is that it becomes more difficult to incorporate greater thicknesses of insulation, the rafters being generally only 100mm deep. Even with higher performance type insulation, this may not comply with the Building Regulations maximum permitted U-Value, especially since, unless you opt for warm-roof construction (*see* page 44) you will still need to leave a ventilation cavity between the insulation and the roof covering. One option is to use a plasterboard laminate with insulation bonded to it, fixed to the underside of the rafters (in all likelihood you would have used plasterboard in any case for the internal surface). The presence of this insulation will have the effect of reducing the head height, which you should take into account when dimensioning the space. Using the plasterboard/ insulation laminate will also address the issues of gaps in the insulation and the relative thermal bridge of the rafters.

Even when using a plasterboard/insulation laminate you should ensure that the insulation between the rafters fits as well as possible. However, another key difference between insulating on the pitch as opposed to on the plane is that rigid board insulation needs to be used since quilts will tend to slump. It

'Warmsqueez' (top) and 'Warmsark' (bottom) from Springvale EPS Ltd. 'Warmsqueez' is designed to fit exactly any given rafter separation, while 'Warmsark' is used in a warm-roof construction to avoid the need to ventilate above the rafters.

Xtratherm 'Polyiso' foil-backed insulation, shown in a ventilated pitched roof. The foil provides a low emissivity layer inhibiting radiative heat loss and also provides some water vapour resistance.

can be difficult to space the joists to exactly the same width each time. Equally, cutting the rigid boards is messy and inaccurate. Therefore rigid boards have tended to be used which are narrower than the rafter separation and held in place with nails driven into the side of the rafters. This is not a satisfactory procedure since gaps can result between the boards and the rafters. A proprietary system which overcomes this problem uses a rigid EPS board with a concertina-type action built-in (*see* the top illustration on page 43) allowing the product to be 'squeezed' into place and held by friction. Side pieces which can easily be broken off (or added) permit the easy use of the product where the rafter separation is not consistent.

There are also rigid board insulation products on the market which incorporate a foil backing, which acts as a low emissivity layer and will also provide a degree of water-vapour resistance. The illustration above shows foil-backed polyisocyanurate insulation in a ventilated pitched roof construction.

Warm-Roof Construction

In a warm-roof construction an additional insulation 'sarking' layer is laid above the rafters (*see* the bottom illustration on page 43). This prevents the outer surfaces of the rafters from becoming cold and thus inhibits condensation, while avoiding the need for a ventilation cavity above the between-rafter insulation. A breathable membrane is then laid on top of the battens shown, over which are placed counter-battens on which to lay the tiles or slates, in the normal way.

Flat Roofs

I would discourage the use of flat roofs in newbuild construction unless it is absolutely necessary, since they do not have the lifespan of a pitched roof (and require much more maintenance). The inevitability of rainwater lying on the roof and the potential for the materials to flex due to cycles of heating up and cooling down make water penetration much more likely in the medium to longer term, even with the best quality systems.

Where a flat roof exists you should give serious consideration to pitching over with a conventional roof. Although a pitched roof will almost certainly be more expensive, if the roof needs to be replaced anyway you need consider only the over-cost compared with the cost of a new flat roof. Whether or not the flat roof needs to be replaced, pitching over could provide additional useful space. This will require planning consent and, especially if it is to be used as habitable space, Building Control approval. Make sure that you can provide the required head height, taking into account the thickness of insulation

required on the pitch; this may necessitate the raising of the external walls. Ensure also that access can be provided, to Building Regulations requirements if necessary (*see* the section on loft conversions in Chapter 5 for more details). If installing a pitched roof is not feasible or is deemed too expensive, a flat roof can also be re-clad or over-clad with a proprietary system incorporating insulation, as the original roof will be likely to have only minimal insulation.

FLOOR INSULATION

In a concrete slab construction, insulation should be incorporated between the slab and the screed in order to avoid excessive thermal mass of the slab. An overall insulation thickness of 100mm would be a good specification, given that the heat loss to the ground is much less than to the air at the critical times (in winter, and particularly at night). Insulation should be laid in two layers, with all joints taped and staggered (*see* the illustration below), to prevent a cold bridge being created by concrete running down between the boards when the screed is being laid. It is especially important, with underfloor heating, to achieve the best possible floor insulation levels, in order to prevent heat-loss from the system.

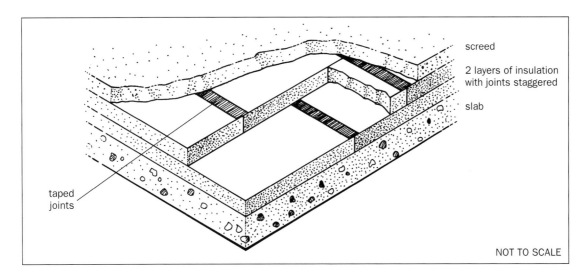

screed

2 layers of insulation with joints staggered

slab

taped joints

NOT TO SCALE

Solid concrete ground-floor insulation should be laid between the slab and screed in two layers, with all joints taped and staggered, to prevent possible cold bridging from concrete running down between the boards when the screed is being laid.

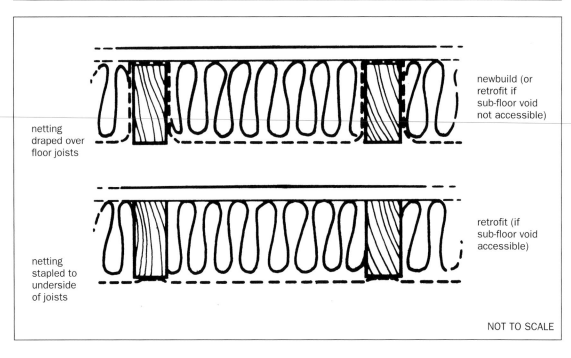

netting draped over floor joists

newbuild (or retrofit if sub-floor void not accessible)

netting stapled to underside of joists

retrofit (if sub-floor void accessible)

NOT TO SCALE

Insulation installed in a suspended timber floor, either new build or retrofit (when all floorboards are lifted) (top) or retrofitted where access can be gained to the sub-floor void (bottom).

A suspended timber ground floor (although not so common these days in newbuild) should be insulated between the floor joists using either an EPS 'squeeze' product, secured against the joist sides or a mineral fibre quilt supported on garden netting laid over the joists (*see* the illustration above). This technique can be used to retrofit insulation into an existing suspended timber floor, although it would involve pulling up the floorboards. Alternatively, if you were not planning this level of disruption and have access to the sub-floor void, the netting can be stapled to the underside of the joists and insulation retained in the same way.

This practice should not cause any problems with interstitial condensation on the timbers (contrary to what some would say), provided that the sub-floor void is ventilated, as it should be in any case. A suspended timber floor will always require vents in the external walls, just below the floor level, to ensure air flow through the void. The cold side of the timbers will be exposed to continuous air movement and thus will not be at risk of condensation forming. It is important that such vents are kept clear and not painted over or otherwise blocked. It is also most important with an existing older property that when building an extension which covers existing air vents you provide sufficient alternative paths for air flow through the sub-floor void.

CHAPTER 3

Methods of Construction

CONSTRUCTION TYPES AND MATERIALS

There are two basic types of construction used in house-building: masonry cavity construction is the most common, with timber frame becoming more and more popular. These are the types of construction you will be most likely to use and therefore are the ones looked at in most detail here. There are also a number of prefabricated and insulated formwork systems, examples of which are described below, which present certain advantages from an energy and environmental viewpoint. Earth-sheltering, green roofs and straw-bale construction are addressed briefly, although other methods such as rammed-earth construction, while interesting, were considered to be outside the scope of this book.

Timber-Frame Construction

Timber-frame construction is making something of a comeback, after having enjoyed a brief period of popularity in the post-energy crisis years of the 1970s to the 1980s. One reason for its wane was concern regarding the risk of interstitial condensation (water vapour condensing within the walls) which could have the potential to rot the structural timbers. A *World in Action* television programme highlighted this issue and precipitated a drop in the uptake of timber-frame construction across many areas of the United Kingdom. Some accused the programme of being biased and sensational – there was even talk afterwards of its having been sponsored from within the masonry construction industry, which would have seen timber frame as a serious threat. Even Granada, the company that broadcast the programme, were not convinced of the risk as another arm of the company continued to use a volumetric timber-frame system for their motorway service-station buildings.

However, the damage was done and it would take years for timber frame to recover from the setback. Interestingly, in Scotland, where the programme was not shown, timber frame has continued to thrive and now represents some 50 per cent of all new dwellings. In Northern Ireland, the Housing Executive (an umbrella social housing organization) built many timber frame houses in the 1970s but stopped almost overnight following the programme. A couple of decades later they opened up the brick outer leaves of a number of timber-frame houses and found the timbers to be in perfect condition. There should be no concern, either, regarding the weatherproofing properties of timber frame, if it can cope with the rigours of the Scottish and Northern Irish weather.

It should be acknowledged, however, that timber frame is less tolerant to defects in build quality than is masonry construction. This is another reason why timber frame has been slow to take off – lack of familiarity with the process did lead to some problems in the early days. The time taken to become familiar with the process also resulted in a failure to achieve the reduced on-site construction time which timber frame should allow and which was used as a key selling point.

Today, a large number of companies all over the United Kingdom and Ireland offer a range of services around timber-frame construction, from delivering the cut timbers for a self-builder, through to a complete design and construction package for the less hands-on (and many options in between).

Advantages of Timber Frame

Advantages
• self-build-friendly – varying degrees of hands-on involvement • high thermal performance for given overall wall thickness • shorter on-site times due to fast construction and elimination of wet trades • improved environmental profile, low embodied energy, natural resource

Thermal Performance

Timber frame has a number of advantages over masonry cavity construction. A greater thickness of insulation can be used for a given total wall thickness. This is due to the fact that the insulation is incorporated within the depth of the structural timber frame. Actually, with timber frame, no cavity is necessary, provided that an appropriate damp-proof membrane is incorporated into the construction. In practice and for aesthetic reasons more than anything else, a brick skin tends to be built outside the timber frame. This inherently provides a cavity, which can even be partially filled, thus increasing the insulation further.

A standard 100mm masonry cavity will usually have a 100mm masonry leaf (brick or block) on either side, totalling a little over 300mm when render/plaster layers are included. Typically, in recent times, this would have included no more than 60mm of partial-fill cavity insulation. A 100mm timber frame stud, with insulation incorporated within the frame, can accommodate 90–100mm insulation. Assuming a 50mm weatherproofing cavity and 100mm facing brick outer leaf, the total wall thickness would be around 250mm – giving a thinner wall with improved thermal performance (*see* the illustration on page 49).

Alternatively, you could use a 150mm stud (insulated) with 50mm cavity and 100mm facing brick outer leaf, or 100m stud (insulated) with 100mm cavity containing 50mm insulation and 100mm facing brick outer leaf (*see* the illustration on page 49). Both these options give a total 300mm thick wall (similar to masonry cavity under current normal practice), although with greatly improved thermal performance.

Shorter On-Site Times

Timber-frame construction should be much quicker than masonry cavity construction, especially if all the timbers are cut off-site under quality-controlled factory conditions and expertly put together on site (*see* 'Care with Timber Frame' on page 50). The absence of wet trades (such as plastering) internally means no drying-out time – again making for quicker construction. Shorter on-site time means a shorter total build programme, which can yield financial benefits, for example, in terms of reduced loan periods.

Embodied Energy and Wider Environmental Benefits

Timber is a natural material and requires less energy to process it into construction materials than do masonry materials, metals or plastics, for example. While growing, timber absorbs carbon dioxide and, while in use, stores the carbon in its cellulose fibres. Even if it is ultimately incinerated, timber is carbon-neutral overall, since the carbon it releases is equal only to that which it has already absorbed. Finally, the recyclability of timber means that it is capable of being reused rather than simply disposed of and, being a renewable material, it also addresses the issue of resource depletion (*see* the sections on 'Embodied Energy' and 'Life-Cycle Assessment' in Chapter 11).

Choice of Outer Skin

Brick Skin

As mentioned above, timber-frame construction tends to have a brick skin built outside the timber structure. This is really an aesthetic choice, or perhaps a psychological one, as the house would then be indistinguishable, to most people, from a masonry structure. Brick-built houses tend to be preferred since they are seen as being more durable, more permanent, more saleable – above all, perhaps, more conventional. The construction industry is very conservative, mirroring our own risk-aversion when

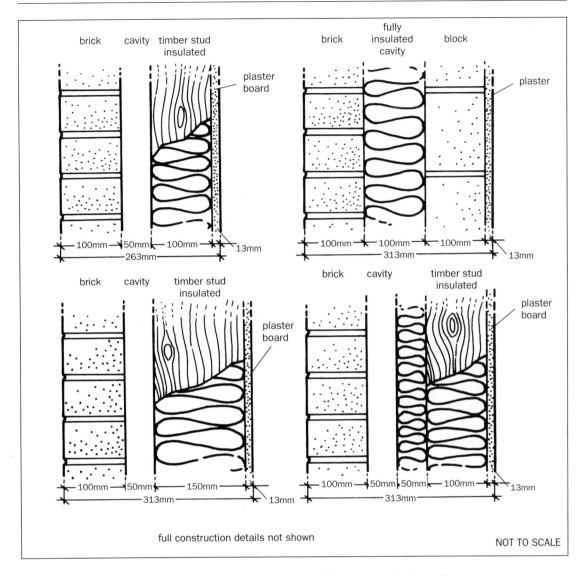

brick   cavity   timber stud insulated

plaster board

brick   fully insulated cavity   block

plaster

— 100mm — 50mm — 100mm — 13mm
— 263mm —

— 100mm — 100mm — 100mm — 13mm
— 313mm —

brick   cavity   timber stud insulated

plaster board

brick   cavity   timber stud insulated

plaster board

— 100mm — 50mm — 150mm — 13mm
— 313mm —

— 100mm — 50mm — 50mm — 100mm — 13mm
— 313mm —

full construction details not shown

NOT TO SCALE

Timber frame versus masonry cavity construction: a thinner wall for the same thickness of insulation or more insulation for the same wall thickness.

making the biggest purchase most of us will ever make. However, as mentioned previously, timber frame can be just as durable as masonry.

It is really not necessary to include a brick skin, even to give a reassuringly masonry-like appearance. The brick skin adds material and labour costs and extends on-site times. It does provide the water-resistance of a cavity and also allows the inclusion of additional insulation in that cavity. However, the correct specification of damp-proof membranes (DPM) will address the water issue, while thicker studs allow for increased insulation more readily and cheaply than would a brick skin and cavity.

Alternatives to Brick Skin
Instead of going to the expense of a brick skin, you can simply use an exterior grade building board, with expanded metal mesh and render applied to the

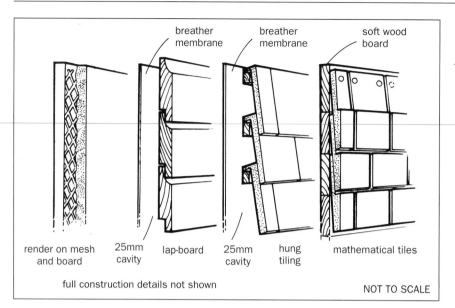

breather membrane breather membrane soft wood board

render on mesh and board | 25mm cavity | lap-board | 25mm cavity | hung tiling | mathematical tiles

full construction details not shown

NOT TO SCALE

Types of external cladding suitable for timber frame construction.

outside. This gives an appearance indistinguishable from that of rendered masonry and just as weatherproof (you can use a couple of courses of brickwork at the foot of the wall to raise the board up off the ground). Alternatively, especially if this is the vernacular style in your area, you could use 'weatherboarding' – lap-board or vertically hung tiling. If you must have the look of brickwork, you could use 'mathematical tiles', a centuries-old technique which has been commonly used in parts of the south of England and gives the appearance of brickwork (*see* the illustration above).

One of the most ridiculous arguments I have heard in favour of a brick skin for timber-frame construction is that, with other options, burglars could gain access through the walls. But would not it still be easier for them to take the traditional route through the doors or windows? Another argument I have encountered is that a colliding vehicle would do more damage to a timber-frame house. This is not necessarily borne out by experience (yes, people have been unfortunate enough to have had that experience) – in one case I heard of, the whole timber structure shifted a couple of inches on impact with a lorry and was later rejigged into position. It was estimated that a masonry structure incurring the same impact would have suffered partial collapse, requiring at least some rebuilding.

Care with Timber Frame

Setting Out

One important factor to be considered with timber-frame construction (and with prefabricated panels too) is that the setting out of the slab needs to be done very accurately. If your levels and angles are not quite right at the base, this can lead to significant gaps at the second-storey eaves level. In masonry construction this would not be serious or even noticeable and could be taken up with wider mortar joints or even additional masonry (although that would indicate a serious gap). However, with timber frame any gaps could compromise the structural integrity of the building. Filling a gap between pre-cut timbers would be unsatisfactory, while cutting a new timber might be little better – the structural integrity relies on clean, square-cut timbers at right angles to each other. Timbers should not need to be cut on site – all cuts should be done precisely under factory quality-controlled conditions. With care in the setting out of the base, the accurately sized timbers will fit together correctly to give a rigid frame with all uprights plumb and angles square.

It is amazing that in many cases in this part of the world hammers are still used for timber-frame construction when nail-guns are available. For speed and accuracy, use a nail-gun to fix timbers. Be sure to follow the manufacturer's/supplier's safety instructions closely. Accidents happen all the time with hammers, although the consequences do not tend to be very severe. A nail-gun, not used correctly, could inflict much more serious injuries.

Interstitial Condensation –
the Five Times Rule

The problems which can potentially arise with timber-frame construction due to moisture condensing on the timbers have been raised above. One further rule should be followed in order to reduce the risk of this happening – known as the 'five times rule'. Provided that the vapour resistance of the layers on the warm side of the insulation (for instance, the plasterboard and vapour-control layer) is at least five times that of the layers on the cold side (for example, sheathing and breather membrane), it should be possible to ensure that moisture is always carried away out of the structure rather than towards the interior. You may find figures quoted for materials in terms of 'vapour diffusivity', in which case the reverse applies – the vapour diffusivity of the cold-side layers must be at least five times that of the warm-side layers. Even if the five times rule is not met, interstitial condensation will not necessarily occur, although more accurate calculations will be needed.

For a comprehensive treatment of all the energy-related issues in timber frame and much more, you need look no further than to the Timber Research and Development Association's (TRADA) book *Energy Efficient Housing – A Timber Frame Approach* (*see* 'Useful Contacts', section 3).

The Segal Method

Pioneered by Walter Segal, this method, based on traditional timber-frame techniques, has been modified and updated to make use of the standard materials available from most builders merchants today. The lightweight method of construction enables people of all ages and abilities to build together, with no previous building or DIY experience. As with other timber-frame methods, the dry method of construction eliminates the need for wet trades such as bricklaying and plastering. The result is an adaptable, environmentally friendly building, designed to the individual requirements of the self-builder.

Advantages of the Segal Method

- simple to build and adaptable to changing family requirements
- individually designed to the occupant's specific requirements
- elimination of specialist wet trades
- suitable for steeply-sloping sites or poor-quality ground conditions
- minimum damage to the surrounding landscape
- environmentally friendly materials
- very energy efficient
- thirty-year defects liability warranty

For more information, contact the Walter Segal Self Build Trust (*see* 'Useful Contacts', section 16).

Steel-frame Construction

Lightweight steel-frame construction is relatively common in North America but has not really caught on here. Its advantages are essentially similar to those of timber-frame construction, that is, reduced on-site times, ability to incorporate high levels of insulation and high strength to weight ratio. Steel does not have the environmental credentials of timber, but it is highly recyclable. Steel-frame systems are more common in non-domestic construction, although they can certainly be used in housing. A conventional appearance is perfectly achievable, as with timber frame, by use of a brick skin (or rendered board or mathematical tiles). However, the advantages of a steel-frame system may be more easily exploited where a non-traditional look or approach is sought, for example, by the use of a metal cladding external leaf. Note that in this case, internal dry-lining will be required to overcome cold-bridging of the frame and the cladding.

MASONRY CAVITY CONSTRUCTION

Today masonry construction generally consists of two masonry leaves (block inner leaf and facing brick or rendered block outer leaf) with a cavity in between. Cavities in masonry construction in the UK have been standardized at 100mm for some years, having been increased from around 80mm in the 1980s. However, in the light of the new Building Regulations thermal requirements, cavity width may well increase again.

The Cavity

Masonry cavities have generally been only partially filled, thus restricting the thickness of the insulation that can be accommodated. There is a reason for cavities not being fully filled. They were introduced initially as a barrier to moisture reaching the internal surfaces from outside, a common problem in older solid-walled houses. Any rainwater penetrating the outer leaf would either remain on its inner surface and evaporate away, or would be shed down that surface. The cavity also improved the thermal performance of the wall by providing a break to the conduction of heat out of the building through the wall and via the insulating affect of the air itself. It was then realized that the thermal performance could be improved yet further by including an insulating material in the cavity. However, a gap was maintained between the insulation and the outer leaf to prevent moisture from tracking across the insulation to the inner leaf.

Forthcoming regulations will make it increasingly difficult to meet thermal requirements with the standard masonry cavity construction. Something will need to change – cavities must be fully filled, different masonry materials used or the cavity width increased, or combinations of any or all three of these.

Full Cavity Insulation

There are certain conditions under which it is not necessary to preserve a clear cavity. First, I know of architects who have routinely specified 100mm of glass fibre batt insulation in a 100mm cavity for the past twenty years or so without any problems – even in Northern Ireland. The risk of moisture penetrating the outer leaf in the first place depends initially on whether the building is on a site exposed to the elements – a sheltered site presents a much lower risk. Furthermore, if the outer leaf is rendered, this presents a very effective barrier to rain penetration (*see* the section on render, below) and cavities can be fully filled with confidence, even in more exposed

locations with a high driving-rain index. Even facing brick, which allows rain penetration when new, has been found to develop imperviousness after a couple of years, although the precise reasons do not seem to be known. In recent years full cavity insulation systems have been designed specifically to overcome fears of moisture penetration, for example, by using carefully detailed, tongued-and-grooved EPS boards (*see* Chapter 2 on 'Insulation').

(It should be noted that the National House Building Council [NHBC] may require a clear cavity to be maintained. This requirement, and any similar that may have implications for building insurance, should be carefully confirmed before you commit to full cavity insulation.)

Choice of Materials

The inner leaf these days is generally of concrete block since it is cheap. And since the wall will be plastered (or dry-lined) on the internal surface in any case, the inner leaf surface finish is unimportant. Most often, medium or dense blocks are used, although lightweight AAC (autoclaved aerated concrete) blocks (*see* page 53) will become more common as thermal requirements increase – and the cost of the AAC blocks will come down. Note that conventional concrete block is not airtight and can contribute to high infiltration levels if the inner surface is not well sealed (*see* the section on air-tightness in Chapter 8).

The outer leaf may be of facing brick or rendered block, again currently usually medium or dense, although AAC block is an alternative. In conservation areas local stone may be used as the outer leaf, although more likely it will be laid as a cladding layer to an outer block leaf. As an alternative to render, several other cladding systems may be used, such as metal panel, timber lap-board or vertical hung tiling, although these would be more common with timber-frame construction.

Fair-faced block can be used as an option for inner and/or outer leaf where plaster/render or dry-lining is not required, although this would be unusual in a dwelling.

A Word About Render

In applying external render to a block wall (or to

'Quinn-lite' AAC block, from Quinn Manufacturing Ltd, can be cut to size accurately by using a special handsaw.

mesh on building board in timber-frame construction) it is essential to use a good quality render, ideally with a significant lime content. Render should act as an excellent weatherproofing layer and allow extra confidence in fully filling cavities, even in exposed locations. Incorrectly mixed renders, however, can actually result, when dry, in a porous layer which will act like a sponge and soak the outer leaf. The inclusion of lime (a traditional method – our forefathers did not use it for hundreds of years for nothing) helps to fill the gaps in the render matrix and seal the layer. Importantly, lime also allows the render layer to breathe, permitting any moisture already in the masonry to escape. Lime has been coming back into fashion lately as builders rediscover its flexibility and weatherproofing properties, and because it is a natural product. Look in local directories for suppliers of lime mortar and render materials.

AAC Blocks

The alternative materials option to improving the thermal properties of masonry cavity construction may be addressed by using AAC blocks. These are made to the same dimensions and strength standards as conventional medium and dense blocks but have the advantage of better insulating properties, as well as being lighter and thus easier to handle on site. This latter advantage should not be underestimated. In the USA these days it is practically impossible to lift anything on site without a mechanical grab, such is the situation regarding litigation surrounding injuries in the construction industry.

As is often the case, the idea is not new, having been developed in Sweden in the 1920s. The inclusion of aluminium filings with the concrete mix causes a chemical reaction with the lime, dispersing tiny air bubbles throughout the material. Steam-curing in an autoclave causes a further reaction which gives the blocks greater strength. Some have questioned the strength of AAC blocks, both in terms of withstanding loads and also allowing chasing to accommodate services. However, the strength to weight ratio of AAC blocks is greater than conventional blocks and there is no evidence that chasing presents a problem when done in accordance with manufacturer's recommendations (*see below*). The blocks can be easily and accurately cut to size if needed by simply using a special saw (*see* the illustration on page 53).

There are certain recommendations that should be followed when using AAC blocks. Masonry hammer drills should not be used, similarly timber nails (flat-sided), expanding metal fixings and vertical twist ties since these may crack or damage the blocks. Chasing should be carried out by using an angle grinder and a purpose-made, sharp hand pick (similar to those used by geologists) rather than a drill (*see* the illustration below).

In addition, contrary to normal practice with concrete blocks, the AAC surface should not be saturated before rendering or plastering. Care should be taken that mortars are of the correct strength (again, suppliers will advise). An overly strong mortar can restrain the blocks, leading to cracking in severe cases. However, as the structure relies upon the compressive strength of the blocks, expert opinion suggests that this issue is probably not too serious from a structural point of view.

Wider Cavities

The third option, and the one which allows the greatest improvement on current norms, is for the cavity width to be increased. This may introduce some structural issues, especially around openings and at junctions. Cills and lintels will need to be deeper and window reveals will also be deeper, either internally or externally, or both. However, cavities up to 300mm should be structurally feasible – if you can

'Quinn-lite' AAC block, from Quinn Manufacturing Ltd, must be 'chased' by using a special hand-pick.

find the wall ties. In some Scandinavian countries, where the colder climate has encouraged a greater focus on fabric insulation, wider cavities are commonplace and longer wall ties are readily available. These tend to be plastic and are thus corrosion-free, although they are also expensive and are required in greater number to provide the structural stability compared with stainless steel. Steel wall ties are readily available from the leading UK-based companies suitable for cavities up to 140mm as standard; longer ties can be provided in consultation with the manufacturers.

Again, a board slightly narrower than the cavity width can be placed on top of the insulation as you go up, to catch any mortar drops and prevent them from falling on the wall ties or gathering at the foot of the cavity. One builder I know routinely leaves out a half-brick at the bottom of the wall at either end. This is to allow a scaffold pole to be pulled through to clear the foot of the cavity, the missing half-bricks are then inserted and the cavity closed. This practice is only feasible with blown-fibre or bonded-bead cavity insulation, installed after the walls have been built.

If a clear cavity is to be maintained and yet more insulation is required than a conventional 100mm cavity can accommodate, a wider cavity may be the only answer. For example, a 140mm cavity would allow for 100mm of insulation with a 40mm clear cavity. Wider cavities also mean a slight reduction in the internal floor area for a given building footprint, or, alternatively, a slightly larger footprint for a given internal floor area. Wider cavities also lead to a greater wall thickness overall, which will have an impact on the appearance of the building. In a rural setting, for example, this could mimic the appearance of an old, solid-walled cottage, which might be desirable. However, if thicker walls are not part of your aesthetic, then the AAC block option (or timber-frame construction) might be preferable.

OTHER CONSTRUCTION TYPES

Insulated Concrete Formwork

Insulated concrete formwork (ICF) is the generic term describing a number of proprietary building systems which all have a common feature – they use rigid insulation boards (such as high-density EPS) as the formwork for poured concrete, which provides the structural element of the building. The EPS is held in place by a plastic framework, providing rigid formwork while the concrete is poured (*see* the illustration on page 56). After the concrete has set, the EPS provides a double layer of insulation with no thermal bridging. A similar process can be used for intermediate floors and flat roofs.

The internal surface can be finished with plasterboard fixed on dabs to the EPS. The external surface may be formed of reinforced render applied to a mesh, or steel cladding, or hung tiles, for example. The key advantages of this type of system are reduced on-site times and high insulation levels. The lightweight internal surfaces mean faster warm-up times and make the system especially suitable for dwellings which are not occupied during the day or are only intermittently occupied.

The continuous concrete core makes for high strength and wind-loading properties – steel reinforcing rods can be used to provide additional strength if required. This type of construction is more common in other parts of Europe and in North America than here, although it is beginning to catch on as the legal minimum thermal requirements become tighter.

Prefabricated Systems

The key advantages of prefabricated systems are reduced on-site construction times and improved build quality. Build quality should be high since quality control can be carried out in factory conditions, while on-site waste is reduced since panels are made-to-measure. On-site supervision is required only while the panels are being erected, although this typically requires a crane, which introduces further costs.

Structural Insulated Panel Systems (SIPS)

Structural insulated panel systems (SIPS) are just what they sound like – composite or laminar panels which provide the structural element of the building and have insulation in-built. Typically, panels comprise inner and outer sheets of oriented strand board (OSB) or similar, with rigid EPS or urethane insulation bonded to the internal surfaces. OSB is

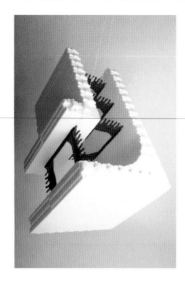

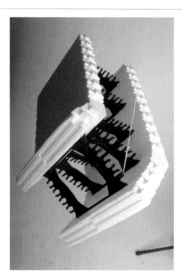

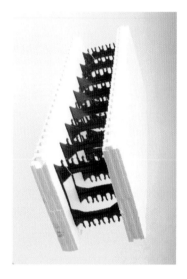

Insulated concrete formwork (ICF) from Amvic Inc. (British agents: Springvale EPS). EPS boards act as formwork for the poured concrete core and as insulation in the finished element.

formed from slivers of low-grade or waste timber, contained within an adhesive matrix and formed into boards under high pressure. The resulting material is strong, cheap and relatively environmentally friendly (*see* below).

Panels incorporating insulation prevent the latter from being incorrectly installed, which can easily happen with masonry construction. In addition, modern jointing techniques can provide an extremely airtight structure (thus further improving energy efficiency) which is particularly required if a mechanical ventilation heat recovery system is proposed (*see* the section on 'Mechanical Ventilation' in Chapter 8). Airtightness will also be one element of compliance

with the forthcoming amendments to the UK-wide Building Regulations. Prefabricated systems using OSB timber panels can also be environmentally-friendly, where the timber comes from sustainable or waste wood sources, non-toxic adhesives are used and the insulation is blown with zero ozone-depletion potential (ODP) gases.

SIP systems may be used to form floors and roofs, as well as walls. The illustration (*see* page 57) shows an example of a SIP system, consisting of OSB with a zero ODP rigid urethane core, which achieves a maximum U-value of $0.2W/m^2K$, easily bettering the new base-case Building Regulations requirements for walls.

Kingspan's 'TEK' structural insulated panel system (SIPS), shown as a wall element and also (overleaf) being installed as a roof panel.

Panelized Roofing Systems

These are less common than prefabricated wall systems, due in part to the extremely cost-competitive roof truss-rafter market, itself a form of offsite prefabrication. However, with room-in-the-roof construction becoming more popular, panelized systems may start to come to the fore, being quick and easy to install and providing good levels of technical performance, including energy efficiency.

Earth-Sheltered Houses

The term earth-sheltered (or 'earth-bermed') houses describes those built into the side of a hill or located partly underground. The reason for putting a house underground usually has less to do with energy efficiency than planning considerations, for example, in a sensitive area or where a view might otherwise be blocked. I know of one example where the owners of a cliff-top house with spectacular sea views built themselves an earth-sheltered house at the bottom of the garden (into the cliff). In this way they still benefited from the same views (or better) as from the old house while not devaluing the market potential of the latter. Strangely, planning authorities have tended not to favour earth-sheltered housing even when these factors have been cited – perhaps due to an in-built conservatism and general unease with anything innovative and unconventional. However, it may be hoped that this starting to change, as environmental issues become more important.

In energy terms, an earth-sheltered house can be favourable as it uses the insulating properties of the earth itself. About a metre underground the temperature hardly varies throughout the year and is always higher, on an average annual basis, than that outside. Of course, there will be other issues to be addressed: how to support, structurally, a mass of earth; how to 'tank' (waterproof) the structure against water ingress; and how to provide sunlight/daylight for a

building which is, in part at least, underground. For more information, contact the British Earth Sheltering Association (BESA); *see* 'Useful Contacts', section 3.

Structure/Tanking
The roof structure will tend to be concrete, either *in situ* cast or pre-cast slab, to provide the mechanical strength needed to support the earth above. Walls

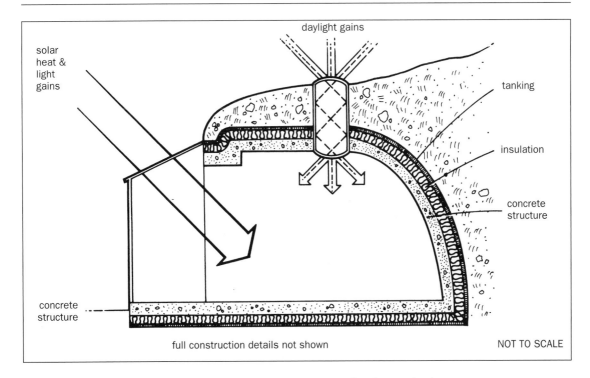

solar heat & light gains

daylight gains

tanking

insulation

concrete structure

concrete structure

full construction details not shown

NOT TO SCALE

Schematic of an earth-bermed structure, indicating the importance of tanking and soil retention as well as the options for providing daylight to the interior of the dwelling.

will need to be retaining walls at the sides bounding the earth. Tanking will need to be provided, not only to the ground floor but to the walls and the roof, to prevent water ingress (*see* the illustration above). This is an extremely important and tricky procedure and is not recommended for the self-builder unless you are previously experienced or under expert guidance. Instead, there are specialist companies that can carry out this work on your behalf – it will be money well-spent and will allow you to proceed with confidence on other parts of the build.

Daylighting/Solar Gains
Where the opportunity arises, an earth-sheltered house should be built into the side of a south-facing slope. This will provide insulation to the north façade and, depending on the geometry of the site, at least parts of the east and the west façade too. The south façade, however, will be opened up to enable solar gains, in the form of passive solar heating and daylighting. The south façade can be quite highly

glazed, while maintaining the Building Regulations requirements for glazing area in relation to floor area, as the other façades are likely to have only minimal glazing (*see* the illustration above).

There is an issue in getting daylight into areas on the north side of the building. While this can be done with roof lights, in the form of light wells capped with glass or plastic domes (*see* the illustration above), it becomes more important than ever to locate the main daytime living areas on the south façade – a key element of passive solar design – while allowing storage, circulation and buffer areas to be located to the north. There is also the matter of providing ventilation to the back of the dwelling. In consequence you are much more likely to opt for a linear plan form rather than a compact one.

In the example cited above, where the building addressed spectacular sea views to the north, an area was excavated behind the south side of the plan to create a courtyard. This provided a suntrap and allowed south-facing windows to be incorporated, for

59

daylight and solar gains. Note that high-performance glazing, for example, double- or triple-glazed, low-E with inert gas fill, would be highly recommended if one were considering large areas of north-facing windows (*see* section on 'Glazing' in Chapter 4).

Green Roofs

If you do not wish to go all the way down the road of earth-sheltering, how about a halfway house – a 'green roof'? The Australian Aboriginals have a saying, which translates something like 'touch the earth lightly' – in other words, try not to have a lasting detrimental impact upon the earth or the way it looks. It is hard to see how even the most environmentally-friendly construction could achieve this. However, a green roof allows you to do two things to redress the balance. First, it provides a habitat for nature and helps to put back into the site some of its biodiversity. Second, it softens the visual impact of the building on the surroundings, especially if it is in an otherwise undeveloped setting.

'Green roofs' are sometimes referred to as 'grass roofs', although, in fact, mosses known as sedums often form the top 'green' layer. Green-roof construction is another specialist operation and not recommended for the self-builder unless already experienced or under expert instruction. The key, as with all roof types, is weatherproofing. Given that, as with earth-sheltering, you are not merely deflecting water off the top surface but encouraging it to be absorbed, your waterproof tanking layers must be excellent and your structure capable of supporting the mass of the roof, especially when it is saturated. A schematic of a typical green roof construction is shown in the illustration below.

The water drainage/retention layer must be carefully designed according to the roof area and the degree of slope to avoid the roots becoming waterlogged while also preventing them from drying out and killing the plants. The separation layer allows for differential movement between the planted layer and the waterproofing below, while the root barrier layer is important to prevent penetration of the waterproofing layers. The insulation must be capable of withstanding water and the pressure from the soil. Finally, the vapour barrier must be well-bonded to the roof deck.

Straw-Bale Construction

Straw has been used as a building material for centuries, in thatched roofing and as a binder in cob construction. In recent years, however, the use of

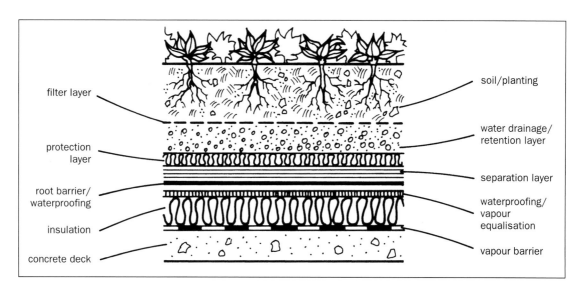

Schematic of a 'green-roof' construction. (Adapted from Brenda and Robert Vale, see 'Useful Contacts', section 2)

straw bales as a walling material has begun to gain a following. Straw-bale construction is not a new idea, having its origins in late nineteenth-century Nebraska, following the introduction of the baling machine. A shortage of timber and the plentiful availability of straw bales led to the latter being used for building. The straw bale houses were usually somewhat makeshift and were seen as temporary accommodation until the occupants could afford a 'real' house. However, they were comfortable and surprisingly durable and, in many cases, became permanent.

For smaller, single-storey structures, the bales can form supporting walls, held together with willow or steel pegs. More usually, in larger structures, the bales are used as infill material, for example, in a post-and-beam, timber-frame construction. Inner and outer walls can be plastered with a lime render, which is flexible and allows the walls to breathe. Bales can be shaped *in situ* with a chainsaw, which can also be used to chase tracks for services. Straw-bale construction provides a high level of insulation and can keep the building warm in winter as well as cool in summer. Straw, being essentially a waste product, also has a very low embodied energy and reduces the need for man-made (and even other natural) construction materials.

There are many different kinds of straw, with varying properties, not all of which are suitable for use in construction. It is also important to ensure that the straw is completely dry and that the bales have the correct density. Although very DIY-friendly, straw-bale construction requires specialist expert guidance. Two key issues that might be of concern are those of attack by fire and by pests. However, the density of the tightly-packed bales means that neither fire nor rodents can easily gain access. Borax-based fire treatment may also kill most potential insects, while rendered surfaces provide good fire protection. Again, expert advice should be sought for confirmation on these issues.

Mortgages may be hard to find since surveyors are often unable to put a value on straw-bale buildings, meaning that the lenders have no basis for their loan. Insurance may prove problematic for similar reasons, although by now there should be a sufficient number of straw-bale buildings both here and in the USA to prove that they can be structurally sound and resistant to fire.

There are many publications on the subject of straw-bale construction as well as organizations providing information and guidance. Contact the British Strawbale Building Association (*see* 'Useful Contacts', section 3) for more information and details of local experts.

Membranes

There are many places where membranes are used in construction. Two of the most important of these are damp-proof membranes in walls and floors and breathable membranes in timber-frame and roof construction.

Damp-Proof Membranes (DPM)

A DPM is essential to prevent the ingress of moisture to the inner surface of the building fabric, for example, beneath solid concrete floors.

Damp-Proof Courses (DPC)

Where laid at the foot of a masonry or timber wall, the term 'DPC' is used. The course is essential to prevent the degradation of the fabric and unsightly dampness and possible mould growth. It also helps to conserve energy since more heat will be lost through a wet element and through the drying out of that element.

Vapour Control (Breathable) Membrane

Breathable water-proof membranes are an essential element of roof and timber-frame construction. There are a number of proprietary products on the market, one of which is shown in the illustration on page 62. The breathability of the product allows moisture to be lost from the structure rather than gathering as condensation and causing problems. In extreme cases, interstitial condensation (as it is called) can lead to the degradation of the building fabric. It is relatively easy to ensure that the membrane is breathable, by simply making it perforated. However, it is essential that the product also has the claimed waterproofing properties otherwise it will simply allow water in instead of out. Ask the manufacturers/suppliers for evidence of recent, independent, rigorous testing showing the properties of the product.

'Protect VP400' breathable, water-proof membrane from Richmond Building Products Ltd, shown in place on a pitched roof under construction.

SUPER-INSULATED HOUSES

This term is used to describe dwellings with much higher than normal amounts of insulation. It can also be used to describe dwellings which are so well insulated that they hardly, if ever, need artificial heating at all. If you can get the heat loss rate down far enough, by using high levels of insulation, you may find that the internal heat gains from the occupants, lighting, other equipment, solar gains and so on can be suffi-

cient to maintain comfort temperatures, certainly at most times of the year. As a rough rule of thumb, this point is reached when overall fabric U-values are below $0.2\mathrm{W/m^2K}$. If you can save altogether on the capital cost of a heating system, as well as the running costs, that improves considerably the economics of extra insulation.

Of course, you do not want to take a chance on this and find out during your first winter that you really did need a heating system after all. It would prove costly and disruptive to retrofit heating after your house is finished. Therefore, if you are going to take this approach, it is well worth first doing some detailed calculations or getting an energy consultant to do so for you. A consultant may be able to use a computer model which can simulate the effect of internal and solar heat gains on internal temperatures, using averaged weather data (such as solar radiation levels and outside temperatures). By building up a mathematical/thermal model of your house, the thermal behaviour of the building fabric can be taken into account and the total heat gains and losses calculated.

At the very least, you should use a U-value calculator (*see* Chapter 2) to estimate the overall U-value of your fabric. The value of $0.2W/m^2K$ should not be taken as an absolute figure; it will vary according to other factors such as the level of internal and solar gains, the desired internal comfort temperature, the location and the exposure level of the site. However, $0.2W/m^2K$ is a useful marker to put down. Your calculations may show the need (or you may feel it prudent) to install a small amount of heating input for times during the mid-heating season – although good design for wintertime passive solar gains will reduce such need (see the section on 'Passive Solar Design' in Chapter 1). In this case you might consider a number of options: first, if your house has a large, central, open-plan area, such as a kitchen/family room or large hall, you may find that a source of heating located here will provide sufficient heat for most occasions. A wood-burning stove might suffice, the advantages of which are that a sustainable fuel is used with no permanent ventilation heat loss route. A source of heating downstairs, especially in an area open to a stairwell, may enable the upper floor areas to be heated too. Normally, such an arrangement would probably not be sufficient to heat the upper floor, but remember that we are talking super-insulation here. Another option would be to install very-low-rated electrical resistance heaters, such as greenhouse heaters. Usually I would not advocate electric heating – it is generally counter-indicative of energy efficiency and environmental friendliness and is not cost-effective in normal circumstances. However, when your heat loss rate is very low and you

require a boost only occasionally, this might be a viable option – and if you have renewables-generated electricity on site (or subscribe to a 'green' tariff), not environmentally unfriendly either. Alternatively, if you are installing a mechanical ventilation with heat recovery (MVHR) system, a small electric heater in the supply air ducting might suffice.

Example Fabric Specification for Super-Insulated Houses

The first point to note is that for an overall super-insulated fabric you need to pay particular attention to the glazing. Windows and doors will always be the weak points thermally and never more so than in a super-insulated dwelling. While for an energy-efficient version of a 'normal' house I would recommend double glazing with a 16mm gap and low-E coating as minimal, for a super-insulated house you should really consider going much further. In a house built to recent Building Regulations standards, even with a fairly low glazing ratio (ratio of window to wall area) you can lose as much heat from your windows as from the whole of the rest of the fabric put together. With a super-insulated fabric, the proportion of the heat lost from glazing could be even higher.

Low-E coated double glazing with a 16mm gap in a wooden frame will give you a glazing U-value of $1.8–2.0W/m^2K$, depending on the type of low-E glazing (*see* the section on 'Glazing' in Chapter 4). However, this will be around ten times the overall target U-value, requiring the walls, floors and roofs to achieve even higher levels. Therefore, it is really worth considering something like triple glazing, with low-E coating and inert gas fill, which would give you a U-value (in a wooden frame) of $1.3–1.5W/m^2K$ (*see* the table in the glazing section in Chapter 4 for a comparison of more options).

Let us take as a starting point a wall U-value of $0.2W/m^2K$ (the new UK-wide Building Regulations base case is $0.35W/m^2K$). With a roof U-value of $0.13W/m^2K$ (base case is $0.25W/m^2K$) and floor U-value of $0.22W/m^2K$ (base case $0.25W/m^2K$) this should give you an overall opaque fabric U-value of around $0.19W/m^2K$, depending on the ratio of wall to roof/floor area (I have assumed a two-storey, detached house of plan area 8m × 6m with roof insulation on the plane). Taking into account glazing

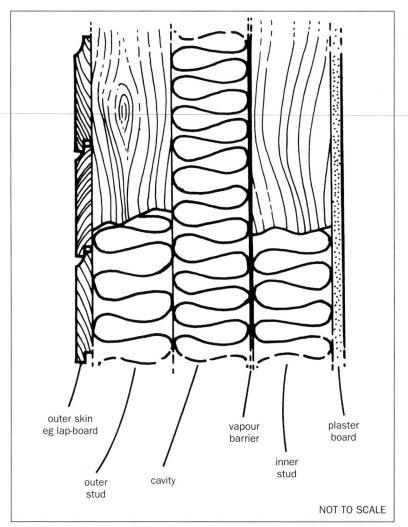

Schematic of a double timber stud construction. (With acknowledgement to Brenda and Robert Vale and the Canadian R-2000 programme. See 'Useful Contacts', section 2)

outer skin
eg lap-board

vapour
barrier

plaster
board

inner
stud

outer
stud

cavity

NOT TO SCALE

with a U-value of 1.5W/m²K and a glazing ratio of 15 per cent, the overall U-value (including glazing) would still be around 0.3W/m²K. With a wall U-value of 0.1W/m²K, the overall U-value, with the same glazing U-value and ratio, would be about 0.25W/m²K. Substituting glazing with a U-value of 1.1W/m²K would bring you down to around 0.22W/m²K. You can see how hard it becomes to make further improvements.

Achieving this level of wall U-value could be done with masonry cavity construction, but would take combinations of AAC block, wider cavities, full-cavity insulation and probably dry-lining too. Alternatively, how about a double timber stud? This approach has been pioneered in Canada (where timber frame is second nature) and has the advantage not only of reducing greatly the cold bridge of the timber studs but also allows much more insulation to be put in. The studs are separated by a gap and connected structurally at the top and bottom, forming the only timber cold bridge. Meanwhile, insulation can be incorporated in the outer stud and in the inner stud – and in the gap in between (*see* the illustration above).

CHAPTER 4

Windows and Doors

Windows and doors ('openings') will always be the thermal weak point in your house, even when they are closed (*see* Chapter 8). With current fabric U-values and a normal 10–20 per cent glazing ratio (proportion of window area to total wall area), the heat loss from your windows can be at least equal to that from your walls. When aiming for an overall highly insulated building, it makes sense therefore to give as much attention to the windows and the doors as to the walls and roof. The most important part of the openings is, of course, the glazing, and this is dealt with in detail in the following sections. However, the window and the door frames and the fabric of the door can also be specified to improve the energy efficiency of the house.

WINDOW SYSTEMS

Existing Frames

Usually, existing frames will be steel or timber with single glazing. Steel window frames are often found in inter-war (1930s) and post-war (1940s–1960s) houses, although these have been found to give problems. Steel requires regular maintenance to avoid rusting. However, successive paint layers result in problems with closing opening lights, necessitating the periodic removal of old paint layers and thus increasing the maintenance liability. The metal itself conducts heat easily from the building, retrofitting double glazing into the frames is impossible (although secondary glazing can be fitted to the window reveals, soffits and cill) and the draught-proofing options are limited. Therefore, steel frames are not a

good choice from an energy viewpoint and generally should be replaced.

Timber frames can be long-lasting and, if in good condition, do not always need to be replaced. It is generally not economically worthwhile, in energy saving terms alone, to replace perfectly good, single-glazed windows, as long as the frames are sound (although there are other potential benefits apart from saving energy – *see* below under single glazing). However, double-glazed, sealed units have been developed specifically for retrofitting into existing timber frames. Provided that the frames are of sufficient depth, the rebates can be extended to accommodate the extra depth of a double-glazed unit – this may be a problem with opening lights, where the rebates are less deep. These retrofit units generally use a narrower pane separation (for example, 6mm) than do normal sealed units (12–16mm), which means that they will not be quite as thermally effective as the latter. However, they will be a good deal better than the single glazing, and less expensive than whole window replacement.

Choice of Replacement Frame
The choice generally comes down to three options: timber, uPVC or aluminium. In operational energy terms there is little to choose between the basic forms of each option. However, there are some differences in the wider energy and environmental properties of each of the above options, as discussed below.

Timber Window Frames
First, let me dispel another myth – that timber is not a durable material for window frames. One has

only to visit old houses, such as stately homes, to see 200-year-old, original timber windows still in place and in good condition. In some derelict old buildings it has been known for the timber window frames, even although unpainted and unprotected from the elements, to survive in fair condition while the rest of the building fabric has decayed. However, these frames typically would be made from hardwoods, in some cases tropical hardwoods, which are not recommended these days on ecological grounds.

The key is first in the quality of the timber. It is true that within the past couple of decades poor quality softwood which had not been properly dried and seasoned was often used for window frames. The timber, being still damp inside, could then rot from the inside out within a matter of a few years, and especially when sealed with coats of gloss paint. This has certainly given timber window frames a bad name although, happily, manufacturers have learned the lessons of the past and timber frame window systems are much improved these days. Frames are available made from good quality European or North American hardwoods, which are replaceable over a reasonable period of time, unlike equatorial hardwoods. There are also good quality softwood window frames on the market, factory pre-treated and primed (*see* the illustration on page 67). Second, it is important to have a maintenance schedule appropriate to the type of material. There is little doubt that timber window frames will need to be painted periodically in order to prolong their lifespan. However, good quality softwood with factory-applied undercoats/primers provides a really good base for top coats of paint, which should last up to ten years, with recoating every five thereafter. Some manufacturers will even guarantee their timber windows for a number of years.

uPVC

PVC, or polyvinyl chloride (the 'u' indicates 'unplasticized'), is now used widely in buildings. From conservatories, windows and doors, to facia-boards, bargeboards, soffits, rainwater goods (gutters, hoppers and downpipes), internal and external piping, flooring, wiring insulation – uPVC is everywhere. Its advantages are versatility, good strength to weight ratio, low maintenance and, of course, cost-competitiveness.

However, there are concerns about PVC as a material which relate to its constituent chemicals, especially chlorine. Chlorine itself is a toxic material which, if released into the atmosphere or water supply, can be very dangerous. Chlorine released during the PVC manufacturing process could combine with other substances in the upper atmosphere to produce compounds such as CFCs (chlorofluorocarbons) which are a major contributor to the hole in the ozone layer. There is also concern regarding the products of combustion released should a building containing PVC ever catch fire or if the material is incinerated post-use. For more on this subject refer to the Greenpeace report *Building the Future* (*see* 'Useful Contacts', section 3). On the plus side, I should mention that applications have been found for recycled uPVC in the manufacture of outdoor furniture for gardens and civic parks and also for children's toys.

The market for uPVC replacement windows has been buoyant in recent years. uPVC is seen as the affordable, low-maintenance option and can readily accommodate double-glazed units and draughtproofing measures to reduce discomfort and heat loss. However, the adage of 'you get what you pay for' is never truer than in the case of uPVC windows. uPVC does not have great mechanical strength properties on its own and frames must be reinforced with a metal sub-frame. There have been some systems on the market, at the cheaper end of the price spectrum, which have not had sufficient metal content and thus the kind of strength and security properties which you would want from your new windows. Furthermore, certain systems have been known to discolour badly on exposure to sunlight, leading a major paint manufacturer to bring out a range of paints specifically for uPVC – which rather puts a dent in its lowmaintenance reputation.

If you are retrofitting uPVC windows into an older or period property you should be aware of the impact

OPPOSITE: Interpane I-plus heat-insulating, inert-gas-filled, low-E-coated, double-glazed units, in Eco-Plus high-performance, borontreated and natural oil-finished timber frames from the Green Building Store – giving excellent energy and environmental performance.

upon the appearance of the dwelling. Due to their lower mechanical strength properties, uPVC frames need to be thicker than timber ones, and the detail found in timber mullions and transoms (respectively, the vertical and the horizontal members separating individual panes in a window sash) cannot be precisely replicated.

In summary, in comparing timber and uPVC, if you go for the top specification of uPVC window you will probably find that you are paying as much as you would for a good quality timber window and then it is all down to aesthetics and wider ecological considerations (plus an acceptance that the timber windows will need to be painted at some point).

Aluminium

Although widely used in commercial, industrial and public buildings, aluminium would be the least common option in a domestic setting since it is usually not seen as compatible with most traditional styles of dwelling. However, aluminium can be an appropriate material in a high-tech, newbuild design.

While aluminium does not rust like steel, it does oxidize, discolour and eventually corrode. Aluminium used for door and window frames, and also rainwater goods, tends to be 'powder coated' – that is, a very durable form of paint is applied to the metal to prevent oxidation. Aluminium is very recyclable, indeed, it is highly likely that any new aluminium used now has some recycled content. However, its recyclability is reduced by the use of powder-coating.

There are also window-frame systems which comprise aluminium (for durability and low maintenance) on the outside and timber (for aesthetic properties) on the inside (*see* the illustration on page 72).

DOOR SYSTEMS

Most external doors are made of solid timber or uPVC. In both cases, with no glazing the U-value is of the order of $3.0 \text{W/m}^2\text{K}$, while half-glazed (double glazing, standard glass) gives around $3.1 \text{W/m}^2\text{K}$ and fully glazed around $3.3 \text{W/m}^2\text{K}$. All such systems now can be provided with good levels of draught-stripping and there is little to choose in thermal terms between the two materials. However, as detailed elsewhere,

---

The Pros and Cons of Window Frame Materials

All three options, at the top ends of the ranges, offer equally good thermal and draught-proofing performance. Other characteristics are as follows:

Timber
- overall good environmental profile (not tropical hardwoods)
- good quality systems likely to be at the top of the price range compared with others
- sympathetic to the architecture of period properties
- will, at some time, require repainting

uPVC
- can be cost-competitive, although lower-cost systems are not as durable/secure
- low-maintenance although can discolour (especially cheaper systems)
- overall poorer environmental profile

Aluminium
- aesthetically suited to modern 'high-tech' look
- likely to be the most expensive option
- environmental profile not as good as that of timber but better than that of uPVC

---

uPVC does not score highly on overall environmental performance, while timber external doors may be made from tropical hardwoods, which are not preferable for wider ecological reasons.

If you are looking for greater energy efficiency there are door systems on the market which offer improved thermal performance without all the environmental disbenefits of uPVC and tropical hardwoods. Steel or fibreglass panel doors, with a polyurethane foam core (*see* the illustration on page 69), can give U-values as low as 0.3 to $0.5 \text{W/m}^2\text{K}$ for a solid door, increasing in proportion to the area of glazing.

The choice of glazing type will become more significant the larger the glazed area. Double glazing would be the common standard, although low-E glass is recommended. Pane separation is likely to be restricted by the depth of the rebate which can be accommodated within the thickness of the door.

Note that the thermal performance of your door will be irrelevant if it is open. The use of draught lobbies on main entrances can greatly reduce the amount of heat lost when entering and leaving the house (*see* Chapter 8).

GLAZING

Single Glazing

If your house already has single glazing and the frames are in good condition, it will not be cost-effective, in purely energy terms, to replace your windows with higher thermal performance systems. However, there are other benefits that might be enjoyed by replacing single glazing, such as a reduction of condensation and down-draughts (see below) and improved acoustic insulation. If you are not suffering from any of these problems, apart from heat loss, then the best and most cost-effective solution is probably a well-fitting set of thick, well-lined curtains. Make sure that the curtains lie against the window architraves without any gap. A pelmet, again with a minimal gap to the curtain, can also help to reduce heat loss at the top of the curtain. At the foot the curtain should lightly touch the edge or top surface of the window cill or, in the case of a full-length curtain, the floor. However, if you have a radiator beneath the window, you certainly should not have full length curtains since the heat will be insulated off from the room and/or directed out through the glazing.

Down-Draughts
'Down-draught' (*see* Chapter 8) is the name given to the air movement which can result from large areas of glazing, especially that of poor thermal performance such as single glazing in metal frames. In many cases, where people claim to experience draughts despite having carried out extensive draught-proofing, the reason may lie in a down-draught from large windows. When air within a room hits a large area of glazing which is relatively cold, the air can cool rapidly. Cold air, being denser, thus falls, creating air movement and the sensation of a draught.

Radiators have tended to be placed beneath windows, partly to combat down-draughts (*see* the section on 'Positioning of Radiators' in Chapter 6).

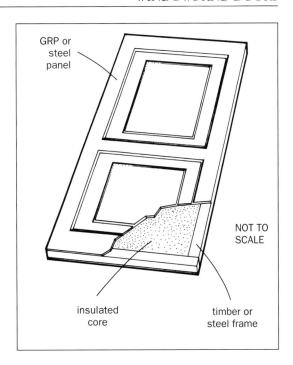

Glass-reinforced plastic (GRP) doors and steel doors, as manufactured by Evergreen Doors Ltd, comprising an insulated core, combine security, durability, good environmental profile and thermal performance.

However, much heat from the radiator is then lost direct through the glazing. A much better approach is to improve the thermal properties of the glazing, thus reducing heat loss and down-draughts.

Secondary Glazing

In an existing house, if your single-glazed window frames are in good condition and are not capable of receiving retrofit sealed, double-glazing units (or you do not want to go to that level of expense and disruption) an alternative is to fit secondary glazing. Proprietary products are available in standard window sizes, comprising a single glazing sheet in a minimal frame. These can be fixed to the existing frames, creating a double layer of glazing. Opening lights can also be treated. One type that allows for easy removal and replacement (for instance, for opening or cleaning windows) comprises a high-transparency Plexiglas sheet with a metal frame, which attaches magnetically to a metal strip fixed to the original window frame. Alternatively, for example, with existing steel window frames, secondary glazing can be fitted to the window reveals, soffit and cill. Secondary glazing can be almost as effective as a sealed, double-glazed unit, provided that it has been correctly installed. Secondary glazing can also be fitted to existing double-glazed frames, and while the thermal improvement would not be as significant, acoustic insulation is improved (*see* below).

Double Glazing

Double glazing is generally standard these days for newbuild and replacement – it really makes no sense to specify anything less. Successive revisions of the Building Regulations thermal requirements in recent years have more or less ruled out single glazing by setting the normal maximum U-value at a level below that which it achieves. The only exception might be replacement in period properties where it may be felt that double glazing would adversely affect the appearance of the building. However, even in this instance it comes down to an aesthetic judgement against clear energy benefits, and you will know what my view is on this.

Specify, as a minimum, dual-sealed units bearing the Kitemark symbol and meeting BS5713:1979. Glazing units should be fitted to BS6262, in accordance with the Glass and Glazing Federation standards (*see* 'Useful Contacts', section 3). In fact, there are a number of ways in which you can improve on standard double glazing (*see below*). Some options have minimal over-costs while others are definitely more expensive in capital cost terms, although they will reduce running costs.

Increased Pane Separation

Sealed double glazing units have tended to be available in two standard formats, 6 and 12mm pane separation. The latter option has become the norm since it is easily accommodated in most framing systems and gives a better thermal performance. The improved thermal performance of the units with the wider pane separation is due to the extra thickness of insulating air. The optimum pane separation has been found, by theory and experiment, to be around 19mm. When you go over 19mm the extra width of

the cavity allows circulating convection currents to be set up which start to accelerate heat loss. A 19mm pane separation would, of course, require a considerable depth of rebate in the frame. However, 16mm units are readily available and can be accommodated within most frames, especially for fixed (non-opening) sashes. The 16mm units should involve little if any over-cost since the only additional expense would be for a small amount of extra material in the spacer at the edge of the unit.

Acoustic Insulation

Incidentally – although this is not really an energy issue – the optimum pane separation for good acoustic insulation is around 150mm. Although this is vastly in excess of the thermal optimum (about 19mm), some acoustic insulation is afforded by standard double glazing units. However, if you are particularly bothered by noise – a busy road or an overhead flight path, for example – it might be worth thinking about installing secondary glazing at a distance of up to 150mm from your existing or proposed windows. This would require the secondary glazing frame to be fitted to the internal window reveals, cill and soffits, which would make it quite intrusive visually. Additionally you would not be able to open windows so easily (not that you might want to, given the circumstances) for ventilation. The use of the magnetic type (*see above*) or sliding sections could allow this, although the latter would be likely to compromise the acoustic performance. In any case, note that permanent background ventilation should be provided either by trickle vents alone or a whole-house ventilation system (*see* Chapter 8 on ventilation).

Insulated Spacers

Glazing U-values tend to be measured mid-pane. In the case of units with multiple glazing this does not take into account the weakest point (thermally) of the unit, that is, the edge, where a spacer is incorporated to maintain the pane separation. Spacers are usually made of aluminium, which conducts heat, thereby creating a cold bridge at the edges of the unit. However, sealed units are available using insulated spacers, which reduce the cold bridge and improve the overall thermal performance of the unit.

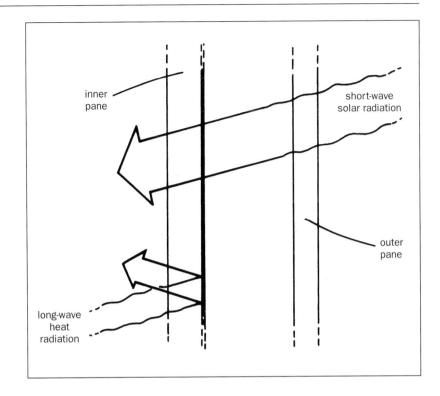

Schematic of low-emissivity (low-E) glazing; the low-E coating inhibits the passage of heat out through the glazing thus improving its thermal performance. Note that not all solar radiation is transmitted, nor long-wave radiation retained.

Low-E Glazing

Low emissivity (or low-E) glazing incorporates a very thin layer of metallic coating applied to the surface. This has the effect of reflecting back some of the heat from inside the house which would otherwise be lost through the glazing (*see* the illustration above). The coating does reduce the level of solar gains transmitted through the glazing, although this effect is not significant when compared with the heat loss saved. The low-E coated surface is positioned on the cavity side of the inner pane in a double-glazing layer in order to protect it from wear. The optical transparency of the glazing is not significantly affected by the low-E coating in most instances, although you may notice a very slight tint at certain times, especially from the outside.

There are two types of low-E coating, hard and soft, the soft coating giving a lower U-value. The only other major difference is that soft-coated glass cannot be toughened or laminated after application, these processes needing to be carried out before the coating, whereas hard-coated glass can be toughened or laminated post-treatment. The over-cost should be modest, especially for the hard-coat option, since anyone who can make up sealed units with standard glass can do so with hard-coat, low-E glazing. Indeed, from time to time glazing companies and suppliers offer (hard) low-E glass at no extra cost over standard glass. In time it is likely that low-E glazing will become the standard. It is most important to note that low E glazed units will come with stickers indicating which side should face outwards.

Inert Gas-Filled Glazing Cavities

Air is a fairly good insulator, but inert gases are better due to their lower thermal conductivity. The most commonly used inert gas in double (and multiple) glazing units is argon, although krypton and xenon (in increasing order of thermal performance) are also found. The amount of inert gas in the cavity will reduce by a few per cent each year because the seals are never 100 per cent perfect; it is simply not

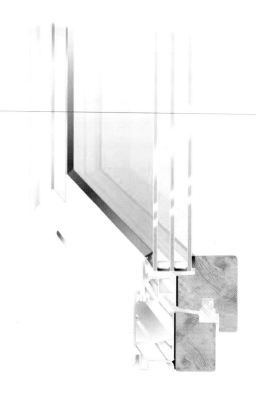

Triple glazing from Swedish Windows – as used in Scandinavia.

possible to produce a perfect seal at the atomic level. This decay will gradually reduce the thermal insulation of the unit, although the gases are not directly harmful either to people or to the environment. Inert-gas fill can increase the cost of the units significantly because of the specialist processes involved. The illustration on page 67 shows a conservatory fitted with inert gas-filled, low-E-coated, double-glazed units, giving a U-value of $1.1 \text{W/m}^2\text{K}$, in high-performance timber frames, treated with environmentally friendly boron preservatives and finished with natural paint oils.

Multiple Glazing Layers

Another option, favoured in Scandinavian countries due to the severe winter climate, is to go for triple or even quadruple glazing layers within the sealed unit (*see* the illustration above). The more glazing layers you have, the more layers of insulating air (or inert gas) and thus the better the thermal performance. Of course, a law of diminishing returns applies whereby you get less value from each successive glazing layer. Also, the frames need to be very deep in order to accommodate successive glazing layers and optical transparency starts to be affected. However, within an overall highly insulated design, multiple glazing may be worth looking at (*see* 'Super-Insulated Houses' in Chapter 3).

Thermal Performance of Different Glazing Types

As mentioned above, the windows will always be the thermally weak point in your building fabric. However, in a totally well-insulated approach, it makes sense to make the windows as thermally efficient as your budget and other considerations will allow. The table opposite gives a comparison of U-values of the several glazing types/systems.

BFRC Rating

The British Fenestration Rating Council (BFRC) has devised a system for comparing the total energy performance of different window systems. The rating system, similar to that for white goods, uses colour-coded letter-ratings, from A (most efficient) to G (least). Energy is also expressed in terms of $\text{kWh/m}^2\text{/yr}$. Most standard systems will have a negative rating, indicating a net heat loss throughout the year. However, some of the higher performance systems can have a positive figure, indicating a net heat flow into the building. At present this system is voluntary, although in time it may replace U-values as the method of expressing the energy performance of glazing systems.

A WINDOW ON THE FUTURE?

At the R&D stage currently are two systems which may have an impact in the near to mid-term future. The first is electrochromic glazing, which can change its light transmission and even U-value characteristics in response to an electric current. Systems which can switch between transparent and opaque are already available commercially and tend to be used internally for privacy reasons. However, the possibility exists of using the same technology to allow or block solar

Indicative U-values (W/m²K) for Glazing Configurations in Wooden Frames			
Single glazing	**4.8**		
Multiple glazing	**Pane separation**		
	6mm	**12mm**	**16mm**
double air-filled	3.1	2.8	2.7
double hard[1] low-E	2.7	2.2–2.3	2.0–2.1
double soft[2] low-E	2.6	2.0–2.1	1.8–1.9
double argon-filled[3]	2.9	2.7	2.6
double argon hard low-E	2.5	2.1	2.0
double argon soft low-E	2.3	1.8–1.9	1.7–1.8
triple air-filled	2.4	2.1	2.0
triple hard low-E	2.1	1.7	1.6
triple soft low-E	1.9–2.0	1.5–1.6	1.4–1.5
triple argon-filled	2.2	2.0	1.9
triple argon hard low-E	1.9	1.6	1.5
triple argon soft low-E	1.7–1.8	1.4	1.3

Notes
1 hard low-E glazing emissivity, 0.15–0.2
2 soft low-E glazing emissivity, 0.05–0.1
3 gas mixture: is 90 per cent argon, 10 per cent air

gains. This could be automated in response to internal temperatures or a given level and direction of solar radiation. Developments in coatings could present further possibilities of changing thermal properties in response to electric current or even, using photochromic coatings, direct solar radiation.

The other system is 'evacuated glazing'. Instead of using air or an inert gas between the panes, a vacuum is formed which gives the best possible barrier to heat loss by convection (although obviously radiation still occurs – think 'the sun' and 'space'). Achieving a high level of vacuum and high quality seal are the main challenges with this technology.

A key benefit of evacuated glazing is that the pane separation does not matter, it can be as little as you like within manufacturing limitations. Therefore, the total thickness of the unit can be greatly reduced compared with multiple-layer and increased pane separation systems, even compared with standard double-glazing units – thus enhancing applicability, especially in a retrofit situation. The problem is that under vacuum the panes distort and, with a narrow gap, can touch, thereby forming a direct conductive path for heat loss and rendering the whole process meaningless. To overcome this problem, tiny metal pillars are placed at regular intervals between the panes to maintain a uniform separation. The pillars themselves do present a route for conduction, although of minimal total area since they are very small. Indeed, the pillars are barely noticeable except in close-up (*see* the illustration on page 74) and do not detract from the visual appearance of the glazing; as one of the developers says: 'You look *through* glazing, not *at* it.' The image shows two units, one on top of the other, having different edge seals. The thinness of the units compared with that of normal double-glazed units can be seen clearly. The technology is about to undergo trials for production feasibility and could be commercially available within the next five years or so.

Finally, current research seeks to marry evacuated glazing with electrochromic technology, creating a triple glazed unit with extremely low heat loss and variable shading characteristics.

Evacuated glazing – currently at the R&D stage at the Centre for Sustainable Technologies, University of Ulster. Two units are shown, with slightly different edge seals. The thinness compared to that of normal double-glazed sealed units can be seen clearly; less obvious are the tiny pillars used to maintain pane separation under vacuum.

CHAPTER 5

Conservatories, Sunrooms and Loft Conversions

CONSERVATORIES AND SUNROOMS

In recent years, conservatories and sunrooms have been among the most common types of extension to a house since they have required minimal planning and Building Control approval and are relatively quick and easy to construct. Technically, a conservatory is defined as having at least 75 per cent glazed roof and at least 50 per cent glazed walls. 'Sunroom' does not have a formal definition as such, but simply describes a room with a higher glazing ratio than a normal room, while having a conventional roof – typically insulated and finished internally on the pitch to enhance the size of the space. Conservatories and sunrooms should always be located on the south side of the house as this is where the sun will be most

of the time. In practice, if this is not possible, then east or west will do, providing the conservatory has one south-facing façade. However, north façades should be avoided.

Basic Types

There are two basic types of conservatory/sunroom, 'free-standing' and 'lean-to'. The first, as the name suggests, is a self-supporting structure, whereas the lean-to type depends upon the structure of the main building for support. Lean-to structures can be accommodated, for example, at the rear of a dwelling between the main body of a two-storey house and the return (*see* the illustration below) and can be relatively simple and cheap to install.

Normally, the roof would be monopitch (sloping

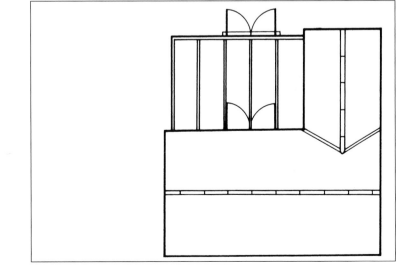

Sketch plan (not to scale) showing a lean-to conservatory accommodated in the return of an existing dwelling. Access doors (which must be of exterior grade) are installed in place of the original window in the adjacent room.

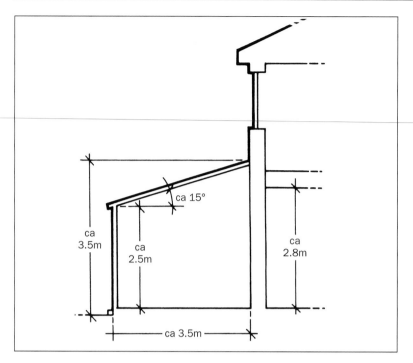

Sketch section (not to scale) showing the constraint on the depth of a lean-to conservatory imposed by roof pitch and head height.

in one direction only), which introduces constraints upon the depth and the head height with respect to the slope of the pitch (*see* the illustration above). In other words, in order to attach the roof to the main body of the house at a point below the existing first floor windows, there will be a maximum depth achievable while maintaining adequate head height at the outer edge of the structure and sufficient pitch angle for water run-off (minimum usually about 15 degrees).

Free-standing structures are more costly to install, but tend to be larger, being able to incorporate dual roof-pitches on either side of a central roof-ridge. Free-standing structures also tend to be more impressive in terms of architectural expression.

A lean-to type structure incorporated in the return has the advantage of reduced exposed wall area and thus reduced heat loss since more of the sides are buffered by the main structure of the house. However, it may not be possible or convenient to accommodate the structure in this way, in which case you are likely to end up with a 'three-sided' or 'peninsular' structure (with three exposed sides), which may be either lean-to or free-standing.

The number of companies supplying and installing conservatories, especially the uPVC type, has increased dramatically in recent years, partly due to the lack of regulatory control over their installation (retrofit conservatories up to 30m² are exempt from Building Regulations in UK). Conservatories as part of newbuild are not included in the thermal analysis, though you must provide thermal breaks and separate heating controls from the main dwelling. In either case, for your own benefit, you should ensure that attention is paid to detail in thermal terms. If you are contracting the building of a conservatory to one of these companies, the general rule applies: do not go for the cheapest option – you get what you pay for.

CONSERVATORIES

Conservatories can serve many purposes such as a pleasant interface between the internal and the external environment; a place to propagate plants (especially non-indigenous species); and as part of a passive solar design strategy. However, they cannot be all things at all times. Unfortunately, having extended the habitable area of your house, the temptation is to use the new space all year round, and in energy terms this can be a disaster. Research by the BRE has shown that a three-sided conservatory (with glazed roof and three exposed sides), even south-facing, when heated can double the annual energy usage of an average, three-bedroom, semi-detached house.

In the case of retrofit conservatories over 30m^2 or newbuild, heated by a radiator, separate zone control must be provided, as required by the Building Regulations. This can be achieved via a thermostatic radiator valve (TRV) on the radiator or by the radiator being on a separately controlled circuit with its own roomstat and programmer channel. If it is not heated by a radiator but used year-round anyway, the default would be electric heating, which is even more costly and less environmentally friendly (unless on a 'green' tariff, *see* the section on these in Chapter 9, or powered by on-site renewables). In either case, the conservatory must also be thermally isolated from the rest of the house via exterior-grade, double-glazed doors.

My advice would be not to heat your conservatory at all – use it not to extend your year-round living space but, rather, to extend either end of the spring and autumn periods. At times when it is too cold (or wet) to sit outside, your conservatory will provide a comfortable, semi-outdoor space, at zero additional energy cost. Overheating in such a conservatory is rarely a problem – if it is too hot to sit in your conservatory it must be warm enough to sit outside.

The ultra-violet (UV) component of direct solar gains can damage certain furnishings and fabrics, so I would recommend keeping all finishes hard and plain, softened by suitable container planting. Remember that the high temperatures may mean that plants need to be watered more frequently in summer – choose hardy, succulent types capable of withstanding high temperatures and periods of drought. You may need to move the plants inside the house in winter, or at least against the wall of the house. Hard finishes, for example, tiled floors (without rugs), also help to absorb excess solar gains and avoid overheating by day while storing useful heat for later in the evening (*see* the section on 'Passive Solar Design' in Chapter 1).

Sunrooms

If you feel that you must use your extended space all year round and therefore wish to heat it, then the answer may be a sunroom. You can still have highly glazed walls, but a conventional roof will greatly reduce the heat losses from the space during the heating season. Typically, the roof is insulated and finished internally on the pitch, either as a warm roof or ventilated (*see* the sections on 'Insulation' in Chapter 2 and 'Loft Conversions', on page 78), with tile or slate covering on battens and sarking felt, on a timber frame. As the inner pitch of the roof is exposed, insulation is incorporated between the roof members, the depth of which will determine the thickness of the insulation. In addition, it is possible to fix rigid insulation to the underside of the roof members and still nail tongue-and-groove timbers (for example) through to form the internal surface. Warm-roof construction will incorporate an insulated sarking layer above the rafters.

Heating should be controllable separately from that of the rest of the house, via TRVs or a separate circuit with roomstat and dedicated programmer channel. As with a conservatory, the sunroom should be thermally isolated from the rest of the house by exterior-grade, double-glazed doors. Bear in mind that there will be no distinction between a sunroom and the rest of the house for Building Control purposes. This will mean that the high level of glazing in the sunroom will need to be compensated for elsewhere, for example, by reducing glazing levels in other parts of the house (newbuild only) or by improved, overall insulation levels.

One thing you should be aware of if you are deciding on a sunroom instead of a conservatory is that the new extension will significantly affect the amount of daylight reaching adjacent areas of the existing house. In the case of a conservatory with a glazed roof, the reduction in light reaching the adjacent areas will be relatively small. If, as is often the case, an existing external window is made into French doors to provide access to the conservatory, the increased area of glazing of the new doors may compensate. If an entirely new opening is made, then the amount of daylight entering the room will surely increase.

However, with a sunroom the opaque roof will greatly reduce the daylight entering adjacent areas. While you will have a bright, well-lit, new space in your sunroom, you may find that parts of your original house become poorly lit, especially in comparison with the sunroom, and suffer as a result. If possible, therefore, it is better to locate your sunroom adjacent to a room with dual-aspect glazing, that is, windows in two walls. In that way, the reduction of daylight in the original house will not be so significant. Alternatively, opt for a conservatory, unheated, but accept less than year-round occupancy.

LOFT CONVERSIONS

Loft (roof space, attic) conversions are probably the most obvious way of extending the living space of an existing house. The space is already there, all you have to do is provide light (artificial and daylight), heat, power and, most importantly, access. First of all, check that there is adequate height in the loft, at the centre and across a sufficient proportion of the floor area to give the head height required. Remember to allow for flooring if it is not already installed, as well as sheeting the inside of the roof pitch. Houses from around the 1930s may have ceiling joists of only 100mm – enough to support the ceiling, but maybe not sufficient to take a floor and associated loading. To satisfy Building Control it may be necessary to re-joist with 150mm timbers. This, in turn, may require new steel purlins to be installed to hang the joists from, since it is unlikely that you will be able to gain access to enough of the wall-plate on which to bear the new joists.

If the rafters are less than 150mm deep you may not be able to accommodate sufficient insulation between them, requiring additional insulation beneath the rafters and thus further reducing head heights. Bear in mind that if you cannot meet the head-height requirements then you will not get Building Control approval. In this case, the loft can still be converted, for example, into a children's playroom; however, it will be sub-standard and classified not as habitable space but as storage space only. The value of the work in resale terms may not be as great, although on the plus side it will mean that the issue of access (*see below*) is not as critical and the costs of the work will be reduced. In any case, you should, of course, satisfy yourself that the proposed works are structurally sound. This may mean getting a structural engineer to look at the job and provide a brief report. This is especially important with a truss roof (indicated by rectangular metal plates joining the roof members).

Access

Lofts can be converted without proper access, but do not then receive Building Control approval and can be classified officially as storage space only. In order to provide proper access, adequate space must be found to install a staircase. When considering possible locations for one, careful calculations are needed to determine what space it will need to occupy. To do this, you will need to work out how many stairs are needed and what depth/height the risers and treads ('goings') should be. Building Regulations govern the maximum height of risers and the allowable ratio of riser height to tread depth. If your upstairs landing is sufficiently wide and you can provide adequate head height between the new stairs and the existing ones, it may be possible to accommodate the new stairs within the existing stairwell, for example via means of 'winders' (*see* the illustration on page 79).

Access to a single room only can allow a reduction on the normal Building Regulations minimum stair width, which may facilitate accommodation within the stairwell. (Note that width in this case refers to 'unobstructed' access width – that is, not including handrails on the wall side, as required to winders under Building Regulations.) If stairs cannot be accommodated within the existing stairwell it may be necessary to sacrifice all or part of one bedroom, for example, the small front bedroom or 'box room' in a conventionally laid-out, semi-detached house. You should then consider the loss of the small bedroom against the gain of extra space in the loft. In either case, remember that you will need to punch through the existing stairwell/bedroom ceiling to accommodate the required head height for the new stairs, which will take up some of the loft floor area (*see* the illustration on page 79).

Roof Lights

Once these issues have been decided, it is time to turn your mind to windows. The most obvious, simple and low-cost choice is a roof light, which is easily installed in the plane of the roof-pitch. Essentially all that is involved is the replacement of tiles/slates, battens and roofing felt with a proprietary

Sketch (not to scale) showing stair winders (plan form) and stairwell (section) that might be required for access to a loft conversion.

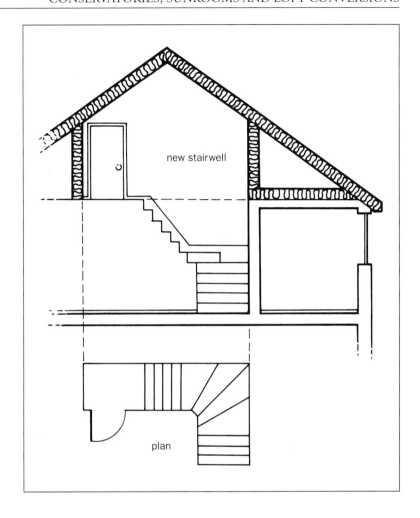

new stairwell

plan

roof light, ensuring that lead flashing is correctly installed around it to provide a weatherproof seal. Usually it will be necessary to remove part of at least one rafter to accommodate a roof light of sufficient size. Extra horizontal timber members are then inserted to brace between the rafters on either side of the gap.

While vertical glazing has the property of being self-shading to some degree (*see* the section on 'Shading' in Chapter 1), inclined glazing will be much more prone to high solar gains and thus the risk of overheating. This should be taken into account when sizing your roof light. Because the roof light 'sees' much more of the sky (*see* the illustration on page 80) you will not need as large an area as you

would for a conventional vertical window in order to provide the same level of daylight and solar heating gains. Also, less of the solar radiation will be reflected back than is the case with vertical glazing.

A blind should always be incorporated, ideally one which comes integral to the unit. A reflective finish on the outer-facing side will allow solar gains to be reflected straight back out through the glazing thus reducing the heat gains. The blind should also be well fitting, to function effectively as a night blind and should be as well insulated as possible to reduce heat loss at night. Heat losses from inclined glazing can be relatively high since more heat is lost by direct radiation to the night sky. Your roof light should therefore have at least the same thermal performance as you

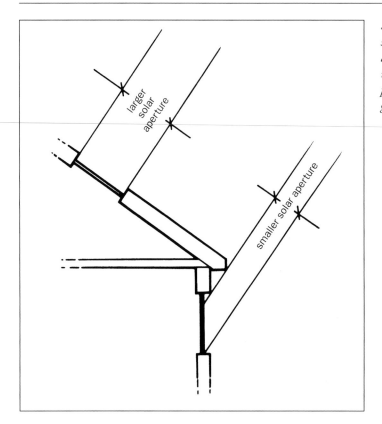

larger solar aperture

smaller solar aperture

Sketch section (not to scale) showing increased 'solar aperture' of inclined glazing over vertical glazing, increasing the potential for overheating and glare in summer.

would specify for new windows, if not higher (*see* section on 'Glazing' in Chapter 4), although this has tended not to be the case in practice.

Windows

Dormer windows would be the other option. While they are obviously more costly, dormers have the advantage of providing a greater area with full head height. Also, the particular heat gain and loss problems of roof lights are avoided and the window can be 'dressed' with conventional curtains or blinds. The dormer roof can be either pitched or flat (in practice, with a slight slope for water run-off). The pitched version will be more expensive although more durable and will probably look better too. However, depending on the position of the opening in relation to the roof-ridge, it may not be possible to accommodate the height of a pitched roof – in this case, a flat roof will be the only option. Remember that flat roofs are inherently a greater maintenance risk and,

bearing in mind accessibility issues, you should go for as good a quality long-life option as possible – incorporating plenty of insulation, obviously. The other weak points, in energy terms, are at the 'cheeks' (sides) of the dormer. Normally, in these areas, reduced element depth makes it harder to incorporate higher levels of insulation. You should therefore select a higher-performance insulation (such as extruded polystyrene or polyurethane/polyisocyanurate) and allow the cheeks to be as thick as is reasonably possible.

Insulation

Some houses are now built with 'room-in-the-roof' construction, anticipating a future loft conversion. This means that the roof is insulated on the slope (pitch), with insulation between the rafters, instead of above (in the plane of) the ceiling, between the ceiling joists. If this is the case, your job will be made much easier since your insulated 'envelope' already includes the loft. If your roof is not already insulated on the pitch, insulation will need to be installed here, to extend the insulated envelope. The first place to insert insulation is between the rafters. Again, you will be constrained by the depth of your rafters in terms of how much insulation can be incorporated and you may wish to use higher-performance insulation materials, such as polyurethane/polyisocyanurate foam or extruded polystyrene. It may be necessary and/or desirable also to incorporate more insulation than can be accommodated between the rafters. In this case, in addition, you can use a plaster-board/insulation laminate, fixed with plaster nails to the underside of the rafters. Note, however, that your head height will be reduced.

The thickness of insulation you can place between the rafters is also constrained by the need to leave a cavity for ventilation above the insulation. This is extremely important since air movement is vital to inhibit condensation on the cold side of the rafters and thus possible degradation of the timbers. Different insulation products may require different depths of ventilation cavity to be left above the insulation – check the manufacturers' literature.

If you are replacing the roof covering, an insulation sarking layer can be laid on top of the rafters, with battens nailed through to the rafters and counter-battens placed on top on which to lay the new roof covering. This form of construction, known as 'warm-roof', keeps the top surface of the rafters from becoming cold and thus inhibits condensation, without the need for a ventilation cavity above the between-rafter insulation. Note that this method will raise the height of your roof and therefore is not suitable for semi-detached or terraced houses – unless your neighbours do likewise. In any case, bargeboards and possibly flashing joints to chimney stacks will need to be repositioned.

Any insulation already in the plane of the ceiling could be removed since the heat rising from the floor(s) below will now be useful in helping to heat the loft. However; especially if the loft is likely to be used in a different way (for example, occupied at different times) from the rooms below, it might be worth retaining the insulation. If the existing insulation projects above the ceiling joists, you could simply lay the flooring boards on top, thus compressing it. While, generally, compressing insulation is inadvisable since it reduces its effectiveness, in this case it would not be a serious issue.

Heating

Heating can be provided readily by extension of an existing radiator system. This is unlikely to present a problem since most boilers will have been oversized and will be able to accommodate extra radiators. In certain cases, a pressure vessel may be recommended to boost the flow of water up to the height of the roof space. Heating pipes can often be run from the bathroom up through the hot water cylinder (HWC) cupboard to minimize disruption. Ensure that any new radiators are fitted with TRVs, to allow for separate heating control of the room. Again, bear in mind the insulation levels of the new space when sizing the radiator, in order not to oversize unnecessarily.

Structural Alterations

One option now being considered increasingly involves a more major structural alteration to the building. If the roof space is such that the head height would be inadequate for conversion, there is the option (with a detached property) of removing the entire roof, timbers and all, raising the walls by a 0.5–1m and installing a complete new roof. This may also require the extension of chimney stacks and will certainly come under the scrutiny of the planners. If this all seems like a huge amount of expense and disruption, remember the phrase 'location, location, location'. Depending on the area, the equity represented in the property may be many times greater than the cost of even this fairly major work, especially if the roof needs to be replaced anyway.

CHAPTER 6

Heating and Hot Water

FUEL/ENERGY TYPES

The fuel/energy types most likely to be used in the house for heating and hot water are natural gas, oil, LPG (liquefied petroleum gas) and electricity (the latter alone, of course, being used for artificial lighting). Natural gas is the most widely used fuel in the United Kingdom as a whole. In Ireland (north and south), however, oil is the most widely used since much of each region is not supplied with natural gas. LPG is also found mainly in areas off the natural gas network. Regarding coal and derivatives, these still have a niche market especially for room heaters, but are rarely used these days for central heating in modern energy-efficient homes.

Electricity can be used for heating and also for hot water, but generally is not recommended on energy and environmental grounds. The reason can be explained in terms of 'primary energy'. Electricity is not a fuel but an energy form, which requires fuels (primary energy) in order to produce it from conventional power stations. These power stations have inherent inefficiencies, from around 35 per cent for a conventional thermal plant to 55 per cent for a modern combined cycle gas turbine (CCGT). There are then further inefficiencies resulting from the transmission and distribution of the electricity to our homes. So although electricity is often very efficient at point-of-use, it may be only 30 to 50 per cent efficient in terms of primary energy. Therefore, while fossil fuels will have a primary energy factor of a little over 1.0, the primary energy factor for electricity may be three times that. Where electricity is generated from renewables, either via a 'green' tariff or on-site, a direct comparison cannot be made, similarly with biomass systems, as they do not involve fossil fuels.

BOILERS

Where to Find an Energy-Efficient Boiler

If you have been in the business of looking for a boiler over the past few years, you will have been amazed at the number of manufacturers and models available, for both gas- and oil-fired types – it could be quite daunting and baffling simply trying to select one boiler from the thousands (literally) on the market. No wonder many of us in the past will have simply taken the advice of the nearest retailer or plumped for the cheapest option; but this is unlikely to be the most energy efficient.

Fortunately, help is at hand in the form of SEDBUK, the Seasonal Efficiency of Domestic Boilers in the United Kingdom (*see* 'Useful Contacts', section 3). The SEDBUK boiler database not only lists over 3,000 boilers but gives details on the fuel (say, gas or oil), type (such as condensing, conventional, combi, modular), mounting position (floor or wall), rated output range (kW), efficiency (per cent) and energy rating (A to G – A being the most efficient). You can also refine your search in terms of any of these factors, as well as the flue type, manufacturer and model name.

So, if you have natural gas available, wish to wall-mount the boiler, want an A-rated boiler and would like to look at a condensing type, you can narrow the search down to about 160 options. Of these you can reduce the options yet further in terms of rated output. For each individual boiler you can also get an estimate (only an estimate, of course) of the annual energy costs for different dwelling types (flat, bungalow, terraced, semi-detached and detached). The SEDBUK website also includes access to the BRE boiler sizing tool, to help you to determine what output you require from your boiler (see below under 'Sizing your Boiler').

Natural gas is available to over 90 per cent of the population of the United Kingdom and is more or less taken as read in England. However, in terms of nationwide geographical coverage, availability is much lower. Large rural areas of Scotland, Wales and Northern Ireland are without access to it. Northern Ireland has had natural gas only in the last ten years or so, mostly concentrated in the Greater Belfast and surrounding areas, and there are large areas of the Province that will never have natural gas. The Republic of Ireland is in a similar situation. Where natural gas is not available, either oil or LPG would be the normal alternative.

Even where natural gas has been introduced recently, conversion from oil is not necessarily an obvious move. Anyone with a perfectly good oil-fired boiler should not convert to natural gas expecting to make big cost savings. If you are replacing a very old oil-fired system, savings would certainly be made, but so they would with a new oil-fired boiler. While the price of oil tends to fluctuate wildly and frequently in response to world events, you will find that natural gas prices tend to track the yearly average oil price quite closely, as it makes economic sense to do so. Natural gas is more convenient in that you do not have to arrange deliveries and it is also more environmentally friendly, kWh for kWh, than oil. However, oil-fired boilers are more efficient than the equivalent natural gas-fired type. LPG is only slightly more environmentally friendly than oil and you still have the issue of delivery. LPG is also more expensive than either natural gas or oil, due to the costs of production, pressurization, containment and transportation. Whatever your choice of fuel, you should aim to get your energy requirement down as low as possible (within budgetary and other constraints). In that way, any price differential between fuels will become less significant.

Existing cast-iron boilers (usually oil-fired) with no insulation can be fitted with a boiler jacket, although you may find that such boilers are over fifteen years old and, unless they are of good quality and regularly serviced, should be considered for replacement anyway.

Sizing Your Boiler

Sizing your boiler is important for a number of reasons. First and most obviously, the boiler must have enough output to meet your maximum heating requirements at the most extreme times of year. For this reason boilers tend to be oversized, to err on the side of caution. While this is perfectly understandable it is not always desirable. An oversized boiler may not only cost you more to buy than the correctly sized one, it will also be running at part-load more frequently, which is generally less efficient (although condensing boilers are actually slightly more efficient at low output). If you want to build in some heating capacity for a future planned extension, then by all means opt for a larger boiler. However, if you are unlikely to be carrying out the extension within the next ten years or so then it is probably not worth oversizing.

Domestic boilers have tended to be sized on rule-of-thumb. This is quick but not at all accurate and does not take into account developments in the energy efficiency of building materials and boilers themselves. Alternatively, there are two more accurate methods available. The BRECSU Whole-house Boiler Sizing Method (which may be accessed via the SEDBUK database) and the HVCA/CIBSE Domestic Heating Design Guide. The latter, produced by the Heating and Ventilation Contractors Association in collaboration with the Chartered Institution of Building Services Engineers, is the most accurate method and the only one which addresses all building and boiler types. However, it is slow and requires a high level of technical knowledge. The BRECSU (Building Research Energy Conservation Support Unit) method is suitable for relatively simple designs incorporating natural gas, oil or LPG conventional boilers up to 25kW, although not for solid fuel nor combi boilers. You may be wondering how you are supposed to know whether your boiler rating will be more than 25kW before you have used

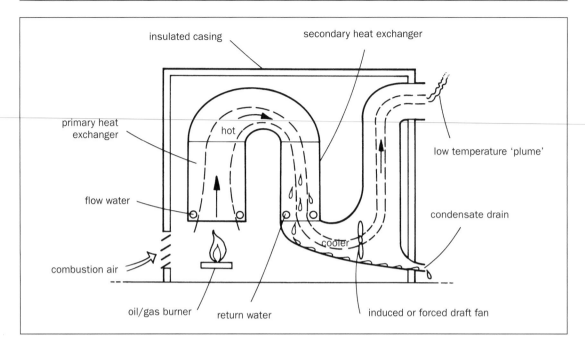

Schematic of a condensing boiler, showing the additional heat exchanger to extract heat from the flue gases and the condensate drain connected to the waste-water system (Courtesy: BRE)

the sizing package. The answer is that 25kW would represent a very large, conventional, domestic boiler and would cover almost all conceivable dwellings – especially those with an energy-efficient fabric.

Condensing Boilers

Soon it will be compulsory, in most cases, to fit condensing boilers in the United Kingdom (this is already a requirement in some other European countries). Condensing boilers differ from conventional ones in that they incorporate a condenser which recovers heat which would otherwise be lost up the flue (*see* the illustration above). This recovered heat then contributes to the heating of water which is pumped round the heating/hot water circuit. As the boiler then needs to use less gas or oil, the system is more efficient and costs less to run.

Although the running costs are reduced, the capital cost of a condensing boiler is higher than that of a conventional one due to the extra components involved. However, as condensing boilers are to become the norm in most cases, not only will this

price differential be irrelevant, but the price should fall in real terms as the manufacturing economies of scale improve. Additional advantages include the ability to install plastic flues, such is the reduction in flue gas temperatures due to the condenser.

When fitting a condensing boiler it is most important that a drainage pipe (known as a 'condensate drain', the slope of which must not be less than 1 in 20) be put in from the condenser to the waste water system. This requirement will be well known to all authorized fitters of gas and oil appliances.

Note that it is compulsory for gas appliances to be fitted by a CORGI (Council of Registered Gas Installers) trained installer. It is advisable to use an OFTEC (Oil-Firing Technical Association) or SNIPEF (Scottish and Northern Ireland Plumbing Employers Federation) approved installer for oil appliances.

In order for the condenser to operate to its maximum effect, the water returning to the boiler needs to be at the correct temperature for the condensation of the flue gases to take place. The required temperature is typically around 50–54°C (however, condensing boilers are still more efficient than conventional types, even when not operating in condensing mode). Lower return temperatures require greater heat loss from the system. For this reason radiators are often oversized compared with normal practice (*see* section on the 'Sizing of Radiators' in this chapter).

In some cases it has been found that, especially when replacing old, cast-iron boilers, a new natural gas condensing boiler can save hundreds of pounds over a relatively short period. Assuming that the old boiler needs to be replaced anyway, only the additional cost of the condensing boiler over a conventional one needs to be taken into account, not the full cost. In this case a condensing boiler can pay back within three to five years, that is, the extra capital cost over a conventional type is offset by the running cost savings over that period. Even if the old boiler does not absolutely need to be replaced, if it is more than fifteen years old a condensing boiler will almost certainly pay for itself (that is, return the full purchase price) in running cost savings well within its lifetime – and will help the environment too.

Condensing boilers are available with natural gas, LPG, or oil, as well as for combination ('combi') boilers, (*see below*). Oil-fired condensing boilers are more expensive than their gas-fired counterparts, because of the use of higher grade materials in the condenser to overcome the higher acidity of the flue gases. However, the highest efficiency boilers available (around 97 per cent) are of the oil-fired condensing type.

Retrofitting Condensing Boilers

When fitting a condensing boiler into an existing heating system, the radiator size will be fixed (unless you want to replace the radiators too). As it happens, radiators will tend to have been oversized anyway, to err on the side of caution, therefore it should still be possible for your condensing boiler to operate mainly in condensing mode. However, you should use a proprietary de-sludging agent to clean the sludge, which inevitably builds up over a period of time, especially in radiators, out of the system since sludge will effectively reduce the surface area for heat emission from your radiators.

Combi Boilers

(*See* also the section on 'Hot Water' on page 96.) Combination (or 'combi') boilers are so called because they provide not only heat to the heating circuit but also hot water direct, without the need for a hot water cylinder (HWC). This saves on the capital cost of the cylinder and associated piping, and also saves space. Running cost savings result from avoiding the cost of heat which is always lost from the HWC and piping (known as 'standing losses'); in effect, you heat only the hot water you actually use (barring standing losses from the pipework to appliances).

Combi boilers are especially well suited to smaller dwellings or ones where large volumes of hot water are not required at any one time, for example, from showers, baths and other hot water appliances being run simultaneously.

Combi Condensing Boilers

These are the ultimate in high-efficiency, quick-response boilers and, while costing a little more than the standard combi, will still pay for their over-cost within a few years. Again, these would be most suitable for smaller dwellings or those with a relatively low hot water requirement at any given time.

Biomass

(*See* also Chapter 9, 'Renewable Energy Technologies'.)

Wood-Pellet boilers

For those who wish to be green yet avoid the cost and intermittency of renewable energy technologies, wood-pellet boilers may be the answer. The pellets, which are manufactured from sustainably-managed or waste timber sources, can be used readily in a dedicated boiler to provide space heating and hot water. The best systems include spark ignition and adjustable feed-rate to provide a turn-down ratio (reduced boiler output in response to reduced demand) allowing control on a roomstat and timer. The uniform pellet size aids the automatic feed as well as efficient combustion, while the low water content results in very little ash. The high density of the pellets reduces the volume needed for fuel storage and systems are designed to meet urban emissions requirements.

Wood Chip Boilers

Wood chips also can be processed from sustainable or waste timber sources but are irregular in shape and have a higher water content and lower density than pellets, thus not lending themselves so well to automated systems. However, their cost is much lower and those in rural areas who can source supplies readily, have the space required for storage and feed, and can accommodate a little more in the way of maintenance (lighting and ash removal, for instance) may find wood chips an economic and environmentally-friendly option.

Cast-Iron Ranges

I am referring here to the traditional farmhouse range which has become much sought after in recent years, especially with people renovating old country houses or seeking to replicate that farmhouse kitchen feel. There are many different types, using different fuels and providing various combinations of heating, hot water and cooking facilities. While their aesthetic merits may be debated, in energy terms they can be something of a disaster.

The old, solid-fuel range which did everything was probably quite effective in an old farmhouse building, which would have lost heat at a high rate through solid stone walls and draughty, single-glazed windows and doors. The range would have been positioned in the kitchen/living area which would have been occupied all day long and may have been the only well heated part of the house. Added to which, the practice of home baking would have meant that the range was in use for cooking for long periods of the day and may even have been kept going constantly. However, in a modern house a range is really not practicable. Where providing heating and hot water, as well as cooking, they are not as efficient or controllable as a modern boiler. If providing cooking only, they also generate considerable levels of heat which, not being part of the controlled boiler heating system, can lead to overheating, especially in a modern, well-insulated house.

If you have been persuaded of the benefits of a modern, efficient boiler for your heating and hot water but still want the look of a range, there are many range-style cookers on the market which use a combination of gas and electricity and will give you all the convenience of a modern cooker.

HEAT PUMPS

Basic Operation

Heat pumps are becoming more widely used these days and have become quite commonplace in parts of the USA and Scandinavia as an alternative to fossil-fuel-fired boilers for providing space heating and/or hot water. A heat pump essentially is a refrigeration circuit where you are not so interested in the cooling effect but instead make use of the heat rejected from the system; think of the back of your refrigerator – this takes heat out of the interior of the cabinet and rejects it via the fins at the back. A heat pump takes heat from a low-grade source (such as the ground, water or the air) and produces useful heat. Due to the physics of the system, the electrical energy input to run the system pump/compressor is outweighed by the thermal energy produced.

The degree to which the thermal energy output exceeds the electrical energy input is expressed in terms of a ratio called coefficient of performance (CoP), typical values of which are of the order of 3.0–4.0. A CoP of 3.0 means that for every kWh of electrical energy used to run the system, 3kWh of heat are produced. If this sounds like something for nothing, it is not quite, since you still need to source your electrical energy from somewhere. If the electrical energy is conventionally generated, this still results in environmental emissions, although the CoP of the system will mean that much better use is made of the electrical energy than would be the case with direct electrical heating. In overall environmental terms, if you consider that the primary energy (see the section on 'Fuel/Energy Types' on page 82) of electricity is around three times that of fossil fuels, a CoP of 3.0 will put the electricity back on a level footing. If renewables-generated electricity is used to power the heat pump, the negative environmental aspect is, of course, removed.

Grants may be available for the installation of a heat pump system – contact your local energy agency (see 'Useful Contacts', section 5).

Components of a Heat Pump System

A heat pump system comprises the following basic components: a circuit containing refrigerant, low-grade heat source, pump, compressor, heat exchanger and expansion valve. The heat source may be either the ground or water (in which case a piping array is required) or, in the case of an air-source heat pump, the air. A ground array will take about 300–400m² area and can be located beneath garden or driveway/parking areas.

A schematic of a ground-source heat pump (the most common type) is shown in the illustration below. The circuit contains a refrigerant, which increases in temperature when it goes through the compressor. This heat is then extracted via the heat exchanger to be used for space heating and/or hot water production. The fluid then passes through the expansion valve and cools further, ready to absorb more heat from the ground. Because the area of the ground array is very large compared with that of the heat exchanger, the heat given to the system should not cause the ground to cool too much. This is a critical area of system design – in extreme cases permafrost conditions can be created in the ground, which is highly undesirable. For this reason, among others, heat pump installation should be regarded as a specialist operation and generally not attempted by the self-builder.

The ground temperature at the depth of the ground array (around 1.0–1.5m) is quite stable, thus allowing the system to be sized with confidence to meet the required heat input to the house. Coils may also be laid in water, if such is available, which avoids costly earthworks; however, caution regarding over-cooling also applies. Another alternative for a ground-source heat pump is to sink a deep borehole. This is a more costly option but may be adopted if adequate space is not available for a ground array or if the underlying rock is too close to the surface. Borehole systems have tended to incorporate an additional heat exchanger between the refrigerant and the fluid pumped into the borehole. However, systems have been developed recently which pump the refrigerant direct into the borehole.

Heat pumps are especially well suited to under-floor heating systems (*see* 'Heating Systems' on page 88), since the latter run at low-flow temperatures, requiring a smaller compressor and thus less electrical input. As with underfloor systems in general, heat pumps should be considered in the context of a very well insulated fabric, so that the heating requirement is low.

Air-source heat pumps may be lower in capital cost but, as the air itself is used as the heat source, the efficiency is lower when you need the heat most, in winter. For this reason, they have tended to be less popular than ground- or water-source heat pumps.

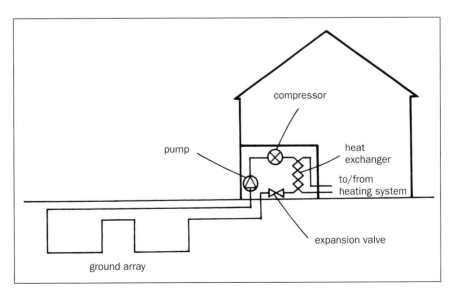

Schematic of a ground-source heat pump, showing the main components.

compressor

pump

heat exchanger

to/from heating system

expansion valve

ground array

However, improvements in heat exchanger technology have resulted in air-source heat pumps once again coming into the picture and, with a very low heat loss building (super-insulated), this type of heat pump might be worth considering.

The key advantages of a heat pump include reliability (how often does your refrigerator break down?) and low maintenance (avoiding boiler servicing, for instance). The heat pump unit itself is contained in a casing about the same size as a domestic boiler and, with appropriate sound-attenuation, should produce no more noise. In running cost terms, at current prices, a CoP of around 3.0 should ensure that a heat pump is no more expensive to run than a fossil-fuel-fired boiler.

HEATING SYSTEMS

Irrespective of which heating system you choose, my advice would be to insulate your house as well as possible in order to get the heating requirement down to a minimum. This will reduce energy use, environmental emissions and running costs over the lifetime of the building and will also 'future-proof' your home against rises in energy costs, which are inevitable over the longer term – indeed, have begun to happen already. Use BS5449 to ensure the appropriate system design temperatures are specified.

With regard to central heating systems there are two basic types: those using water and those using air. 'Wet' systems pump heated water round piping circuits, while 'warm air' systems distribute heated air by way of ducts and grilles. The former are by far the more common and can be sub-divided into those using radiators as the heat emitters and those using underfloor pipes. Confusingly, radiators actually deliver most of their heat by convection, whereas underfloor systems are fully radiant.

Heating System Controls

Irrespective of which type of boiler and heating system you choose and which fuel, the overall efficiency of your system will be greatly influenced by the level of control. Building Regulations in the United Kingdom already require a good level of control, and whether you are planning a newbuild or a boiler/heating system replacement, the Regulations

will apply. If, however, you have an existing heating system which is relatively new but not well-controlled it will certainly be worth upgrading, even although there may be no regulatory obligation to do so. Relevant information may be found in the Central Heating System Specification (CHeSS) publication (*see* 'Useful Contacts', section 13).

Thermostats and Programmer/Timers
The controls should provide what is termed 'boiler interlock', that is, the boiler will not fire unless there is a demand for heat in the house. That may sound obvious, although there are poorly controlled systems which allow boilers to fire simply to maintain their own internal thermostat settings when there is no requirement for heat in the house. The demand should be signalled from a room thermostat (for heating) or a hot water cylinder thermostat (for hot water) which has registered that the room/water temperature has fallen below its setpoint.

The other essential component is a programmer/timer; make sure that you get at least a two-channel, seven-day programmer. This will allow you to set a number of on/off periods for each day of the week, separately for heating and hot water. Therefore, only when the heating or hot water circuit is within its timed 'on' period *and* the thermostat is calling for heat will the boiler fire.

Each channel of the programmer/timer is attached to a thermostat and also to a motorized, two-port valve on the particular circuit. When the thermostat calls for heat, provided that the channel is timed 'on', the two-part valve will open to allow water to flow round the circuit, the pump will start and the boiler will fire. As soon as the thermostat setpoint is reached, or the 'on' period ends, the boiler will cease firing. The two-port valve will close when the pump stops running. Typically, a short run-on period is set for the pump in order to make use of heat already generated.

Location of Room Thermostats
Room thermostats (or 'roomstats', for short) must be located somewhere which is representative of the temperature requirements and conditions of the rest of the house since the whole heating system is usually controlled on this one thermostat. Places to avoid

A typical two-channel, seven-day programmer/timer, allowing separate time control of heating and hot water for different periods each day, depending on need. Image courtesy of Danfoss.

Thermostatic radiator valves (TRVs), such as these from Danfoss, allow control of individual radiators; they come in a range of finishes.

are: living rooms with secondary heating sources such as open fires, electric fires or coal-effect gas fires, since the heat from these will influence the roomstat; places subject to direct solar gains or excessive draughts, which again will influence the reading – close to windows and doors is therefore not suitable; and other areas of higher heat gain, such as kitchens. In fact, unless your main living room has no secondary heating, in which case that is a good location for the roomstat, the only other suitable place tends to be in the hall, as close as possible to the centre of the house. If you have two heating circuits you will need a roomstat for each. For example, if the upstairs is controlled on a separate circuit (requiring a separate channel on your programmer/timer) the roomstat might be located on the landing or in a bedroom, again subject to the conditions mentioned above.

Remember: turning your roomstat down just 1°C can save up to 10 per cent of heating costs.

Thermostatic Radiator Valves (TRVs)

TRVs incorporate a thermostat which senses the air temperature in the room, causing the hot water flow to the radiator to be reduced progressively as the room temperature rises. When the room temperature drops, the valve opens up allowing water to flow through the radiator and thus heat the room. TRVs generally have about six settings, corresponding to different valve positions from fully closed to fully open. Be careful to install the TRV in the direction of the flow indicated (by an arrow) on the device, otherwise you will surely get 'water-hammer' (a loud knocking sound resulting from pulsations being set up in the water in the pipes). This may mean placing the TRV on either the flow side or the return side of the radiator (although there are some types now on the market which are reversible simply by twisting the head). Avoid mounting the TRV in a vertical position since it can then be influenced by heat from the pipework below, instead of sensing only the room temperature. As in most cases, do not be tempted to go for the cheapest option – these may have a particular weakness in the form of a small pin which is an integral part of the mechanism and which can stick, rendering the TRV inoperative.

Zone Control

The concept of a heating zone in a building may be defined by, for example, its particular temperature requirements, expected solar or internal gains, or occupancy patterns. The living room is often regarded as a separate zone since comfort temperatures are generally a little higher here. Alternatively, bedrooms, not occupied during the day, could be seen as a separate zone. TRVs can give effective zone control but do not provide boiler interlock (*see above*) – this requires a roomstat. The roomstat will provide the basic control for the boiler, with the TRVs allowing closer control of individual rooms.

TRVs will need to be turned up and down every time you want to change the temperature in the room. In certain cases this may be inconvenient, in which case a couple of options are available. First, you can get a programmer with multiple channels connected up via two-port valves to different heating circuits, representing different zones. For example, the upstairs could be on one circuit and downstairs on another; but always remember to leave a channel for the HWC (unless using a combi boiler). In this way the upstairs circuit could be switched off during the day and the downstairs at night, for example, without having to go round turning TRVs up or down. This option is most feasible in a newbuild situation or where extensive works are being carried out. Another option is to install a system which incorporates additional two-port valves which may be opened or closed from a central control panel. Wiring needs to be installed between each valve and the controller and to the 12V power supply unit (*see the illustration on page 91*).

Radiator Systems

Sizing of Radiators

Advice on the location of radiators is given in the following section. Regarding the sizing of the radiators, this is usually left to the plumber/fitter who would use rules-of-thumb based on the floor area of a room. It is important that you make the plumber aware if you have a well-insulated house since the rules-of-thumb will then tend to oversize your radiators. While this is not necessarily a serious matter in terms of energy consumption, you do not want radiators bigger than they need to be, from an aesthetic

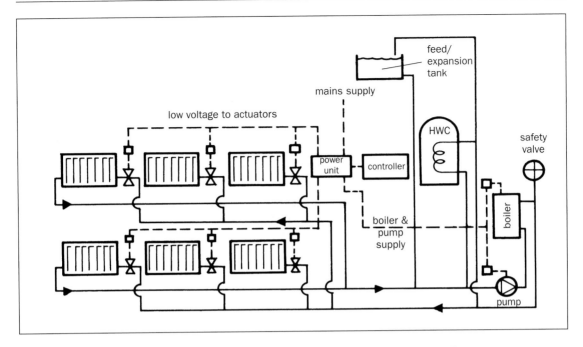

Schematic of a radiator control system allowing each radiator to be controlled from a central keypad. (Courtesy: Lakeview Developments)

or a capital cost viewpoint. If in doubt, especially with a new house, it may be worthwhile asking a building services (mechanical) engineer to calculate the actual heat loss rate from the building, taking full account of the insulation levels, of course, and to recommend suitable radiator sizes for each room.

There is one more factor to take into account regarding radiator sizing. Soon it will become compulsory for most boilers fitted in the UK to be of the condensing type (*see* above under 'Boilers') which require a lower water return temperature in order to function in condensing mode. This requires more heat loss from the system, which would suggest larger radiators. However, as most radiators will tend to have been oversized in the first place, to err on the side of caution, this may not actually result in their needing to be any larger than normal. Again, a building services engineer (or perhaps a well-informed plumber/fitter) will be able to calculate the size of radiators needed for the required return water temperature and which also will provide an effective heating output for a given flow temperature.

Positioning of Radiators

As you might expect, there is no simple answer to the question 'what is the best position for a radiator?' Radiators have tended to be located beneath windows, for various reasons. Two thermally-related reasons are as follows:

- rising warm air helps to reduce condensation by raising the glazing inner surface temperature – this was especially significant when single glazing was commonplace
- rising warm air also helps to combat downdraughts – again, more of an issue with single glazing.

The obvious disadvantage is that heat rising from the radiator (by convection) can be lost straight through the glazing, without ever contributing to heating the room. Incidentally, the term 'radiator' is something of a misnomer since typically less than a third of the heating effect comes from direct radiation from the surface of the radiator, the rest coming from convection – that is, warm air rising from the surfaces of the radiator and being carried into the room. This is even more true with double-panel radiators with multiple fins on each panel.

However, another (and possibly compelling) reason is to do with interior design and the use of space. The wall beneath a window tends not to be useful for anything else, such as placing furniture, whereas a radiator placed on an open wall will compromise the positioning of furniture such as bookcases or dressers. Chairs or sofas placed facing the centre of a room with their backs to a radiator will not permit benefit from its radiative output. This was perhaps more of an issue with the old unfinned, single-panel radiators where more of the useful heating output was by direct radiation and should not be so relevant these days.

The ideal location for a radiator, in thermal terms, is on a wall at right angles to a window wall. In this way, convection currents can be set up which allow air movement parallel to the plane of the window, which will minimize heat loss through the window (*see* the illustration below). In a large room, two radiators on opposite walls may be required. However, as usual, the optimum thermal scenario must be reconciled with aesthetic and practical issues to do with how the room looks and how it will be used.

If the radiator *must* be located beneath a window, ensure that the inner sill projects over the top of the radiator, but not too close, about 150mm should do, and not too far beyond the inside edge of the radiator, about 50mm should suffice. This will help to prevent heat from the radiator being carried to the glazing surface and being lost before it has had a chance to circulate round the room. Also, fit curtains that lightly touch the top or the front edge of the sill, not full-length ones that will block off the radiator.

Radiators located on an external wall, especially in older, solid-walled houses, may be fitted with reflective panels (foils) behind, to reduce heat loss to the wall. Products are available at DIY outlets and are reasonably simple to fit – you do not have to disconnect the radiator. Alternatively, a budget version could be made by using kitchen aluminium foil.

UNDERFLOOR HEATING SYSTEMS

Underfloor heating systems have become much more popular in recent years, principally because they do away with radiators, which can compromise room layout and are seen by many to affect interior design adversely (although many manufacturers make radiators of all shapes, sizes and colours which are designed to make an internal architectural statement).

Underfloor heating is certainly simple to install and, although this has not always been the experience in practice, should be no more expensive than radiators. Underfloor systems, by introducing heat at floor level, can provide a more even temperature gradient from floor to ceiling. More heat at a lower level, where it is often most needed, can also give improved comfort conditions.

Underfloor heating works well with condensing boilers (*see* page 84) since it operates at lower water flow temperatures, which improves the efficiency of

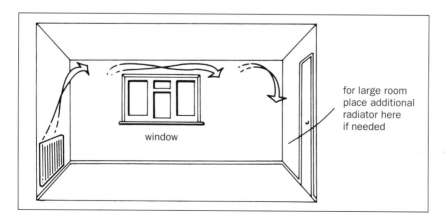

for large room place additional radiator here if needed

window

Optimum positioning of a radiator, from a thermal and energy-efficiency viewpoint.

the boilers. Electric underfloor heating systems are also available, although are not recommended on environmental grounds unless you have a plentiful supply of renewables-generated electricity – and, otherwise, will also be expensive to run. More and more now, underfloor heating is being seen in association with heat pumps (*see* page 86). The low flow temperature of an underfloor system means that the heat pump does not require as much electrical input to raise the temperature of the water, thus improving the coefficient of performance (CoP).

Underfloor heating can also be used on upper floors, which will require some modification compared with normal suspended timber floors. The pipes can be laid in a dry mortar screed resting on timber or concrete formwork, which is then sheeted over and the flooring laid on top. However, it is less likely that underfloor heating would be used on upper floors as radiators tend to conflict less with bedroom and bathroom interior design. Also, the soft floor coverings usually found in bedrooms are less suitable for underfloor heating (*see below*).

The main downside with underfloor heating is the response time of the system (*see* the section on 'Passive Solar Design' in Chapter 1). Response time simply describes the time taken between introducing heat into a room and comfort temperatures being reached. To demonstrate this point, consider three heating systems: a warm air system, a wet system with radiators and a wet system with underfloor heating. The warm air system will have the quickest response time since it heats the very air which is fed into the room. A radiator system will take about 30min to an hour (depending on various factors, including the thermal properties of the building), while the underfloor system would take several hours. Underfloor heating systems thus tend to be run continuously (not timer-controlled) because the response time is otherwise too long.

Suitable Flooring for Underfloor Heating

The response time of the underfloor heating system will also be affected significantly by the floor covering. A thick carpet will have the effect of blocking heat from entering the room. For this reason, hard finishes are recommended, such as wooden or slate floors or ceramic tiles. In addition,

the top surface should be thermally well connected to the floor screed in which the heating pipes are laid. This can raise a problem where wooden floors require an intermediate layer (for instance, where fixing with nails is proposed). British Standard BSEN1264 relating to underfloor heating with solid/timber floors, recommends a maximum floor covering resistance (above the screed) of 1.5 tog or 0.15m²K/W. This indicates that the wooden floor should be laid direct using a special adhesive onto the screed, which therefore must be very smooth and flat. Proprietary, self-levelling compounds can be used to achieve this finish. Tiles laid on a mortar bed will be thermally well connected, provided that there are a minimum of gaps in the mortar.

Control of Underfloor Heating

The best form of control for an underfloor heating system is to use the floor temperature as the control parameter. Radiator systems use air temperature sensors located at around head height. However, this type of control will not be so good for an underfloor system since by the time the air has reached a given temperature the heat built up in the floor slab will mean that heat continues to be delivered into the room. Sensing floor temperature allows equilibrium to be maintained between the floor and the room. The thermostat setting can be adjusted to provide the desired room comfort temperature.

*Optimum Construction and Configuration
for Underfloor Heating*

Piping is generally plastic, laid in loops in the screed layer of a solid concrete floor (*see* the illustration on page 94). Of course, you should make particularly sure that the floor is well insulated below the screed so that heat from the pipes is not lost to the floor slab and below. A floor U-value of around 0.15W/m²K should be readily achievable with a suitable thickness of insulation, such as high-density polystyrene, having the right load-bearing capacity for the screed and floor covering. The precise thickness will depend upon the type of insulation, but a figure of 100mm, in two staggered 50mm layers with joints taped, would be a good marker.

Underfloor heating is best used with a highly insulated fabric where the heat requirement is very low.

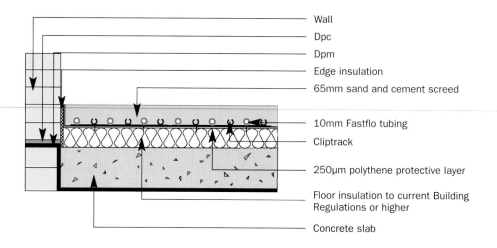

- Wall
- Dpc
- Dpm
- Edge insulation
- 65mm sand and cement screed
- 10mm Fastflo tubing
- Cliptrack
- 250µm polythene protective layer
- Floor insulation to current Building Regulations or higher
- Concrete slab

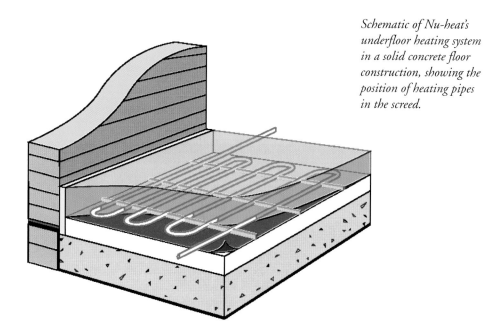

Schematic of Nu-heat's underfloor heating system in a solid concrete floor construction, showing the position of heating pipes in the screed.

Heat can then be trickled in gently by the underfloor system and, if correctly controlled as described above, should not lead to overheating, while the low heat loss rate of the fabric will ensure that the system is not expensive to run. Floor surfaces should be hard, such as timber or stone/ceramic, and should be well connected thermally to the screed.

Warm Air Heating Systems

A warm air heating system incorporates a heating unit, which essentially does a similar job to that of a wet system boiler, although it heats air instead of water. Systems fired on natural gas or LPG may be direct or indirect (that is, involving a heat exchanger), with oil-fired systems being indirect only.

Systems may also be supplied with integrated water heaters.

The heating unit is usually located centrally and comprises a burner and a fan. The air is warmed as it comes into contact with the flame (or heat exchanger surface in an indirect system) and is circulated through ducts located around the house. Grilles at the ends of the ducts in each room then supply air into the rooms. The air is moved around the system by the fan, similarly to a pump circulating water in a wet system. Air is recirculated back to the unit, requiring vents, typically located in the internal doors. This return air is then filtered, reheated and circulated round the system again. Depending on the system and the way it is set up, you can have either 100 per cent recirculation with ventilation air from trickle vents, or you can link in with a mechanical ventilation and heat recovery (MVHR) system to provide the fresh air component.

The advantages of warm air systems include very quick start-up times from cold and low running costs. This can be a significant advantage in an intermittently occupied dwelling with thermally lightweight internal surfaces. The system fan may also be run without the burner during the summer to circulate air through the building.

Many of these systems were installed in the 1960s and the 1970s, although they are rarely seen now. Part of the reason seems to be that people felt that the air was too dry and found the air movement uncomfortable. Those with respiratory problems such as asthma were especially critical. However, now, with heating loads much lower due to improved insulation levels, lower volumes of air, possibly at a lower temperature and velocity, would need to be supplied to maintain comfort temperatures. Indeed, it is now possible to get warm air systems fitted with electrostatic air filters which can significantly reduce odours and airborne particles, which is good news for asthma sufferers. Warm air systems can only be considered realistically in a newbuild situation (or a very extensive refurbishment) since space must be found in walls or cupboards and floor and ceiling voids to accommodate the distribution ducts, which are larger nearer the central unit, reducing in diameter as they get further away.

Electric Storage Heating

Electric storage heaters should never be chosen unless all other options are technically impracticable. In this case you should opt for the highest possible insulation levels in order to bring the heat requirement down to a minimum. Storage heaters are uncontrollable at the point of use, the amount of heating capacity available during the day being determined by the charging rate the previous night (although systems have been developed which use weather-forecasting to determine the charging rate). Even if the somewhat rudimentary input/output controls are used correctly, the amount of heat output available will decrease throughout the day, reaching a minimum when you need it most, in the late evening. While being relatively cheap to install, storage heating systems are also expensive to run (even though off-peak electricity is used), especially taking into account supplementary heating (which is almost invariably peak rate electric). Finally, where the electricity is generated from fossil fuels, electric storage heating is also environmentally unfriendly. Where storage heaters exist, serious consideration should be given to their replacement with a wet or warm air system, fed from an efficient boiler/heating unit. This will involve considerable disruption and therefore, where possible, should be carried out during other major works.

Focal-Point Fires

Focal-point fires have become more popular in recent years as more houses are built without open fires or as people use the open fires they have less often. Electric focal-point fires are often found placed in front of an unused fireplace, while gas-fired, coal-effect fires have become increasingly common in new houses as well as being retrofitted into existing ones. In energy terms these too are something of a disaster – especially the electric bar fire variety, which use peak rate electricity and are expensive as well as environmentally unfriendly (assuming the use of conventionally generated electricity). The gas type is little better since it represents a heating source which is outside the controlled boiler heating system. If you insist on putting in a focal-point fire, select the lowest energy-rated option available – and then try not to use it.

Open Fires

A television set might be said to have taken the place of the open fire in today's houses, being not only a source of information and entertainment (replacing the fireside chat) but also a reassuring glow in the corner. Though the appeal of a real fire is still great for many of us – maybe it strikes a chord with our inner caveman – open fires are really not practicable these days. Also they can result in very high heat loss through air being drawn up the chimney, equivalent to a window left open permanently.

If you cannot conceive of a house without a real fire, get a closed-in fire such as a wood-burning stove. In rural areas these can be a useful means of disposing of waste wood from felled or pruned trees. In urban areas, where smoke-control requirements are in force, pelletized wood stoves can be used, which give rise to very little smoke or ash (*see* the sections on 'Biomass' in Chapters 6 and 9). And finally, if you simply must have an open fire, ensure that it is fitted with a damper plate which can be slid into place across the foot of the chimney to reduce ventilative heat loss. For existing open fires, there are proprietary products available (for example, inflatable devices) which can be used to block the chimney when it is not in use – but take care not to attempt to light the fire when the chimney is blocked. The lack of draw up the chimney will probably make it hard to light and, if you do succeed, you will get a reminder when the room starts to fill with smoke.

HOT WATER

Hot Water Cylinder

Generally, hot water is provided from the same boiler that serves the heating system. Most commonly, a hot water cylinder (HWC) is fed by a piping circuit, similar in principle to the radiator circuit. Hot water from the boiler passes through a heating coil which runs through the centre of the HWC and transfers heat to the water stored in it. As hot water is used, it leaves from the top of the HWC and cold water (usually from the roof space cold water storage [CWS] tank) flows in to replace it, thus requiring more output from the boiler circuit to bring the HWC up to temperature again. Even when hot water is not being used, heat is lost from water standing in the HWC and pipes – even when these are well lagged (insulated). These losses, known as 'standing losses', are unavoidable with HWCs and are a consequence of having a volume of hot water readily on tap.

There are more efficient types of HWC, incorporating larger heating coils, which reduce recovery time, thus boiler cycling (on/off) and fuel use. BS1566 and BS7206 provide a useful minimum standard, improving considerably on the performance of typical 'medium duty' cylinders, which should be avoided. There are also 'high-performance' cylinders available, which should have a reheat time of no more than 20min per 120ltr.

Lagging

There are ways of maximizing the efficiency of your HWC. First and foremost is to ensure that it is well insulated. Today most HWCs come ready insulated with factory-applied foam insulation – select the option with the most insulation available. Existing HWCs may be not be pre-insulated and then require a lagging jacket. These are readily available from hardware and DIY stores and come in the form of strips of nylon-wrapped lagging (insulation) which, when secured with ties around the HWC, provide a complete jacket. Again, opt for the thickest available and ensure that it is well fitted with no gaps between the strips. The bottom of the tank will not be insulated, although this is not serious since most heat will be lost from the top. Therefore make sure that the insulation fits well at the top of the HWC. People may tell you that an unlagged HWC makes for a warmer airing cupboard (or hot press). However, there will still be adequate heat due to the standing losses even from a lagged HWC to keep linens, towels and so on dry; any more heat is a waste of energy and money.

Pipes likewise should be well lagged, including both the flow (into the HWC) and return (out of the HWC) from the boiler circuit and the pipe leaving the top of the HWC. It has been common practice in many instances to leave unlagged those hot water pipes which are within occupied spaces, on the basis that the heat gains are still useful. However, such gains are not part of a well-controlled heating system and, moreover, can lead to overheating in summer, when hot water is still required but not heating.

Controls

Good controls are essential for the efficient production of hot water. For a new house, the Building Regulations will require separate control of the heating and hot water circuits. For an older house without separate circuits, it is well worth installing them, especially if you are having some other work done anyway. The hot water circuit should be on a separate channel of a seven-day programmer/timer, which will allow a number of 'on' periods to be set within each day of the week. A thermostat (sometimes called a cylinder stat) on the HWC will ensure that only when the temperature in the HWC falls below a predetermined level will the boiler fire up to feed the domestic hot water (DHW) circuit (provided that it is within a timed 'on' period). The optimum temperature to which to set the HWC thermostat is 60°C ±2.5°, in other words, 57.5° to 62.5°C. The reason for this is that at lower temperatures there is an increased risk of *Legionella* formation, while higher temperatures simply waste energy.

Combi Boilers

(*See* the section on 'Boilers', on page 82.) Combi boilers provide hot water direct, rather than from a storage tank (HWC). You may remember the old gas hot water geysers that used to hang on (on more commonly off) the wall above the kitchen sink? Put such things out of your mind – the principle may be similar but the technology has, thankfully, moved on apace. Combi boilers heat water on demand as it flows through the boiler, their firing being activated by the flow of water, for example, in response to a tap being opened. Consequently, a combi boiler will not provide large volumes of hot water in a short space of time – such as might be required from multiple baths or showers (or other hot water appliances) being run simultaneously. However, standing losses are virtually eliminated because of the absence of a storage tank and associated pipework, resulting in high efficiency. Combi boilers, therefore, are generally most suited to smaller dwellings, such as one- or two-bedroom flats or small bungalows, rather than larger family houses. But note that combi boilers are incompatible with solar water heating systems (*see below*), which require a hot water storage tank.

Solar Water Heaters

These are dealt with in much more detail in Chapter 9 on renewable energy technologies. Briefly, a solar collector, mounted on a south(ish)-facing roof, traps heat from the sun and transfers it to water which is fed to a storage tank ready for use. Solar water heating systems are compatible with most conventional boiler systems and HWCs, although not (as mentioned above) combi boilers, which do not require a storage tank. A solar water heater, with a collector area of about 0.7–1.0m^2 for each occupant of the house, could provide around 50 per cent of your annual hot water load. Naturally, you will get most of the benefit in the summer, when 80–90 per cent of your hot water demands could be provided via the solar system, significantly reducing the use of your boiler. In the winter, perhaps only 15–20 per cent of hot water needs will be met.

Solar water heaters are becoming more economically viable as the price of systems falls and as the cost of conventional energy rises. The payback period (the time taken for savings from the system to equal its capital cost) will depend not only on the level of hot water demand but on the type of fuel which the solar system displaces. For a correctly sized system in a house with normal demand patterns and an oil- or gas-fired boiler, the payback period (at today's energy prices) will usually be of the order of 10–15 years – well within the maintainable lifespan of the system. And just think of the 'feel-good factor' you would get every time the sun shines down on your collector – knowing that you are harnessing nature's energy and doing your bit to reduce environmental pollution… what price can you put on that?

MICRO-CHP

CHP, or combined heat and power, is the practice of simultaneously generating electricity and producing useful heat. All electricity generation produces heat, especially that from generators connected to engines, such as in central electricity generating plant (power stations). Unfortunately, that heat is usually just dumped into the atmosphere. This fact, along with other inevitable mechanical inefficiencies, makes conventional central electricity generation only about 35 per cent efficient. CHP, on the other hand, can be almost twice as efficient, by recovering heat from the engine cooling system and the flue gases to heat water. CHP has hitherto been confined mainly to larger industrial and commercial buildings, or buildings with high year-round hot water demand such as 'wet' leisure centres. However, lately, smaller units have been developed, the smallest and most recent of which is micro-CHP. Trials of the technology should be completed by the time this book is published and a number of manufacturers are poised to move into the market.

Micro-CHP units are powered by natural gas and provide the space heating and domestic hot water normally supplied by a central heating boiler, as well as about 1–3kW of electrical output, depending on the type and size of the system. The lower end of the range might be sufficient to cover standby (continuous background) electrical loads while the upper end could meet a significant proportion of total electricity loads. Sources from within the micro-CHP industry (and thus with a vested interest) estimate that ultimately the technology could supply as much as 20 per cent of British domestic electricity.

The blue box is a WhisperGen micro-CHP unit, which contains a heating part (as in a boiler) plus a Stirling engine to generate electricity. It is made by WhisperTech (see 'Useful Contacts', section 1). The original gas-fired boiler (the wall-mounted white box) is retained as back-up, since this was a pilot scheme under the NIE Smart Programme.

CHAPTER 7

Lighting

ARTIFICIAL LIGHTING

Lighting is one of the most difficult things to get right, from an aesthetic point of view as well as from that regarding the energy it uses. The aesthetics are all important since lighting can play a major part in the interior design of your house. This can be seen both in terms of the illumination of the features of the house and also in the design of the fittings themselves. However, lighting can be also one of the major portions of energy costs, being 100 per cent

electricity – generally at peak rates. It makes sense, therefore, to look at ways of providing your lighting more efficiently and at lower cost.

Lamp Types

The term 'lamp' is used here in its technical sense – that is, not a 'table lamp' nor a 'bedside lamp', but the 'bulb' that goes into it. In reality, the 'bulb' may not be a bulb, it may be a tube – hence the term lamp, which covers all types of light emitter.

Examples of the range of compact fluorescent lamps (CFLs) now available. Image provided by the Energy Saving Trust (EST), which maintains a database of tested and approved long-life quality CFLs.

Compact Fluorescent Lamps (CFL)

These are, in effect, thin fluorescent tubes coiled up. Mounted on a bayonet or screw fixing, they can fit into a standard domestic fitting. Alternatively they can come with two- or four-pin connectors (PL types) which are compatible with a dedicated fitting only. The electric current 'excites' gas molecules within the tube, causing them to fluoresce. While early CFLs all had a high colour temperature (*see below*) and thus produced a very white light, there are CFLs available now which have lower colour temperatures. This, combined with instant warm-up and reduced flicker on start (further disadvantages of early CFLs), mean that they are now much more acceptable in a domestic setting. In addition, while early CFLs were bulky and often not compatible with light fittings, there is a much greater range of CFLs now available in different sizes and formats (*see* the illustration on page 99), from reflector lamps, to candle-type and even a glass-enveloped type, resembling (and hardly any bigger than) a conventional 'light bulb'.

Advantages of CFLs

The advantages of CFLs are two-fold. First, they last much longer, generally at least eight times longer than conventional 'light bulbs'. Second, they use much less energy – typically a fifth of the energy used by a tungsten filament lamp giving the same light output. While they also cost much more (at present) the over-cost will be saved many times over during the lifetime of the lamp due to its lower energy usage and longer lamp life. I started using CFLs in my own home ten years ago and, only recently, have had to replace just one for the first time. A simple illustration of the economics follows, you can argue with the figures and even put your own ones in, but the outcome is the same, CFLs are cheaper in the long run – and not that long either.

Take a 20W CFL priced at £10 and a 100W GLS (conventional 'light bulb'; *see* 'Tungsten Filament Lamps', on page 101) priced at 50p. The GLS will typically last for 1,000hr, thus consuming 100kWh of electricity, costing £10 (at 10p/kWh). The CFL will use a fifth of the electricity, thus costing £2 to run per 1,000hr or £16 over its lifetime of 8,000hr. However, the GLS will need to be replaced about eight times over the lifetime of a CFL, giving a running cost for the GLS of £80. You will also need to spend eight times 50p (not allowing for inflation!) on GLS lamps over the period, totalling £4 purchase costs. Over 8,000hr, the CFL will thus cost a total of £26, while the GLS will cost you £84. The CFL will actually pay for itself within around 2,000 operational hours, which would be typically around one to two years for the more frequently used fittings.

To get the most out of CFLs, it pays to buy the better quality lamps, which are usually rather more expensive than the lowest priced ones since the latter do not have the same lamp-life and therefore will not give you such good savings. The Energy Saving Trust (*see* 'Useful Contacts') maintains a list of approved lamps which have been tested for quality and lifespan.

Self-Ballasted and Non-Self-Ballasted Types

CFLs come in two basic forms. One has the control gear integrated into the lamp (self-ballasted) while in the other (non-self-ballasted) it is incorporated into the fitting. The self-ballasted type (depending on the end-cap) can be installed into either a conventional bayonet or screw fitting. The non-self-ballasted PL type, with a two- or four-pin end cap, requires a dedicated fitting which cannot accept a conventional end-cap. The self-ballasted type is obviously the one to choose if you wish to use existing conventional fittings. However, if you are starting from scratch, a dedicated fitting accepting only a non-self-ballasted lamp should be considered. Currently there is a far greater range of self-ballasted lamps available (*see above*) offering a variety of shapes, light output levels and colour temperatures. However, a disadvantage of the self-ballasted type is that if either the tube or the controls fail, the whole unit must be replaced, and the incorporation of the control gear makes for a more bulky lamp. Recently there has been a requirement, in the England and Wales Building Regulations, for a minimum of two dedicated fittings to be installed in every new house. This requirement is now being extended UK-wide to cover a minimum proportion of fixed fittings. The range of these dedicated fittings has started to expand, with pendant fittings now available and is likely to increase further in the future following the legislative moves described.

Tungsten Filament Lamps

These include the conventional 'light bulb', sometimes referred to as GLS (general lighting service). Other types include R80 and R100 reflector lamps and also halogen lamps. Light is produced by passing an electric current through a very thin filament of wire such that it glows. The filament is protected from the air (and thus combustion) by a vacuum or a neutral gas in the glass envelope. However, over time the filament will degrade and burn out, hence the frequent need to replace the lamps. The relative inefficiency of these lamps is due to the fact that less than 10 per cent of their energy consumption results in light output; the rest is heat.

Halogen Lamps

Tungsten halogen lamps, which have been used in vehicle headlights for some years, have become common in domestic as well as retail and commercial settings, due to the intensely bright light they produce from a very compact lamp. This means they can be used in fittings which could not possibly accommodate a GLS or a CFL and can thus more easily contribute to the interior design themselves – not only by the light they produce but by their very form. Two types are typically found, the linear type (as used in outside security lighting) and the conical

type. Low voltage versions (of the conical type) can be used safely in areas such as bathrooms and kitchens where moisture is more likely. However, a downside in safety terms is that the lamps run at the high operating temperature required for the 'halogen cycle'. The halogen cycle is the process whereby tungsten from the filament is burnt off and combines with the halogen gas during operation, being deposited back on the filament on cooling. The high operating temperature raises safety issues, especially where small children are concerned, and also contributes to the potential overheating of spaces.

In energy terms, moreover, halogen lamps are not to be commended. Even the low-voltage conical types are not low energy since the current is raised to compensate for the lower voltage, giving the same power consumption (wattage) as the mains voltage type – typically around 50W. Due to the high operating temperature much energy is wasted as heat and the lamp life is relatively short, especially when the heat is not able to escape from around the lamp. If recessing halogen lamps into a ceiling void, for example in an upstairs bathroom, insulation should be removed immediately above the lamp fitting and transformer (in the case of low voltage types). Because they are quite expensive to replace, the total operational costs of halogen lamps are high.

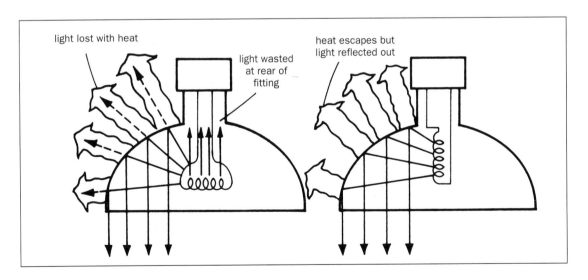

If using low-voltage-type halogen lamps, make sure you opt for the axial filament type with dichroic reflector.

If you are replacing low-voltage type conical halogen lamps in an existing fitting, use the most efficient types available. First, the type with an axial filament (*see* the illustration on page 101) allows more light to be emitted from the lamp. Second, a dichroic reflector allows heat to escape from the sides of the lamp, while light is directed out through the lens. A newer type with an infra-red coating actually reflects heat back into the lamp, thus maintaining the required high operating temperature at a lower energy consumption – typically 35W for an equivalent 50W basic conical halogen type.

Induction Lamps
Induction lamps can be used as replacements for R80 and R100 tungsten filament spot lamps. While they would be more common in a commercial setting, there may be domestic situations where an induction lamp would be favourable. The key advantage of induction lamps is their extremely long lamp life (typically 16,000hr), hence they might be considered for inaccessible locations. However, the purchase price is high.

LEDs

Light-emitting diode (LED) light sources are poised to make a major impact on lighting in buildings. You will have noticed LEDs in use in traffic lights and rear lights of buses and certain cars, applications requiring only luminance (being seen). LEDs have also begun to make an appearance in buildings, though again they have been used mainly for their luminance – for example to indicate circulation routes and on stair treads. However, due to recent breakthroughs in brightness and efficiency of white LEDs, these are now beginning to compete with incandescent and fluorescent lighting sources in terms of illuminance (lighting of spaces).

The basic LED is a solid state device containing a chemical compound which emits coloured or white light when an electric current passes through it. Though LEDs have been around for at least 30 years, their use has been limited to applications such as electronic indicators, displays and toys. These recent advances however have led to predictions of a doubling of the global market from £2.1 billion to £4.1 billion by 2009.

Using a tenth of the energy of an incandescent lamp of comparable brightness, LEDs could reduce global electricity consumption for lighting by 50% over the next 20 years. Additional benefits include longevity, durability and compactness as well as minimal heat production.

Colour Temperature and Colour Rendering

Lighting manufacturers and designers speak of the 'colour temperature' of a lamp, which refers to the temperature to which a 'black body' object must be heated until the colour of the light is matched. Yellower and pinker light thus has a lower colour temperature (below 3,000K), while that of bluer and whiter light is higher (over 4,000K). Tungsten filament lamps therefore have a lower colour temperature than fluorescent tubes. This is contrary to the way we think of the quality of light from incandescent sources, which appears warmer and that from fluorescent sources, which appears cooler. (Daylight has a colour temperature in the mid-range.) Fluorescent tubes are often seen as looking too commercial for a domestic setting, owing partly to their bulk and partly to the quality of light produced. While early CFLs all had a high colour temperature and thus produced a 'cool' light, there are CFLs available now which have lower colour temperatures, from 2,600 to 3,000K.

A term sometimes confused with colour temperature is 'colour rendering', which describes the accuracy with which a light source shows the true tone of a colour (based on daylight rendering). Some lamps give a better colour rendering than others, although not always across the whole spectrum. Fluorescent lamps tend not to give good colour rendering – you have probably at some time stepped outside a shop to see the true colour of a garment. However, full spectrum lamps are available, at a cost premium, which give excellent colour rendering.

Switching and Control

There is generally no need for elaborate lighting controls in a domestic setting since it should be a simple matter to switch lights on and off manually as you need them. However, it may be worthwhile to consider installing an extra switch where you have, say, two ceiling fittings in the same room, or ceiling and wall fittings. The cost of the extra wiring at the construction stage will be negligible, while the potential savings over the lifetime of the building may be considerable. This may be especially worthwhile if, say, one fitting is in an area well served with daylight. You then have the choice of having either lamp on at any given time, instead of having to have the light on in the part of the room well lit by daylight when it is not needed, just because the other part of the room requires light. These days infra-red (IR) switches and fittings are available which do away with wires altogether. They may be especially worth thinking about in a retrofit situation, although the units will require batteries.

By the way, most dimmer switches work not by reducing the energy consumption of a lamp but by diverting it, via an electrical resistance. Thus the lamp will use just as much energy when dimmed as it does at full brightness. Instead of relying on dimmer switches, think in terms of providing light from, for instance, different locations – wall fittings, standard uplighters and central ceiling rose fittings. If you then have these fittings separately switched, you may adjust the overall lighting levels and distribution in the room – and thus the 'mood' – without the need for dimmer switches. Provide wall and ceiling fittings first where possible, separately switched from beside the door so that they may be more easily turned off when leaving the room. Incidentally, I am often asked whether it takes more energy to switch a light off then on again, than to leave it on. The short answer is no – and I shall explain why. I think the origins of this myth may have arisen in one of two ways. First, fluorescent lamps draw more current on starting up. Second, tungsten filament lamps do not last as long with frequent switching since the cycle of heating up and cooling down degrades the filament (this does not have a bearing on the energy consumption, but might have led to the assumption that it was better to leave lights on than switch them off). Overall, I think common sense should prevail in this matter. If you are leaving the room to make a cup of tea it is probably not worth switching off the lights; if, however, you are going to have your dinner, then it is worth it. In areas where lights are likely to be left on for a long time make sure that you use a low-energy lamp – that way you will not incur such high energy usage and costs.

External Lighting

Bulkhead fittings can always be fitted with CFLs, to which there are unlikely to be any aesthetic objections. Photocell/daylight control is an option, to prevent operation during daylight hours. Security lighting, which is usually controlled on a photocell and PIR (passive infra-red) or other type of motion/presence detector, is almost always of the linear halogen type – this should be limited to 150W, which is quite sufficient in most domestic situations.

DAYLIGHTING

Daylight is the best form of lighting – any lighting expert will tell you that. Daylight covers the full visible spectrum and thus has excellent colour rendering, although at either end of the day, especially in the evening, it will often show colours in a yellowish hue. Of course, daylight is not always available in sufficient amount when and where we need it. However, it makes sense to try to design a new house in order to maximize the availability of daylight (especially in mainly daytime occupied areas) relative to other factors such as heat loss, privacy and architectural design. Larger window areas will allow more daylight to enter the space, but will also incur higher heat losses. The use of higher performance glazing (*see* the section on 'Glazing' in Chapter 4), as well as shutters and well-fitting, well-lined, thick curtains, can help to reduce such heat loss, thus balancing the negative impact of larger windows.

As regards the window area, a good starting point is an overall glazing ratio (ratio of window area to total wall area) of 20 per cent, ideally 60–70 per cent of which should be on the south side, for solar heating gains. The north-facing glazing area should be as low as possible to prevent heat loss while allowing adequate daylighting. A figure of 10 per cent of room floor area will probably suffice, much less than this and the room will start to appear gloomy and unwelcoming. As a rough rule of thumb, daylighting will generally penetrate sufficiently into a room to a depth of around 2 to 2½ times the head height of the window. Thus for a window head height of 2.0m, daylight will reach about 4.0–5.0m into the room – sufficient in most cases, although the daylight levels will drop off markedly as you go deeper into the room. Clearly, the daylight level will be greatest opposite the midpoint of the window. The extent to which daylight is provided across the width of the room will also depend upon the overall width and location of the windows.

Another slightly more complicated rule-of-thumb relationship can be applied, for a single aspect room (windows on one side only). For a room of width (W), and depth (L), with window head height (H) and average surface reflectance at the rear of the room (Rb), the following relationship applies:

$$[(L/W) + (L/H)] \leq 2/(1-Rb)$$

L should not be greater than the maximum value which allows the equation to hold true, that is, for the left-hand side to be equal to or less than the right-hand side. An average value for Rb, for a relatively light-coloured room, is 0.5, making the right-hand side of the equation equal to 4. For a room of 4.0m width (W) and a window head height (H) of 2.0m, the maximum value of depth (L) is thus around 5.25m. Beyond this depth, daylighting is likely to be insufficient and artificial lighting may be needed even in the daytime.

Where dual aspect daylighting is available, this will not only enhance total daylighting levels, but will also improve the quality of light by providing daylight from two different directions, thus illuminating surfaces and objects more evenly. Roof lights provide higher levels of daylighting for a given glazing area and also a more even distribution of daylight throughout a room. However, they tend not to provide views and can lead to excessive solar heat gains and higher heat losses too.

Specific Daylighting Technologies
Light Pipes
In areas where direct daylight is unavailable or insufficient, a number of techniques can be used to transmit daylight into the space. The simplest of these consists of a plastic dome mounted on the roof, connected by a highly polished, reflective tube to a diffuser in the ceiling (*see* the illustration below).

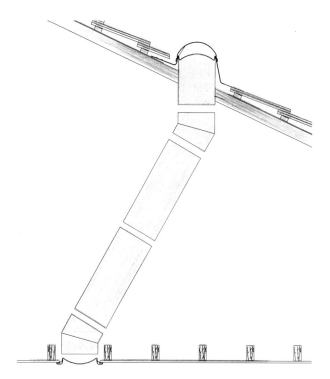

Glidevale's 'Sunscoop' lightpipe can provide daylight to poorly daylit or 'landlocked' areas. Daylight collected by the external dome is transmitted via multiple reflections through the highly polished tube to the internal diffuser.

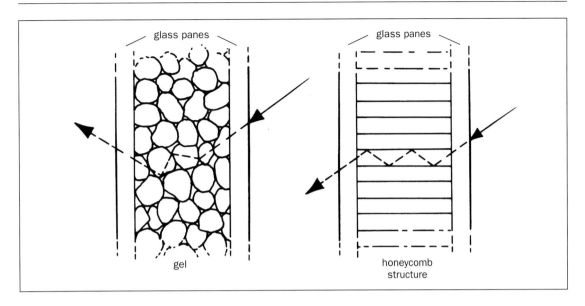

Two types of transparent insulation material (TIM), the honeycomb type and the gel type, which combine translucency with insulation properties and can be used where daylight is required but not optical transparency.

Daylight is thus 'collected' by the dome, transmitted by multiple reflections down the tube and is emitted into the space at the diffuser. The most obvious application would be for a top floor landing, which may well be without windows and is close to the roof.

Obviously, the further away the diffuser is from the dome, the longer the tube and the less effective the system will be, although manufacturers claim a very low loss of performance for distances of up to a few metres. Such systems are not cheap, but can be justified in terms of the aesthetic quality of the light provided and cost savings on energy and lamp replacement over artificial lighting. Of course, some artificial lighting will still be required for periods outside daylight hours.

Transparent Insulation Materials (TIM)

The term transparent insulation material (TIM) describes a range of materials which have insulating properties but which are also transparent to daylight. TIMs are not optically transparent, that is, you cannot see through them, but they allow diffused daylight to enter a space while having vastly greater heat-retaining properties than glass. The two main types are the gel type and the honeycomb type (*see* the illustration on page 105). The material is quite new and certainly has a high-tech appearance, which might compliment a modern design of dwelling.

Approximate Outdoor Surface Reflectances*	
Material	**Percentage**
water	7
earth (dry)	10
gravel	13
vegetation	25
brick/concrete	40
white paint (old)	55
white paint (fresh)	75

Note
*figures from McNichol and Lewis (*see* 'Useful Contacts', section 2)

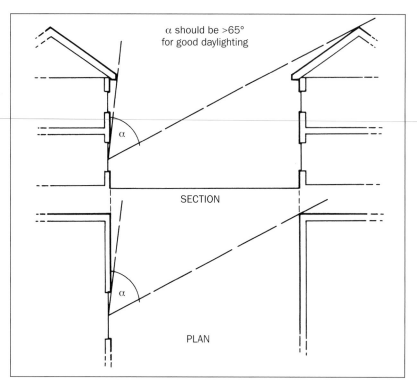

α should be >65°
for good daylighting

α

SECTION

α

PLAN

Estimation of sky angle: an indicator of daylight availability in a room. (Adapted from EcoHomes (BRE), see Useful Contacts, section 1)

Recommended Internal Surface Reflectances*	
Surface	**Reflectance**
ceilings	0.7–0.85
window walls	0.6–0.7
other walls	0.4–0.5
floors	0.15–0.3

Note
* figures from McNichol and Lewis (*see* 'Useful Contacts', section 2)

Maximizing Daylight

Obviously the bigger your windows, the more daylight they will let in. However, there is clearly a conflict in energy terms between avoiding electric lighting and allowing too much heat to escape through the glazing. Fortunately there are other ways of getting the most, in daylighting terms, out of a given area of window. First, to function most

effectively the window head height should be as great as possible. This will increase the sky angle (the angle to the vertical that the mid-point of the window makes with any nearby obstructions – see the accompanying illustration on page 106) and will also reduce the risk of a dark region at the junction of the window wall and ceiling, which can create visual discomfort. Second, surfaces around the window (sills and reveals, inside and out) should be light-coloured and reflective (within reason, avoiding glare). Areas outside the window, especially if not well-served by direct sunlight, should also be light-coloured, in order to reflect as much light as possible into the room. The reflectance of a surface can differ greatly, from around 7 per cent for water to 75 per cent for fresh white paint. There are also pearlescent paints on the market which reflect light better, or you can make a DIY version by mixing tiny glass balls into white paint.

Surfaces inside the room should also be light, in order to transmit daylight more effectively into the room. Recommended values of reflectance for different internal surfaces are given below.

BS8206 and CIBSE-Recommended Daylight Factors

	Average (%)	Minimum (%)
living room	1.5	0.5
bedroom	1.0	0.3
kitchen	2.0	0.6

In terms of what colours will provide these levels of reflectance, a smooth wall, freshly painted white can reflect up to 85 per cent of daylight, dropping to around 75 per cent for cream and 65 per cent for yellow. Darker colours absorb more light, although colours such as terracotta and deep yellow can create an impression of warmth. Incidentally, the above principles regarding reflectance apply for artificial lighting as well as for daylighting.

Daylight Factor

The daylight factor is a means of quantifying the amount of daylight available in a space. The factor, expressed as a percentage, is the fraction of daylight entering the room compared with the level of daylight outside from an unobstructed, uniformly overcast sky (think of the middle of a playing field on a bright but overcast day). The overcast sky is used as the basis since the distribution is even from all directions. The Chartered Institution of Building Services Engineers (CIBSE) and British Standard BS8206: Part 2 give recommended daylight factors for different rooms, as shown above.

The values tabled above reflect the different re-quirements for daylight and general lighting levels in different rooms of the house. However, a daylight factor of 2 per cent is a generally recommended, minimum aesthetic level for daytime-occupied spaces, while a value of 4 per cent can displace elec-tric lighting at most times of day.

Be wary, though, that if the daylight factor is very high on one side of the room and much lower on the other, this can lead to visual discomfort, due to the contrast between the two parts of the room. For visual comfort, a uniformity ratio of not less than 0.4 is often recommended – that is, the lowest value

should not be less than 0.4 of the highest (although BS8206 and CIBSE recommended values represent a uniformity ratio of only 0.3–0.33). This may suggest balancing a large area of glazing on one façade with a smaller area on another.

Daylight Factor Calculation
A sample calculation for daylight factor, applied to a whole room, is as follows:

daylight factor = $T \times A_w \times \theta / [A \times (1 - R^2)]$,
where T is glazing transmittance (0.84 for clean single glazing, 0.72 for clean double glazing),
A_w is net glazing area (that is, not including frame) m^2,
θ is the visible sky angle (measured in degrees between the vertical and a line from the centre of the window to the top of the furthest obstacle – see previous illustration on page 106),
A is the total area of room surfaces (including the window wall and window itself) m^2, and
R is the average reflectance of surfaces in the room (0.5 for a light room).

So, say you have a room 4m wide by 5m long by 3m high, with a double-glazed window of clear glazing area $2m^2$ with no obstructions, then:

daylight factor is $0.72 \times 2 \times 90/[94 \times 0.75] = 1.84$ per cent

This tells you that the average daylight factor is just on the border of good daylighting levels.

If you were to add another window of the same area, the result would be:

daylight factor is $0.72 \times 4 \times 90/[94 \times 0.75] = 3.68$

So doubling the area of your windows will, not surprisingly perhaps, double your daylight factor. A value of 3.68 would allow you to avoid using electric lighting during most if not all periods of the day. The equation can be rearranged to tell you what area of glazing you would need in order to achieve a given daylight factor (DF), as follows:

glazing area $A_w = [A \times (1 - R^2) \times DF]/(T \times \theta)$

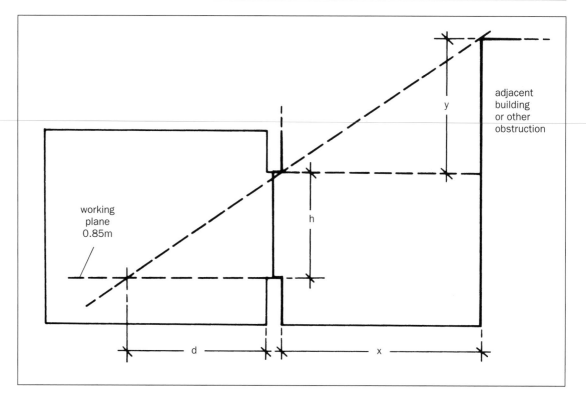

Estimation of the 'no-sky line': the point in the room (at the working plane, 0.85m) at which the sky can no longer be seen – an indicator of daylight availability. (Adapted from EcoHomes (BRE), see Useful Contacts, section 1)

View of Sky

The point in a room at which the sky is no longer visible is termed the 'no-sky line'. For practical purposes, the reference height in the room is taken as that of the working plane, that is, 0.85m. Where rooms are very deep or there are neighbouring buildings or tall trees close by, the no-sky line may leave a significant part of the room without direct daylight (not to be confused with direct solar radiation, which depends upon orientation too). Areas beyond the no-sky line may appear gloomy when compared with other parts of the room. The position of the no-sky line thus gives an indication of the daylight distribu-

tion in the room. The no-sky line may be calculated as follows (*see* the illustration above): if h is the window head height above the working plane, y is the height of the obstruction above the window head, x is the distance of the obstruction from the window and d the distance into the room of the no-sky line, then: $d = x\,h/y$. If d is greater than the depth of the room, then some sky can be seen at the working plane from any part of the room. However, if d is less than the room depth, thought should be given to resizing the room, relocating the building further away from obstacles or raising the window head height (which may mean raising the ceiling height, too).

CHAPTER 8

Ventilation

Ventilation has become an increasing area of focus in building design in recent years. Successive revisions of the Building Regulations in the United Kingdom and Ireland have increased fabric insulation requirements to the extent that ventilation now represents a significant proportion of overall heat loss. However, modern window systems in particular have reduced infiltration (accidental ventilation, *see below*) to much lower levels than those experienced in older houses, especially those with single-glazed vertical sliding sash windows (often referred to simply as 'sash windows'). Refer to the relevant Building Regulations document (Part F in England and Wales and also in the Republic of Ireland, part K in Northern Ireland, part 3 in Scotland) for more information on the legal requirements for ventilation in dwellings.

While being a source of heat loss, ventilation is essential for the health and comfort of occupants and for the preservation of the building fabric. We all need fresh air to sustain life functions. A certain number of 'air changes per hour' (the replacement of stale air with fresh) is also needed to remove odours and to preserve air quality. Ventilation is also one means of removing moisture and combating condensation, which can not only give rise to unsightly, unhealthy and potentially damaging mould growth but can also rot timbers.

Other sources of 'pollution' in the home which can be addressed with adequate ventilation are shown in the accompanying box.

The term 'ventilation' is used to describe deliberate, designed-in air changes, while those occurring accidentally, due to leaks in the fabric, are termed 'infiltration'.

NATURAL VENTILATION

Ventilation by natural means (no fans) is the norm in most dwellings, except in kitchens and bathrooms, and even in these areas it is possible to make use of passive ventilation (*see* page 114). The most obvious means of ventilating a room is by opening a window. Natural ventilation is effective up to a depth of twice the room height for a single aspect room (with opening windows on one side only) and up to four times the room height for cross-flow ventilation. You will also circulate some ventilation air every time you leave or enter the house or a room. However, to rely on opening windows is not very satisfactory, especially in winter. Either the windows will be open too long, in which case much heat will be lost, or they will remain closed, in which case there may be insufficient ventilation. Correctly designed, permanent background ventilation is best.

Sources of Pollution in the Home
moisture
allergens (such as dust mites)
VOCs (from carpets and furniture)
oxides of carbon and nitrogen (combustion products)
odours
tobacco smoke

Trickle Vents

The first and easiest way to introduce permanent background ventilation is via narrow openings, usually located in the window frame and known as trickle vents. New window systems should have these now – UK-wide Building Regulations require a certain area of permanent background ventilation per square metre of floor area. It is possible to retrofit trickle vents, although some existing frames may not have sufficient space to accommodate them. In this case it is possible to fit the vents into an external wall, although this is a more difficult operation; another option would be into an external door. The vents can be shut off, although this is not recommended since you may then not have the ventilation you need. Some types of trickle vent do not close altogether, so that even when you think they are closed, they are not. Do not on any account block the vents with newspaper or anything else, unless you are confident that adequate ventilation is provided by other means.

MECHANICAL VENTILATION

Extract Fans

Extract fans are a means of enhancing ventilation, for example, in areas where there are no opening windows or where there are particular requirements for increased air changes, such as in kitchens and bathrooms where moist air is generated.

Care should be taken with the positioning of the fans. They should be sited away from internal doors and should be close to the source of moisture production. A backdraught shutter should be installed on the external grille to avoid wind being blown back down the duct when the fan is not running. In very windy locations it may be worth fitting a solenoid-operated shutter which opens and closes (tightly) on the operation of the fan. Take care also if you have open-flued appliances in your house since the extract fan can cause the 'spilling' of gases from the flue, even if the flued appliance is in a different room. If in doubt, consult your local Building Control office.

Kitchens and Bathrooms

It is vital to provide sufficient ventilation in bathrooms and kitchens since these are the areas where the most warm, humid air is produced. Water vapour in the air will condense on cold surfaces (for instance, the mirror in the bathroom) unless it is removed. Opening a window can provide effective ventilation, but will also result in high heat loss and relies on manual control. Extract fans can provide the necessary air change rates without excessive heat loss, especially when linked to a heat recovery system (*see* page 111). In either case, especially in bathrooms, low wattage fans can be specified (the bathroom fan should be low voltage, in any case, for safety reasons).

Bathrooms

Extract fans in bathrooms are often linked to lights and controlled on a run-back timer to operate for 15min after the light is switched off. This form of control assumes that the light is switched on in all cases. The 15min run-on period is reckoned to remove effectively sufficient water vapour from the room as would result from a bath or a shower. This run-on period can be a nuisance, especially at night, and people often disable the fans for that reason. Such a practice is most inadvisable, especially in a bathroom with no opening windows. Instead, you could install a time delay (say, 3min) during which the fan does not operate, allowing quick night-time visits to avoid the noisy 15min run-on. Low noise fans can also be specified, which are less likely to cause nuisance.

Humidistat Control

Alternatively, options are available where the fan is controlled by a humidity sensor (or humidistat). Therefore, instead of running every time the light is turned on, the fan operates only if the humidity reaches a certain level, thus addressing the root need for the ventilation. In addition, where the bathroom has sufficient daylight, it is then not necessary to turn on the light just to work the fan (although these should have been switched separately in any case where daylight is available). Humidistat control can also be used with passive ventilation systems (*see* page 114).

Kitchens

In kitchens, extract ventilation is often provided via a cooker hood. This is effective where the hood is ducted direct to outside. Where air is simply recirculated, by a filter to remove odours, a separate extract fan should be considered. Again, the lowest wattage fan which is recommended by the suppliers for the purpose should be used. Humidistat control can also be used in kitchens, with manual override for the removal of odours or smoke.

Clothes Drying

Drying clothes is one of the greatest potential sources of moisture. On no account should you rely on drying clothes on radiators. As well as being questionable aesthetically, this practice raises humidity levels and can encourage dust mites, exacerbating respiratory conditions such as asthma. Alternatives include tumble driers, which are available either electric- or natural gas-powered, although these use much energy. A better solution would be to use an unheated utility room in which the boiler is located. You will probably find that the residual heat from the boiler is sufficient to provide comfort conditions for short periods (such as the room would be used for) as well as drying clothes over a reasonable period (a day or two). The room should have ventilation, to remove moist air, although this can be humidistat-controlled to avoid excessive loss of heat and thus drying capacity.

Heat Recovery Ventilation

While ventilation is essential and some heat loss inevitable, the amount of heat lost can be reduced by the use of a heat recovery system. This can be done on a whole-house basis or in individual rooms.

Single-Room Heat Recovery Ventilation

Individual rooms can be fitted with heat recovery fans, which combine an extract fan with a fresh air supply fan. A heat exchanger allows some of the heat from the extracted air to be transferred to the incoming fresh air, thus preheating it. Most types have two settings, a low flow rate designed for constant use and a high one for intermittent use, controlled on a humidistat if required. These units can be as effective as extract fans in removing humid and stale air, while also providing fresh air and recovering up to 60 per cent of the heat otherwise lost. It should be noted, however, that concern has been voiced regarding the ability of these systems to operate effectively other than in still air. Claims have been made that any degree of wind movement renders the fan incapable of extracting. Look for independent, rigorous testing of systems in typical wind speeds in the United Kingdom and Ireland of 4–5m/sec.

Whole-House Mechanical Ventilation with Heat Recovery (MVHR)

In general, the scale of domestic buildings means that it is not necessary to introduce mechanical ventilation, except in the specific areas as covered above, natural ventilation being effective in most cases. However, there may be circumstances in which you would wish to consider mechanical ventilation for your whole house. For example, if you had no permanent background ventilation in an existing house and particular air quality requirements for health reasons or if you were aiming for a very airtight fabric in the case of a new building (a prerequisite for these systems in any case).

There are a number of such systems now on the market. Some use trickle vents as the supply air source, but then do not include heat recovery. Most share common features, an extract system and a fresh air supply system (each with fan and ducts) and a heat exchanger. Heat is recovered from waste air extracted from areas such as bathrooms and transferred to incoming fresh air supplied to other habitable rooms (*see* the illustration on page 112). The 'tempered' air provided can reduce cold draughts that may result from other systems, improving comfort levels, while up to 80 per cent of heat can be recovered from the waste air streams. A system with variable extract rate will be better able to cope with high levels of moisture production. If the kitchen is included, a regularly changed filter should be installed since grease will foul the heat exchanger's heat transfer surfaces.

The advantages of this kind of system are clear: guaranteed sufficient ventilation (assuming correct design and sizing) with reduced heat loss and improved comfort conditions. Such systems may also help to combat dust mites and thus improve conditions for asthma sufferers (*see* page 117). The disadvantages include capital costs and running costs, and also maintenance liability.

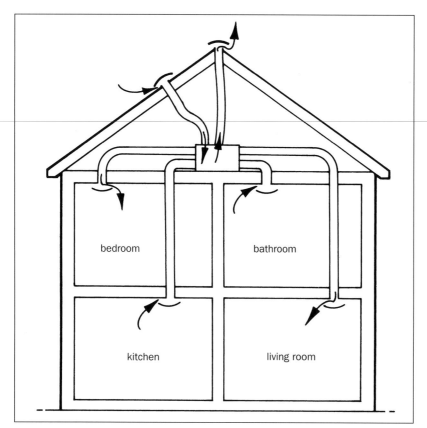

Whole-house mechanical ventilation with heat recovery (MVHR) – one method of designing-in ventilation levels – requires an airtight building envelope. (Courtesy: BRE)

Airtightness

Whole-house ventilation systems will work most successfully with an airtight fabric, so that ventilation is provided by the system rather than by infiltration. Forthcoming proposed amendments to the Building Regulations in England and Wales, and also in Scotland and Northern Ireland, will require dwellings to be designed to minimum standards of airtightness and in most cases to undergo pressure testing on completion to confirm that design standards have been met. This does not apply to existing buildings being refurbished, nor to extensions since the existing building would affect the result.

The normal minimum airtightness level for new dwellings in the UK is $10m^3/(hr.m^2)$ at 50Pa (Pascals, or N/m^2). However, a figure of $7m^3/(hr.m^2)$ is readily achievable. This means that, when the dwelling is pressurized (via use of a door fan, *see* page 113) to a pressure of 50Pa, no more than $7m^3$ of air should leave the building each hour for every m^2 of envelope (walls, floor and roof). For a detached house this would equate to around seven air changes per hour (ach) at 50Pa and, for a semi-detached house, about 5 ach. The current average value for new UK dwellings is about 14 ach at 50Pa, equivalent to an average infiltration rate at normal pressure of about 0.7 ach. A good value for an energy efficient home would be around 0.35 ach at normal pressure.

Airtightness Testing

A high level of workmanship is necessary to achieve an airtight building – it is not enough simply to rely on well-draught-sealed windows and doors. With newbuild, if working to a target air-tightness level (such as $7m^3/(hr.m^2)$ at 50Pa), it is important to advise all tradesmen and sub-contractors that you may have coming on site, especially those whose operations are likely to influence airtightness, that

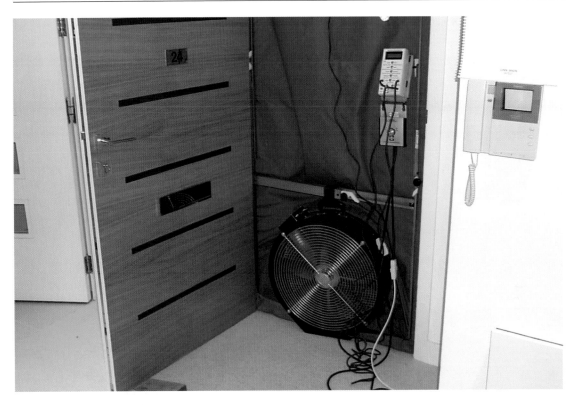

Airtightness testing using a door fan. (Image provided by the Building Research Establishment [BRE])

this is an integral part of your design. But how will you know if you have achieved the target? The only way to tell for sure is to carry out a fan pressurization test. This is a specialized operation involving expertise and the right kit. More companies are moving into this area as interest increases and in anticipation of legislative changes.

On a domestic scale, one or two fans mounted in a door-sized frame are used to blow air into the house (*see* the illustration above). The door fan is sealed in the door frame and all windows and specific ventilators (such as fans and trickle vents) are sealed off. In this way only infiltration is measured, not designed ventilation. The fans are then allowed to run until a pressure of 50Pa is reached and a measurement is taken of the airflow through the fan required to maintain that pressure. Different readings may also be taken at different pressures.

The rate of airflow across the fan will indicate the level of leakiness – the greater the airflow required to maintain the pressure, the more leaky the building. A smoke pen (available from scientific instrument suppliers) can also be used to pinpoint local areas of air leakage, for example, around window frames and at skirtings, in order for remedial measures to be taken if necessary. Relatively small gaps can be sealed with expanding foam or even flexible sealants. Larger gaps may need something more substantial, such as insulation or mortar.

It is a good idea to carry out the pressurization test before installing fitted kitchens, for example, in case remedial measures are needed. However, if water appliances are installed, ensure that water traps are filled or in some way blocked, otherwise a false reading will be given. Pressurization tests can also be carried out on existing houses, although the presence of fitted units may make remedial measures impracticable.

It is also possible to use smoke pens to identify leaks without pressurizing the house, although they will work much better with a higher pressure difference between inside and out – a windy day might suffice.

Passive Stack Ventilation

If you want designed-in ventilation but without the energy consumption and running costs, you should consider passive stack ventilation (PSV) (*see* the illustration below). 'Stack' in this case refers to the 'stack effect' – a term for the well-known physical property of warm air to rise. In fact, it is not only the stack effect that is used here, but also the 'chimney effect' – that of air passing over the top of the duct drawing in air at the bottom. Care should be taken to avoid down-draughts by correct termination at roof level. System manufacturers and suppliers will be able to advise you on this and other matters regarding installation.

PSV, in conjunction with trickle vents, can provide ventilation in kitchens and bathrooms. With the appropriate location of transfer grilles between these and other rooms having trickle vents, it is possible to provide ventilation to these other rooms too. Ceiling grilles are connected via ducts, as straight and vertical as possible, to terminals, usually located at the roof ridge since this will provide the longest possible run for the maximum stack effect. If bends cannot be avoided these should be as shallow as possible – ideally no more than 30 degrees (45 degrees as an absolute maximum) to the vertical.

The advantages of PSV are the absence of energy loads, running costs and noise and also reduced maintenance requirement. Disadvantages include variable ventilation rate and the requirement for straight, vertical duct runs, which are not always easily incorporated. Additional extract fans can be installed if required to cover periods of high moisture and humidistat-controlled dampers can be used at the ceiling grilles. More advice on PSV may be found in BRE Information Paper IP13/94 (*see* 'Useful Contacts', section 13).

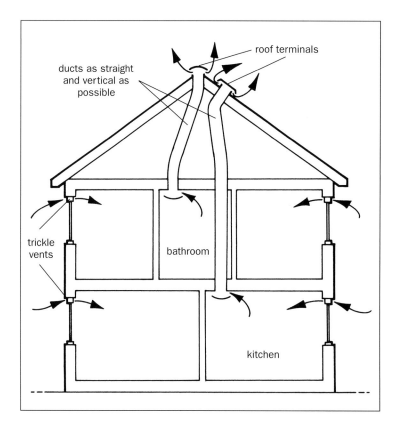

Schematic of PSV system providing whole-house ventilation without fans – can be humidistat controlled. (Courtesy: Passivent Ltd)

An Innovative, Low-Energy Window System

Trials are under way in Northern Ireland, Poland and Denmark of an innovative window system which seeks to address the problems of inadequate ventilation and excessive heat loss often encountered, respectively, in new and old buildings. The project is a collaboration between Cambridge University, University College Dublin and the Northern Ireland Housing Executive (*see* 'Useful Contacts', section 1). Two single-glazed frames are placed close together to form a double-glazed unit. However, instead of being hermetically sealed, the gap is ventilated through openings at the bottom of the outer frame and at the top of the inner one. This allows air to enter the gap from outside, gain heat and rise up under solar action, entering the room by the upper vent. The vents are automatically controlled according to the air quality inside the house and low-E glazing is used to reduce heat loss from the room. The efficiency of the system, which preliminary indications show can save 10–15 per cent of heating costs, is better with a very airtight fabric.

Reducing the Sources of Moisture

Extract fans, or PSV grilles, should be located close to the source of the moisture (such as close to a shower head). Moisture produced during cooking can be reduced by covering pans with lids. Closing internal doors, especially to bathrooms, will reduce the spread of moisture to other parts of the house. Avoid unvented heating appliances (such as LPG or paraffin heaters and some natural gas heaters). Avoid drying clothes in unventilated rooms and vent tumble dryers to the outside where possible.

Reducing the Sources of Moisture

- locate extract fans close to source of moisture
- cover cooking pans with lids
- keep internal doors closed especially to bathrooms
- avoid use of unvented heaters
- avoid drying clothes in unventilated rooms
- vent tumble-dryers to outside

Common Sources of Infiltration

- around doors and window opening lights
- chimneys
- around services (pipes, cables, for instance)
- loft hatches
- skirting
- gaps around joist ends
- suspended timber floors
- electrical boxes
- ceiling light fittings
- porous materials (such as concrete blocks)

INFILTRATION

As defined above, 'infiltration' describes air changes which occur accidentally, due to leaks in the building fabric rather than those which are deliberately designed-in, which are termed 'ventilation'. Infiltration used to be almost synonymous with ventilation. In older houses, there is usually enough infiltration to provide sufficient air changes without any specific ventilation. Sometimes the level of infiltration is too high – indeed, there is an industry built up around reducing it by the use of draught-proofing and draught-sealing products.

The Nature and the Scale of the Problem

Infiltration can occur in a large number of places. Sometimes its source is clear, for example a gap at the bottom of a door or an open chimney. In other cases, the source may not be obvious. You may feel a draught, but may not be able to pinpoint where it is coming from. Where the source is obvious, for example gaps between opening window sashes or doors and their frames, draught-stripping measures can be effective (*see* page 116). Where the source is not so obvious you may have to turn detective to find the cause and employ a wider range of draught-proofing techniques. It is worth bearing in mind that if you were to aggregate all the cracks and gaps in your house and represent their total area in your living room wall, you would typically have a hole of at least one square metre. Of course, the actual effect of all the cracks and gaps is not the same as such a hole in one wall – the analogy is used simply to illustrate the scale of the problem.

Air can enter the external leaf through gaps, even cracks in mortar courses, or gaps around waste pipes, for example, and find its way into the interior of the house through gaps around joist ends and under skirtings, along waste pipes, through gaps in floorboards and other such routes. Furthermore, which may surprise you – most types of concrete block are not actually airtight. A good layer of plaster will form an airtight layer, but air can still enter the house where the plaster stops (typically before the bottom of the wall since skirting would be anticipated). A dry-lined internal block wall may be quite leaky unless joints are well taped and sealed and/or plaster dabs (where used) laid continuously around the perimeter of the boards.

I know of cases where, even in new houses, the occupants have experienced discomfort due to draughts which they have not been able to explain. Problems seem to occur particularly in stairwells. The draught may be due to air infiltration through a significant proportion of the combined area of gaps and cracks in the upper floor. This air finds its way to the stairwell by any or all of the routes mentioned above and, being cooler and thus denser, will literally fall down the stairs, creating accelerated air movement. However, there is also another possible explanation – the 'down-draught effect'.

The Down-Draught Effect

There is a possibility that draughts occurring in places such as the stairwell may be due to what is termed the down-draught effect. This is the sensation of a draught caused by a large volume of air suddenly cooling and thus falling, creating air movement. This can happen where there is a large area of glazing, especially single glazing. In extreme cases a large area of uninsulated wall or ceiling may have a similar effect. Thus, while there may not be any actual air infiltration, a draught is felt which causes discomfort. Installing secondary or double glazing (or insulation, as appropriate) will improve the situation.

Preventing Draughts

Draught-Stripping/Proofing

In older houses, where infiltration levels can not only provide sufficient ventilation but can be excessive, causing unnecessary heat loss, draught-stripping and draught-proofing can be effective. The two terms are almost identical, although perhaps the former might describe the application of strips of flexible spacing material, while the latter might be seen as a general term covering not only draught-stripping but also such techniques as the application of 'brushes' beneath doors and sealing around other gaps. The practice is well known and understood and is therefore not dwelled upon here. However, to ensure a good quality product the draught seal should conform to BS7386:1997. Complementary advice on ventilation is provided in BS7880:1997.

Draught-stripping can be very effective in taking up gaps between doors and door frames, or between window frames and opening lights, for example. Sliding sashes are more difficult to treat since the movement of the sash across the seal would be likely to break it down; in effect, the seal is not maintained once the sash is opened. However, new products have been introduced recently which allow the seal to be maintained when the sashes, having been opened, are returned to a closed position. Brushes can be fixed to the bottom of a door, to provide an effective seal when the door is closed. The advantage of a brush is that it is flexible, tolerant to movement and can also take up irregularities in the surface of the floor and threshold.

Draught Lobbies

Think of the heat lost from your house when you stand on the doorstep bidding farewell to guests. This could be avoided by the use of a draught lobby, which is formed from two sets of doors at the main entrances. Many Victorian and Edwardian houses have two sets of doors on the front entrance – the Victorians knew a thing or two.

But in order to be effective, only one set of doors can be open at any one time – like an air-lock – the idea being that only a small volume of air is displaced each time the entrances are used. To be officially termed a draught lobby, the two sets of doors should be separated by a space at least 2m² in area, this being the area deemed sufficient to wheel a pram or buggy into the lobby without needing both sets of doors to be open at once. Draught lobbies do take up space and can also interfere with wheelchair access (unless made sufficiently large, in which case they take up even more space). However, the lobby can also form a useful place to remove muddy boots and leave wet umbrellas to dry, for example.

Wider Health Issues

Asthma

As well as being essential for respiration, ventilation can also be a significant factor for specific medical conditions. High concentrations of dust mites, which thrive on humid conditions, can exacerbate symptoms in asthma sufferers. Provision of adequate ventilation, by whatever method, is therefore important in maintaining a healthy internal environment, especially for the very young, the old and those with respiratory or allergic conditions.

Radon Protection

If you live in an area with high ground radon levels you may be recommended to take measures to prevent its build up in the house. The risk is related to the underlying geology of the area, especially with rocks such as granite. One method is to ensure adequate ventilation, to move radon gas emissions out of the house. Another method, which may be used simultaneously, is to install a radon barrier membrane. Plastic membranes are likely to be perforated during the construction process and a better option is a good layer of pitch (about 12mm). Your local Building Control office or the Health Protection Agency (now incorporating the former National Radiological Protection Board) or, in the Republic of Ireland, the Radiological Protection Institute of Ireland, will be able to advise further (*see* 'Useful Contacts', section 3).

Enhancing Natural Ventilation

Hedges, rows of trees or even high fencing can be used to good effect to attract, deflect or accelerate winds in the vicinity of the building (*see* the illustration on page 14 in Chapter 1). Generally you should be wary of channelling winds towards your building. However, for a very sheltered site, you might wish to enhance favourable south-westerly winds for summer ventilative cooling.

Hedging or 'side-fins' can also be effective. Side-fins could comprise specific elements of construction (resembling buttressing) or adjacent wings of the building. The illustration below shows good and bad configurations for encouraging cross-ventilation. The 'good' configuration provides positive pressure on one side of the space and negative pressure on the other, thus enhancing cross-flow. The 'bad'

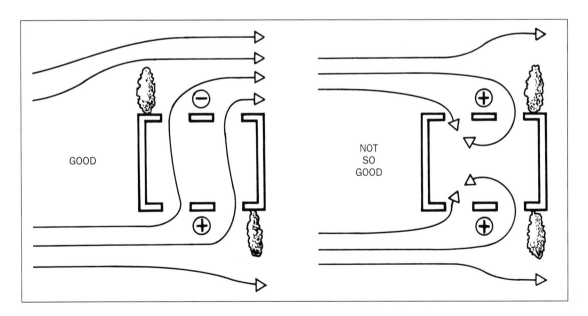

Examples of good and bad cross-ventilation, showing areas of positive and negative pressure.

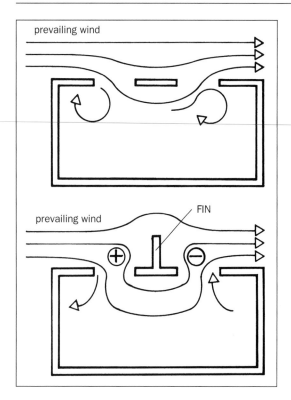

Enhancing single-side ventilation using side fins.

configuration introduces positive pressure on both sides, resulting in stagnation. Side-fins and hedging can also be used to effect in single-sided ventilation, as shown in the accompanying illustration above, again producing positive and negative pressures in the right places.

CONDENSATION AND MOULD GROWTH

One hopes that this is becoming a thing of the past; mould on walls and ceilings indicates moisture, which may come from either of two sources – damp penetration from the outside or condensation of water vapour from internal air. In either case the cause of the problem may be a point in the structure where there is a direct physical connection between the inside and the outside surfaces. Such a connection may act as a route for water to track across from the outer leaf of a cavity construction to the inner leaf. It may also act as what is termed a 'thermal bridge' or 'cold bridge', which is a path of higher heat loss rate causing a lower temperature on the relevant part of the internal surface. As this area will be colder, compared with other surfaces in the room, condensation will happen here first.

In older, solid-walled houses, a physical connection exists throughout the walls. It is especially important therefore to ensure that all mortar joints are well pointed against driving rain penetration. It is also important that there are no leaks from rainwater goods (gutters, hoppers or downspouts) which could cause soaking of the outer surface and increase the risk of damp penetration. There are products on the market which claim to seal brickwork against water penetration. However, it is more important to attend to the matters mentioned above – mortar joints and rainwater goods. In cavity-walled houses and on ceilings, condensation can also occur at points where insulation is missing, as this part of the surface will be relatively cold.

Condensation is not uncommon on windows, especially in winter on single-glazed windows, and is a consequence of water vapour from warm humid air inside the house condensing on the cold window surface. The internal surface of single glazing will be colder than that of double glazing due to the poorer insulating properties. The reduction of condensation is therefore one benefit often cited for the replacement of single glazing with double glazing.

Condensation on glazing can be aesthetically displeasing, although it need not be more serious than that, provided that the moisture is mopped up promptly and prevented from soaking into wooden window frames or sills (for example, via a good paint layer – choose a 'microporous' type so that the wood can breathe). However, if condensation occurs on other surfaces, such as walls or ceilings, this can be a very serious matter. Dampness can attract mould growth which, as well as being unsightly, can be detrimental to health. Inhalation of the spores released by the mould can cause problems, especially in those with respiratory conditions.

Combating Condensation

There are two ways in which condensation can be

discouraged. First, try to increase the surface temperature of the affected area. For a wall this might be done by installing cavity wall insulation, for example, or by insulating internally with dry-lining (external insulation could also be effective but is less likely to be aesthetically acceptable). Where a cold bridge is known to exist, internal insulation may be the only answer. In the case of a ceiling, loft insulation should be checked and installed/increased as necessary.

Increasing the surface temperatures may address only half the problem. If there is humid air in the room it will condense on any surface that is below its dew-point (defined as the temperature at which water vapour in air condenses). The other way in which condensation can be deterred is by improving ventilation. Adequate ventilation can ensure that the humid air is moved out of the dwelling thus reducing the likelihood of condensation. Condensation and mould growth are most often encountered in bathrooms and kitchens because of the high moisture content of the air. It is therefore most important to ensure adequate ventilation in these areas (*see* sections on 'Bathrooms' and 'Kitchens', on page 110). Bathrooms which are located in single-storey extensions or otherwise bounded by three external walls may be particularly prone to condensation owing to high heat loss, especially where the fabric insulation is poor.

Interstitial Condensation Risk Assessment

In newbuild there are situations in which you might need to predict whether condensation is likely to occur in a given construction. Fortunately there are computer packages available that will do this (*see* 'Useful Contacts', section 12). The user enters the materials of the various construction layers and their dimensions – an in-built database will contain the most likely materials and their relevant physical properties. The package will predict whether condensation is likely to occur and, if so, at what point in the structure. Possible remedial measures are also suggested.

It is unlikely that interstitial condensation will be a problem in most conventional constructions. With certain timber-frame constructions there may be the possibility and since the consequences could be serious, it may be worth carrying out the test. One situation where the risk can be significant is with flat roof constructions involving metal cladding outer surfaces. Generally, Building Control should pick this up, and, if concerned, they may request that a condensation risk assessment be carried out.

CHAPTER 9

Renewable Energy Technologies

SOLAR WATER HEATING

Solar water heaters come in several different types, all of which have in common a collector which traps solar energy, thereby heating water, which is fed to a storage tank ready for use. Solar water heating systems are compatible with most conventional boiler systems and HWCs, although not combi boilers since these do not involve a storage tank. Different systems may be defined by the collector type (for instance, flat plate or evacuated tube) and whether they are direct or indirect (*see* page 121).

Solar water heaters are becoming more economically viable as the price of systems falls and the cost of conventional energy rises. The payback period (the time taken for savings from the system to equal its capital cost) will depend not only on the level of hot water demand but on the type of fuel which the solar system displaces. If you are displacing peak rate electricity (at around 10p/kWh) the payback period will be much less than for gas or oil (at, say, 3p/kWh). For a correctly sized system in a house with normal demand patterns and a natural gas- or oil-fired boiler, the payback period (at today's energy prices) will usually be of the order of 10–15 years – well within the maintainable lifespan of the system.

Sizing the Collector

It is rarely possible or economical to size a solar energy system for 100 per cent of a given load in the United Kingdom or Ireland. This is because a system sized for solar radiation levels during the winter (even if sufficient solar energy were available) would be grossly oversized for the summer, and vice versa. The economic optimum size of a system will provide around 50 per cent of hot water requirements over the year. Naturally, you will get most of the benefit in the summer, when 80–90 per cent of your hot water demands could be provided via the solar system, significantly reducing the use of your boiler. In the winter, perhaps only 15–20 per cent of hot water needs could be met.

As a rule of thumb, you should allow around $0.7\mathrm{m}^2$ of evacuated tube collector or $1\mathrm{m}^2$ flat plate collector per person in the house. Manufacturers of particular systems will also give guidance on optimum sizing. While the sizing of evacuated tube systems can be fine-tuned by the addition of successive tubes, flat plate systems come in modules of fixed size.

Locating the Collector

The collector part of the system is usually located on a south-(ish)-facing pitched roof, in order to receive as much direct solar radiation as possible. The collector will be most effective when the angle of the sun is at right angles to the plane of the collector. Of course, the solar angle changes throughout the day and the year. On average over the year, the optimum inclination angle for the collector in the United Kingdom and Ireland is about 30–40 degrees, which, happily, is the normal pitch of a roof in this part of the world. A south-facing roof will give the maximum exposure to the strongest solar radiation throughout the day at all times of the year. However, any orientation between south-east and south-west can give satisfactory performance.

If a flat roof is available a frame can be fashioned to provide the optimum inclination and also positioned for optimum orientation. However, be careful to provide adequate ballast or mechanical fixings to overcome the wind-loading. Note that fixing into a flat roof is never to be commended since the last thing you want to do is to perforate it, thus inviting water ingress, while if you are using ballast you must ensure that the structure of the roof is adequate to withstand its weight.

Flat Plate Collectors

These are the simplest and cheapest systems, although the efficiency will not be as great as that of an evacuated tube type (*see* page 122). The collector consists of an absorber plate, painted matt black for the optimum absorption of solar radiation, behind which runs a pipe containing water (in the case of a direct system) or an antifreeze mixture (in the case of an indirect system). The pipe, being in contact with the absorber plate, heats up and transmits heat to the water or antifreeze mixture.

Direct systems actually circulate the water from the body of the hot water cylinder (*see* the illustration below) and have the advantage that an additional storage tank (or new tank with additional secondary circulation coil) is not required; this can be especially important in a retrofit situation where space is tight and disruption to be kept to a minimum. Hot water from the collector is trickled into the top of the HWC where it remains due to its natural thermal buoyancy. However, such systems do not have frost protection inherently and must rely on the coefficient of expansion of plastic tubing to prevent the pipes from bursting.

Copper pipes in the collector will transmit heat more effectively but need to be used with an indirect system. An indirect system circulates an antifreeze mixture through the collector and a heat exchanger is used to transmit the heat to the water in the HWC. This could be done by the use of a further secondary

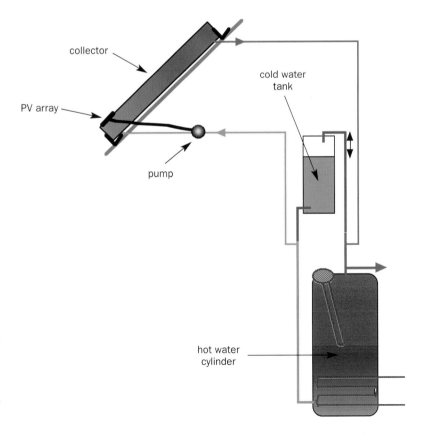

Schematic of Solartwin flat-plate, solar water heater, which can be easily retrofitted into an existing house and which requires no electrical connections.

circulation coil in the HWC (in addition to that from the conventional boiler circuit) or, alternatively, via an additional HWC.

A big advantage with flat plate collectors is that they are relatively simple for DIY installation, especially the direct type, which can connect into an existing HWC. The collectors themselves come in one piece and are not too heavy – a couple of people should be able to install them easily, provided that access is available to the roof. Grants may be available for the installation of solar water heating – contact your local energy agency (*see* 'Useful Contacts', section 5). However, to avail yourself of grants, approved installers are generally required to be used.

Evacuated Tube Collectors

These have a higher efficiency than flat plate collectors and, importantly, are able to make significant use of 'diffuse' solar radiation – in other words, the type we get with an overcast sky – whereas flat plate collectors are really productive only with direct solar radiation (clear sky conditions). However, as might be expected, evacuated tube collectors are more expensive than flat plate ones, being a more complex technology and involving additional components and assembly costs. For this reason also installation does not lend itself to DIY (plus, as mentioned previously, grant-aiding schemes generally require approved installers to be used). Contact your local energy agency for more information about grants.

Evacuated tube collectors are always of the indirect type. Solar radiation is collected on the absorber fins in the tubes and raises the temperature of a low-freezing-point heat transfer fluid. The fluid rises by natural circulation up a pipe in the centre of the fin and gives up its heat, at a condenser, to water circulating through an insulated manifold at the end of the tubes. The water from the manifold may then be

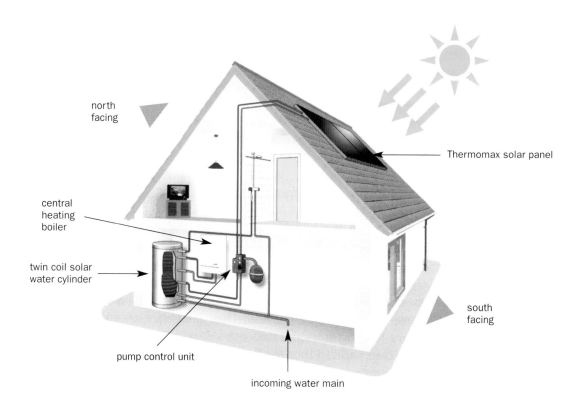

north facing

Thermomax solar panel

central heating boiler

twin coil solar water cylinder

pump control unit

south facing

incoming water main

Schematic of Thermomax evacuated tube, solar water heater.

Thermomax evacuated tube, solar water heater retrofitted onto a house in Bangor, Northern Ireland.

Close-up of the small photovoltaic (PV) array which powers the circuit pump of a Solartwin flat-plate, solar water heater, thus avoiding need for mains electrical connection and usage/cost.

fed to a secondary circulation coil in an HWC and back to the manifold (*see* the illustration on page 122). The top illustration on page 123 shows an evacuated tube array in position on the roof of a house.

Additional Components

Solar hot water heaters generally require a pump to ensure the correct flow of water and non-return valves to prevent reverse circulation. One system (*see* the bottom illustration on page 123) uses a small photovoltaic (PV) array to power the pump. This avoids your having to connect the pump to an electricity supply and, of course, avoids the (albeit small) electrical load normally incurred by the pump. Of course, the PV needs solar energy to work, but then so does the solar water heater – if there is enough for one then there is enough for the other.

PHOTOVOLTAIC CELLS

Photovoltaic (PV) cells are so called because they convert light direct into electricity. There are two types of cell, crystalline and thin film. Crystalline systems use the electronic properties of crystals to generate a current from light, while thin film systems rely on semi-conductor technology for the current flow. Crystalline systems are the more efficient, although more expensive since they require the actual growth of crystals of suitable quality. Thin film systems can be manufactured much more quickly and cheaply and their efficiencies are improving.

As with other solar technologies, PV should be south-facing as far as possible, although the normal location on a roof pitch means that an orientation off due south is not critical – even on a north-facing roof pitch PV can produce 60 per cent of its maximum output. A conventional roof pitch of 30 to 40 degrees also means that the PV cells will be placed at a favourable angle to the incoming solar radiation when it is most available in the United Kingdom and Ireland. In summer, with a sun angle of 50–60 degrees, a 30–40-degree pitch will give an angle of incidence close to 90 degrees, ideal for the maximum intensity of solar radiation and maximum potential output from the system. Installation is not generally a DIY-friendly operation – in any case, to avail yourself of grants currently available you will need, as mentioned before, to use an approved installer. Contact your local energy agency for information on grants (*see* 'Useful Contacts', section 5).

PVs have no moving parts, make no noise and have no parasitic loads (for instance, from pumps). The biggest problem with PVs is how to use them. Solar water heaters produce hot water which can be stored and for which there will always be a demand; PVs produce electricity, for which an immediate end-use must be identified, the alternatives being to export it to the grid, which requires grid-synchronization equipment (a further cost) or to store the output in batteries (also an additional cost and maintenance). A low voltage circuit can be run direct off batteries, although mains voltage appliances will need an inverter.

As regards the optimum size of a PV installation, grid-linked systems should be at least 8–10m^2 in size. This is because larger systems are proportionally less expensive than smaller ones and the economics are influenced by the amount of electricity you can export (as well, of course, as its price). Stand-alone systems should be sized according to the loads they are proposed to meet.

You may have noticed PV cells powering illuminated road signs and navigation buoys at sea. In these kinds of application, where grid connection is costly or does not exist, PV is most viable. In a normal domestic setting, however, of all the renewable technologies, PV is probably the hardest to justify economically at the time this book is being written. However, grants may be available which can meet up to 50 per cent or more of capital costs, making PV a much more attractive proposition. Economic viability is likely to improve in the future as the cost of grid electricity rises and the capital cost of systems continues to come down (although the latter is not a factor for someone installing a system now).

PV Arrays

Cells are generally arranged in modular arrays (*see* the illustration on page 125) which can be up to almost any size, depending on the area of roof available (and your budget). With newbuild or when re-roofing, PV arrays can take the place of the conventional roof covering (tiles or slates). This allows the array to be

Array of retrofitted PV cells from solarcentury.com.

more aesthetically integrated into the roof-scape and also avoids your having to penetrate the roof covering with fixings. The frame of the array must be well sealed at the joint with the roof covering. In a retrofit situation, you will generally retain the existing roof covering, but systems come complete with rubber grommets to ensure a good seal post-installation.

PVs can also be mounted on a frame on a flat roof. In this case the orientation of the house itself is not an issue since the frame can be placed in any direction. However, you will need to provide adequate ballasting or mechanical fixings to overcome the wind-loading. Penetrating a flat roof is never something one likes to contemplate. Alternatively, the roof itself would need to be structurally capable of taking the weight of the frame, panels and the ballast.

Tiles/Shingles

Developments in PV technology that further improve integration into the building fabric are PV tiles or shingles. These products are used in place of conventional tiles and can form all or part of the roof covering (*see* the illustration on page 126). Currently

C21 PV tiles from solarcentury.com, being installed in a new-build situation; the tiles enhance architectural integration compared with a standard PV array.

costs are around twice those of PV arrays for the same output. Electrical connections are made between the tiles and thence to the batteries or inverter. Modules are available as single tiles, or in larger panels. In both cases the products can blend in well with conventional roof coverings.

BIOMASS

This term covers any system which uses plant matter (including timber) as the fuel in a combustion (or gasification, *see below*) system, for example, wood chips, wood pellets, willow and miscanthus grass. Generally, on a domestic scale, this means wood chips or pellets burned to heat water, much as oil or gas in a conventional boiler. For those wishing to be green, yet avoid the high additional cost and intermittency of renewable energy technologies, biomass may be the answer. It is effectively carbon-neutral since the carbon emitted during use has been absorbed as carbon dioxide during its growth. If from forest residue or timber-processing waste, for example, the emissions would have been released during the decay process in any case. Sustainable sources specifically planted are replaced, thus ensuring the absorption of more carbon.

Combustion or Gasification?

Most domestic-scale systems will be used only to raise heat, to feed a 'wet' heating system and to provide domestic hot water (DHW). In this case, the biomass will simply be combusted to heat the water, much in the same way as with a gas- or oil-fired boiler. This is the type of system referred to in the following sections on wood-pellet and wood-chip boilers.

However, larger installations could possibly use the process of gasification, whereby the biomass is partially combusted under controlled conditions, producing a combustible gas. This gas can then be fed into a combined heat and power (CHP) unit to generate electricity on site as well as feeding the heating and the hot water system. The CHP unit comprises an engine which drives a generator to produce electricity while heat is recovered from the engine cooling system as well as from the flue (*see* section on CHP in Chapter 6).

Wood-Pellet Boilers

(*See* section on 'Boilers' in Chapter 6.) Wood pellets are manufactured generally from sustainably-managed or waste timber sources. They are more expensive to buy than wood chips but are much denser and have a lower moisture content, which means that less space is required for storage and there is less ash production. Automation is simpler as the pellets are of uniform size and systems can be controlled on timers in much the same way as a conventional boiler system. Systems are designed to meet urban emissions requirements.

Wood-Chip Boilers

(*See* section on 'Boilers' in Chapter 6.) Wood chips also can be processed from sustainable or waste timber sources but are irregular in shape and have a higher water content and lower density than pellets, thus not lending themselves so well to automated systems. However, the cost is much lower and those in rural areas who can source supplies readily, have the space required for storage and feed and can accommodate a little more in the way of maintenance (ash removal, for example) may find wood chips an economic and environmentally friendly option.

WIND TURBINES

For a number of reasons, planning and safety restrictions being among them, wind turbines are a less likely option for most dwellings, especially in built-up areas. However, if your house is in a rural area, with sufficient land available in order to distance a turbine from yourself and your nearest neighbours, then wind energy may be an option. There is also a new type of wind turbine on the market which simply 'plugs in' to the mains and, being small, is designed to be mounted on the side of a house (*see* 'Windsave', on page 128). However, you should consult your local planning office in any case. There are various configurations outlined here, some of which are more viable than others. Before considering a technology, however, there are two important steps to be taken, namely, determining the amount of wind available at your site and also obtaining planning permission for the turbine.

Wind Resource

The first step is to determine whether there is sufficient wind resource at your location. The British Wind Energy Association website (*see* 'Useful Contacts', section 3) has a service which enables you to find out the average annual wind speed at your location. Values are not absolute with regard to each given dwelling or precise location, but are based on an estimated average per kilometre square grid. The values of wind speed in metres per second (m/sec) are given at heights of 10, 25 and 45m above ground level. As a rough guide, wind turbines start producing an output at a wind speed of about 4–5m/sec, and an annual average of around 6m/sec is usually reckoned to be the minimum required for effective operation. Certain systems can shut down if the speed is too high, so select a system that complements the wind availability at your location.

Planning

The next step is to approach your local planning office since you will ultimately get nowhere until you have done this. The output from the system will be dependent upon the size of the turbine and the wind speed available. Wind speeds are higher at greater heights above ground level, but this will require a taller tower, which is likely to raise greater concerns with planners. A lower tower is thus more likely to be approved. A set fee is applicable for any planning application. If you are simultaneously making an application for other work, you could include the wind turbine in that application. However, it is possible that the wind turbine element will result in the whole application taking a longer time. It may be preferable to submit the wind turbine application separately and pay the additional fee in order to allow the application for the main works to proceed more quickly. Again, your local planning office will advise.

Stand-alone or Grid-Linked?

A wind turbine can be used either in connection with the grid or stand-alone; for example, feeding a dedicated circuit or where no grid connection exists, in which case battery storage will be required. Where the wind turbine is not supplemented by the grid (or some other system such as a diesel generator) the batteries are generally sized to provide three or four days' worth of normal consumption, in order to bridge gaps in wind availability. Depending on the storage capacity and load patterns, it may be necessary, from time to time, to defer non-essential activities when battery reserves are low. A wind turbine, with battery storage, feeding a dedicated circuit, can be relatively straightforward. A low voltage circuit (say, for lighting) would be one option. However, batteries are expensive to buy and maintain and attention is turning increasingly to using the electricity grid as back-up. The problem has been that the interfacing and signal conditioning equipment required is expensive, although recent developments have come along for smaller systems which reduce these costs (*see* 'Windsave', below).

A further option is to use the grid not only for back-up but also to export surplus electricity. This is the most complex and costly option, requiring the greatest amount of interfacing equipment and is not generally economically suitable for most domestic scale systems. Currently, most electrical utilities will pay only a low rate for electricity exported to the grid. However, developments such as 'net-metering' (paying producers the going rate for exported electricity), or even enhanced unit rates (such as have been seen in certain European countries such as Germany), would make grid-linked systems more attractive. Contact your Electricity Regulator (*see* 'Useful Contacts', section 4) for more information on forthcoming developments in this area.

Direct Water Heating

In this configuration the wind turbine is simply connected to an electric immersion heater. One advantage of this is that optimum use is made of the fluctuating output from the wind turbine. Also, back-up is readily provided via a fossil-fuel-powered boiler circuit or a conventional electric immersion heater. The output from the system, hot water, is always useful and the lower capital cost will improve the overall viability. However, the economics will be most favourable if the system displaces grid electricity rather than relatively cheap gas or oil.

Windsave

This is a recent development which makes wind energy much more accessible for most people. The system is small, relatively inexpensive and can be mounted on the side of a house – like a slightly over-sized television aerial. The most important feature of the Windsave system, however, is its interface with the mains electricity system, which allows it to be simply plugged in to offset electricity consumption (*see* 'Useful Contacts', section 3).

Micro-Hydro

For those fortunate enough to have a water course of sufficient and reliable flow on their property, a micro-hydro turbine may be an option. Similar issues arise to those with wind turbines in terms of how to use the output. Also, you should bear in mind that the output from the system may be subject to alterations to the water course made upstream.

GREEN ELECTRICITY TARIFFS

An alternative to renewables-generated electricity on site is to sign up to a 'green' electricity tariff. Most electricity suppliers now offer one for electricity generated from renewable energy, usually from large-scale wind turbines. Some suppliers simply repackage existing renewable generating capacity, but the best tariffs guarantee new renewables-generated capacity. There is no change involved to the grid connection nor disruption of any kind – and, of course, you do not actually get supplied exclusively with renewables-generated electricity – there are no 'green' or 'brown' electrons.

The way it works is this: an assumption is made of the average electricity consumption for a domestic household (say 3,500–4,000kWh per year). The electricity supplier then guarantees to purchase sufficient renewables-generated electricity in a given year to meet that average demand, multiplied by the number of people on the tariff. Some tariffs offer different levels of 'green' input, for example 10, 50 or 100 per cent. In cases other than 100 per cent the assumed average consumption is modified accordingly to arrive at the total renewables-contracted figure. Therefore, in effect, you can claim that all your electricity (or a percentage, depending on the terms of the tariff) is green. Not only that but, on the best tariffs, you can say that you are supporting new renewable energy installations.

CHAPTER 10

Appliances and Housekeeping

APPLIANCES AND GADGETS

White Goods

EU Energy Label

You have probably noticed, if you have been in an electrical store during the past five years or so, that all 'white goods' now carry letter ratings from A++ (most efficient) to G. The ratings used to go from A to G, but some manufacturers, at least in part no doubt encouraged by the recognition the rating process gave to more efficient products, began to produce even more efficient appliances. The description 'white goods' covers cold appliances such as refrigerators and freezers, and also laundry appliances (washing machines and tumble dryers) and dishwashers.

The rating system, introduced by the European Union in 1995, enables potential buyers to compare not only the purchase price and specification but also running costs of different makes and models. In addition to the letter-rating, a representative energy-consumption figure is shown; for example, for a washing machine, the kWh per cycle or, for a refrigerator, the kWh per year (*see* the illustration opposite). Laundry appliances and dishwashers also give the ratings for wash, spin and dry cycles. Some manufacturers provide information on other factors such as the capacity and noise.

Energy Saving Trust 'Energy Saving Recommended' Scheme

The Energy Saving Trust (EST) also has its own 'Energy Saving Recommended' labelling scheme (*see* the illustration on page 131) and maintains a database of appliances and suppliers on its website (*see* 'Useful Contacts', section 1).

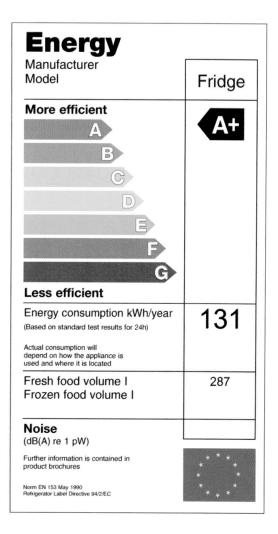

EU energy label for domestic white goods appliances.

Ecolabel

A voluntary Ecolabel scheme applies to washing machines and some other household appliances. The Ecolabel indicates that the product has passed tests on several key environmental issues, including energy efficiency, making it among the best in its class. Look for the 'daisy' symbol (*see* the illustration opposite).

Hot or Cold Fill

Washing machines are always plumbed for hot and cold water fill. However, you may find that certain appliances, such as dishwashers, are plumbed with one connection only. Most plumbers will connect this to the cold water supply, thus leaving the appliance to heat water from as low as 4°C to the operating temperature (about 90°C) using its internal electric immersion heater. This is costly and wasteful since the chances are that you have a cylinder full of hot water (at around 60°C) in your airing cupboard, sitting doing nothing most of the time. Subject to water hardness conditions, you should be able to connect the dishwasher to the hot water supply and reduce energy costs.

Tumble Dryers

The use of a tumble dryer is preferable to drying clothes on radiators, from an air quality as well as an aesthetic viewpoint. However, whether of the electric or gas-powered type, tumble dryers use a lot of energy (although the latter are cheaper to run). If you have the opportunity, you might think of building a drying room or using a utility room instead. The room would need to be ventilated but this could be controlled on a humidistat to reduce excessive heat loss. The room would not necessarily need to be heated if, say, the boiler were located there (*see* Chapter 8 on 'Ventilation').

Choose Wisely

There is no general correlation between purchase price and running costs. Some of the more expensive top-of-the-range brands, as well as lasting longer, are also the most energy efficient, although there are others, especially those that trade on image, of which the same could not necessarily be said. You may not base your purchasing decision entirely on energy effi-

Energy Saving Trust (EST) 'Energy Saving Recommended' logo; look out for this on all kinds of energy-consuming equipment.

EU Ecolabel 'Daisy' symbol indicating that an appliance is among the best in its class across a range of key environmental factors. (Defra)

ciency – it may not even be high on your list of priorities – but at least take it into account, especially when comparing a number of otherwise similar options. Lower energy consumption not only means lower running costs but is also likely to mean relatively low maintenance, since motors, heating elements and other components are run for shorter periods, although frequency of use will be an equally if not more significant factor.

Household Gadgets

Despite houses becoming more energy efficient in terms of heating systems and insulation, domestic energy use has actually been rising steadily over recent years. It may not be surprising that total domestic energy consumption is up, since so is the number of dwellings. However, the average use per household has also been on the increase. Partly this may be explained by houses now being larger on average than in the past. However, another reason is the increase in electricity consumption, much of which can be explained by the sheer number of electrical appliances in use around the home.

In the Kitchen
Cast an eye around your kitchen – you will probably see up to a dozen electrical appliances. In addition to the white goods and maybe the cooker, you may also have a microwave oven, an electric kettle, toaster, coffee machine, food processor, blender and electric deep fryer – and that's just for starters. You may also have an electric slow-cooker, electric grill, ice-cream maker, bread-maker, yogurt maker, coffee grinder, electric scales, electric juice extractor, electric carving knife, electric can opener, electric egg boiler – and one I came across only recently – an electric parmesan grater. Many of these are useful and could not be easily replaced. However, some (mostly towards the end of the list) smack of laziness or gadget mania.

We seem to be obsessed with electrical gadgets. Just because an automatic or electrical version of a tool exists does not mean that it does the job any better than the original, manual version. Manufacturers and retailers exploit our gadget mania to convince us that we need things when we really do not. These devices are often marketed as labour- and time-saving. But after you have assembled,

dismantled, cleaned and reassembled the electric version, is it really any quicker or less effort than the manual one? Perhaps we should just stop and think before buying our next electrical kitchen gadget – do we really need it? You may argue that many of these machines do not use much energy since they are not used very often – so in that case are they really worth buying in the first place? And it does not stop in the kitchen …

Throughout the House
Move into the living room and you may see a television, video player/recorder and/or DVD player/recorder and CD/tape player, and, more often than not these days, there will also be at least one satellite/cable box. Many of these appliances are designed to be left on standby so that they may be activated at the touch of a button from the comfort of your armchair. Did you know that televisions and video players use at least half as much energy on standby as when in use (whereas they use none when switched off)? Is your sitting room really that big that you cannot take a couple of extra steps on entering it to push the television set on/off button, and likewise on leaving the room?

Moving on through the house, we may find vacuum cleaners, personal computers and peripherals (printers, home network routers, for instance), mobile telephone chargers, telephone answering machines, more televisions/video/CD players, video games, hair-dryers, curling tongs, electric toothbrushes, electric razors, electrically-heated towel rails, convector heaters, fans, electric blankets … You get the picture.

'Energy Vampires'
Some appliances (such as the set-top boxes) do not even have an off button – you have to switch them off at the socket, which is often inaccessible and may involve reaching down or round behind furniture. And so we leave them on – not running, not being used, but still on. These are the 'energy vampires', which slowly drain energy away during the night, while we lie sleeping unaware of the energy consumption that we committed ourselves to when buying them in the first place. Responsible manufacturers should enable their appliances to be used in an energy-efficient way – surely that starts with an

on/off button. Perhaps we should all boycott appliances which do not have one? Manufacturers take note.

In the Garden

Moving out of the house, things do not get much better. You may have an electric lawn-mower, an electric strimmer, electric hedge-cutters and 'garden-vac'. If you are elderly or your mobility is impaired, then you may have every need of such devices, in which case I hope that you will excuse my rage against these machines. However, for those of us who are lucky enough to be able-bodied, a little hedge-clipping with shears or sweeping up of leaves with a yard-brush would not do any harm – indeed, it might do us some good – like a free work-out. Petrol mowers are not much better in energy terms. Added to which, concern has been raised recently regarding the health affects of breathing in the exhaust fumes from a petrol mower, an occupational hazard for gardeners. If your lawn is not too large, you might consider one of the old-fashioned, mechanical lawn-mowers instead.

Patio Heaters

One garden appliance which deserves special mention is the so-called 'patio heater', generally fuelled by a propane gas (LPG) cylinder, although also available in an electric form. My simple advice regarding these appliances is, 'Do not buy one'! They may heat your patio, but they heat a lot else besides – the outside air, the atmosphere. They are not just patio heaters, they are global warmers. Patio heaters remind me of being in the southern USA some years ago and walking out of an air-conditioned mall under a canopied walkway. Expecting a blast of warm air, I was surprised to be hit by a cool breeze, straight from an air-conditioning unit! This device was effectively trying to cool the outside air – much in the same (or perhaps opposite) way as a patio heater trying to heat it.

SUMMARY OF GOOD HOUSEKEEPING TIPS

Heating/Insulation
- turn room thermostats down 1°C and save up to 10 per cent of heating costs

- make sure curtains are well lined and well fitting and close them at dusk to keep heat in
- do not install full-length curtains where they would cover a radiator
- use your programmer/timer to provide heating/hot water only when needed
- during the day, turn down TRVs in rooms not occupied
- do not heat your conservatory, use it to extend the summer season, not all year-round

Hot Water
- take showers instead of baths; they normally use less than half the water
- set your cylinderstat no higher than 60°C
- fix dripping taps promptly, especially hot water taps
- always use the plug when running hot water into a sink or basin
- use low-flow showers with aerating heads instead of power showers

Draught-Proofing
- block gaps beneath skirting boards and around pipes penetrating external walls
- block chimneys when not in use (proprietary products are available for this)

In the Kitchen
- put lids on pans to reduce moisture and also save energy by turning down the ring
- use the right size pan; the base of the pan should just cover the ring/flames
- do not fill your kettle full for just one cup of tea
- cook more than one meal in the oven at a time and put the extra in the refrigerator/freezer; do not put warm food in the refrigerator/freezer, let it cool down first
- reheat food in a microwave oven
- do not have the refrigerator/freezer next to the cooker, you will only make it work harder
- keep refrigerators and freezers at least half full and defrost regularly
- avoid leaving the refrigerator/freezer door open for longer than necessary
- think twice before using electrical gadgets

Lighting/Power
- keep curtains and blinds fully open during the day to let plenty of light in
- make sure clothes are well spun/wrung out before putting them into a tumble dryer
- every time a conventional light bulb blows, replace it with a low energy lamp (CFL)
- always switch off lights unless you are leaving the room only for a couple of minutes
- do not leave televisions, etc. on standby, switch off at the appliance or socket
- try a low-temperature cycle for washing machines and dishwashers

LOW COST MEASURES TO IMPROVE ENERGY EFFICIENCY

Heating/Hot Water
- install loft insulation up to 270mm (grants may be available)
- insulate all hot water pipes within the house, especially those not normally visible
- fit a minimum two-channel, seven-day programmer/timer linked to roomstat and cylinderstat
- have your boiler serviced, ideally yearly and at least once every two years
- fit TRVs where not already present (except in areas where roomstats are located)
- upgrade existing controls to include roomstat, cylinderstat, programmer/timer and TRVs
- install a boiler jacket on older cast-iron boilers with no insulation
- fit insulation to your hot water cylinder or improve existing insulation if incomplete
- fit a thermostatic shower to automatically mix water to the right temperature

Insulation/Draught-Proofing
- install floor insulation to suspended timber floors, especially during other works
- fit secondary glazing to existing single glazing where frames are sound
- install cavity wall insulation where appropriate (grants may be available)
- install radiator foils on external walls, especially in solid walled houses
- draught-proof windows, doors, loft hatches and letter boxes

Other
- fit low-energy lamps (CFLs) to the most-used light fittings, use the EST database
- ask your local energy agency for a free energy check
- have a SAP rating carried out on your home and assess the affect of remedial measures

CHECKLIST FOR NEW EQUIPMENT

- select A-rated white goods (refrigerators/freezers, washing machines, dishwashers, etc.)
- replace boilers over fifteen years old with new condensing boilers where possible
- select combi boilers for smaller dwellings
- use the Ecolabel and EST 'Energy Saving Recommended' schemes for new appliances
- use the BRECSU boiler-sizing method to size a new boiler correctly
- use the SEDBUK database to identify the most efficient boilers available
- do not buy that latest gadget unless you really need it

CHAPTER 11

Energy/Environmental Rating and Legal Framework

SAP ENERGY RATING

For some years it has been a legal requirement, under the Building Regulations in the UK, to have a SAP Energy Rating carried out for all new dwellings. SAP stands for Standard Assessment Procedure (for Energy Rating of Dwellings) and is a method of assessing the energy efficiency of a dwelling. SAP is based on BREDEM (Building Research Establishment Domestic Energy Model), which takes user-input data on the dimensions and construction of a proposed (or existing) dwelling, plus the heating system and fuel type, and provides an estimate of the annual heating and hot water energy consumption, costs and CO_2 emissions. In addition, a rating is applied for easy comparison with other dwellings or alternative design options.

Energy consumption due to heating and hot water production only have been included in the SAP since these are largely determined by the characteristics of the building fabric and the boiler heating system (with the underlying assumptions in BREDEM regarding internal temperatures and occupancy patterns). Energy consumption caused by lights and appliances has not been included in the SAP rating since these are liable to vary greatly from one house to another and are not necessarily related to the design of the house. Current versions of SAP however, include allowances for dedicated low-energy lighting fittings (the type which cannot accept a conventional bayonet or screw end-cap). Some SAP software packages (*see* page 137) include additional modules which allow lighting and appliances to be taken into account.

Because the assessment is carried out long before the sale of a house, and also because SAP has only applied to new dwellings, most people will not have been aware of it. However, all this is set to change. New EU legislation requires all buildings, at point of lease or sale, to have an energy rating certificate produced and made available to the purchaser. In the case of dwellings in the UK, the energy rating will be provided via an updated version of SAP. In the Republic of Ireland the Building Energy Rating (BER) certificate has been introduced, based on the DEAP (Dwellings Energy Assessment Procedure — similar to SAP), initially for new dwellings with existing housing to follow.

In addition, the 'whole building' compliance route for UK Building Regulations thermal requirements is based on SAP. Previously there has been no requirement to achieve a minimum SAP rating (except at a time in England and Wales where one route to compliance was to achieve a SAP of 85). Now, however, SAP is used as the basis for compliance. Maximum long-stop elemental U-values have been set, along with minimum boiler efficiency and air-tightness levels, with an overall target based on dwelling size and shape and fuel type. Fabric thermal performance, boiler efficiency and air-tightness, amongst other factors such as deployment of low or zero carbon technologies, are balanced to achieve the target.

Also, the rating will form part of a package of information provided for a prospective purchaser. In this way, the energy rating of different purchase options can be compared, along with other criteria such as number of bedrooms, price and location. That is not to say that energy efficiency will be viewed necessarily with the same importance as these other factors. However, when comparing two otherwise similar options, it might be a deciding factor. Moreover, it will give some idea of the annual cost of providing heating and hot water for the house in question (*see* the illustration on page 136).

DESIGN INPUT AND RESULTS

Reference No: 1248
Property: 24 Galwally Avenue
Belfast, BT8 7AJ

Issued on	1 August 2005
SAP Rating:	**98**
SAP Value:	98.21
Fuel Bill:	£247.61
CO$_2$ Emissions:	4.5 tonnes per annum
Energy used:	59.5 GJ per annum

Surveyor: 2082–01, Patrick Waterfield, Tel: 028 9022 3545, Fax: 028 9022 3545
Address: 24 Galwally Avenue, Belfast, BT8 7AJ, N. Ireland
Client:
Software Version: EES SAP 99.01.4060-LA-D UnID, October 2000, BRE SAP Worksheet 9.60

SUMMARY OF INPUT DATA:

1.0	Property Type		H House, S Semi-Detached
2.0	Number of Storeys		3
3.0	Date Built		1938
4.0	Sheltered Sides		2
5.0	Sunlight/Shade		Average
6.0	Internal Walls Perimeter		20.00m, 28.00m, 13.00m
7.0	Internal Floor Area		48.00m^2, 68.00m^2, 20.00m^2
8.0	Living Area		20.00
9.0	Average Storey Height		2.80m, 2.60m, 2.60m
10.0	External Doors		U: 3.10 A: 1.89m^2, U:3.30 A: 3.15m^2 Semi, U: 3.10 A: 1.89m^2 Semi
11.0	Windows:	Type 1	D Double glazed S South U; 3.00 A: 1.50m^2
		Type 2	D Double glazed S South U: 2.20 A: 3.00m^2
		Type 3	D Double glazed N North U: 3.00 A: 4.00m^2
		Type 4	D Double glazed N North U: 2.20 A: 1,00m^2
		Type 5	D Double glazed W West U: 3.00 A: 3.00m^2
		Type 6	D Double glazed W West U: 2.20 A: 2.50m^2
		Type 7	
		Type 8	
12.0	Roof Lights:	Type 1	
		Type 2	
13.0	Draught Proofing		100%
14.0	Solar Water Heating		0
15.0	Pressure Test		
16.0	Mechanical Ventilation		None
17.0	Fans, Chimneys, Flues		1, 0, 0
18.0	Main Wall Type		U: 0.35 A: X Timber frame: 20%
	Other Wall Types		U: 0.30 A: 35.00m^2
19.0	Plane Roofs		U: 0.25 A: 68.00m^2
	Slope/Flat Roofs		
20.0	Lower Floor Type		U: 0.35 A: 48.00m^2
	Other Floor Types		Timber Floor: 68.00m^2, sealed
21.0	Main Heating		BOC Oil Standard boiler, 1998 or later. Pumped: pump in unheated space
	Heating Controls		CBD Program and roomstat and TRVs
	Secondary Heating		RCJ Coal open fire in grate
	Hot Water Heating		HWP From the primary heating system
22.0	Underfloor Heating		None
23.0	Thermal Store		None
24.0	Hot Water Cylinder		Yes, with stat
	Insulation		Foam, thickness: 38mm, pipes insulated
	Volume		110 litres
25.0	Community Heating		None
	CHP Unit		
26.0	Electricity Tariff		S-Standard
27.0	MHS Efficiency		79% (Value from the SAP worksheet table 4a/4b)
	SAP rating Complience		Pass

SAP energy rating printout from Elmhurst Energy Services Ltd – one of the UK government-approved SAP energy rating software and training organizations.

Self-builders, being involved during the design stage of the project, will have been more aware than most people of the SAP rating. However, there is also another way in which the self-builder can use SAP during the design process and that is to compare different design options. For example, you could compare, say, the relative impacts of increasing the insulation and installing solar water heating, or of a higher efficiency boiler compared with high-performance glazing. The SAP assessment will allow you to compare options in terms of energy consumption, energy cost and CO_2 emissions. By then factoring in the capital costs of the various options you can determine the most cost-effective way of achieving a given SAP rating.

Carbon Index

Originally, SAP was heavily influenced by energy/fuel prices and its primary focus was on encouraging energy efficiency by a reduction in costs. Later, the fuel cost factor was reduced in significance and energy consumption and CO_2 emissions became the key indicators. However, the latest development is the introduction of a carbon index figure. On a scale of 0–10, a low figure indicates high carbon emissions (or poor performance) and a high figure indicates low emissions (or high performance). The fuel type, together with the building fabric and heating system, will determine the overall carbon index. The introduction of such an index makes sense since the driver for all the energy-efficiency legislation is targets for the reduction of carbon dioxide emissions. The simple 0–10 scale should also make for easier understanding.

Approved SAP Energy Rating Software and Training Providers

When the legislation comes into force requiring energy rating certificates to be produced, this will need to be done by a suitably qualified person. As previously, you do not have to be a registered assessor to provide a SAP rating. However, as the certificate is based on SAP, it is likely that registered assessors will be used. To use the approved software you need to be registered with one of the three approved companies providing SAP software and training (see below). SAP assessments from registered assessors are generally accepted more readily by Building Control than submissions from other sources.

The three companies now licensed to provide SAP Energy Ratings are: Elmhurst Energy Services Ltd, NHER and MVM Starpoint (see 'Useful Contacts', section 10). There is also an umbrella organization called FAERO, the Federation of Authorized Energy Rating Organizations (again, see 'Useful Contacts', section 10), from whom up-to-date details can be obtained.

BENCHMARKS FOR ENERGY EFFICIENT/ENVIRONMENTAL DESIGN

EcoHomes: An Environmental Rating for Homes

You might think that it is hard enough trying to juggle all the many aspects of self-build or refurbishment – aesthetic, functional, economic, legal and so on, without having to think about energy and environmental matters too – and you would probably be right. There is a bewildering assortment of technologies and products now on the market that make reference to energy efficiency and environmental

---

EcoHomes Issues

- energy: CO_2 emissions, insulation, energy-labelled appliances, low-energy lighting
- transport: access to public transport and other amenities, cycle storage, provision of home office
- pollution: zero ODP insulation, renewable energy, low NOx burners
- materials: sustainable timber, storage for recyclable waste, building elements having the Green Guide for Housing Design 'A-rating' (see 'Useful Contacts')
- water: water-saving appliances and alternatives to mains water
- ecology and land use: preserving/enhancing ecological features, compact plan form
- health and well-being: daylighting to BS8206:2, sound insulation, semi/private external space
- management: energy/environment manual, site impacts, security

EcoHomes

EcoHomes …

… addresses the impact on the external environment …

… and the provision of healthy internal environments …

… in new housing.

credentials. You may start out with good intentions, but, at the end of the build, how will you know whether you have an environmentally friendly house? One way is to get the approval of an independent expert, in the form of an EcoHomes accreditation (*see* the illustration on page 138).

EcoHomes is a means of applying a total environmental rating to a proposed house design. A wide range of issues is covered, under the broad headings of energy, transport, pollution, materials, water, ecology and land use, health and well-being and management. The scheme was designed and is operated by the BRE. The *EcoHomes Guidance* is freely available from the EcoHomes website (*see* 'Useful Contacts', section 3).

EcoHomes recognizes that it is not always possible to achieve the same level of environmental performance in all aspects of the building, there will be constraints in terms of function, cost, aesthetics and aspects related to what the site offers. Credits are given for each issue addressed satisfactorily, the number of credits being in proportion to the importance of the issue or the need to encourage it to be addressed. A weighting is also applied to each category, again reflecting its significance. However, it is not necessary to gain credits for each and every issue. The numbers of credits, with weighting applied, are totalled up and a percentage calculated. A rating is given depending on the total percentage, as follows: a 'pass' requires 36 per cent, 'good' requires 48, 'very good' requires 58, and 'excellent' requires 70. The 'pass' level can be achieved by just about any dwelling meeting Building Regulations minimum legal requirements – it is more or less simply a matter of recording information on the specification of the dwelling; the 'good' rating can often be achieved with little if any increase in the specification or capital outlay over and above normal good practice; the 'very good' level will require more specific measures and may involve more significant additional costs; and finally, the 'excellent' rating is quite challenging and will require a significant departure from normal practice – renewable energy technologies and water economy measures, for example. As you can see, with the 'excellent' rating starting at 70 per cent, there is plenty of scope built in for future developments.

The BRE maintains a list of licensed, approved experts from which you may select an assessor. A workbook is issued for the development in which relevant information is entered. The assessor checks the information and determines the rating achieved. The assessor's recommendation is then returned to the BRE for quality assurance and certification; a fee is payable for this. As EcoHomes is designed principally with multi-dwelling developments in mind, the fee would be relatively high for a single dwelling – probably around £600. However, you might consider this good value for confirmation of an eco-friendly design. For up-to-date information, contact the EcoHomes office at the BRE (*see* 'Useful Contacts', section 3).

The *Green Guide to Housing Specification*

This sister publication to *EcoHomes Guidance* is described as 'an environmental profiling system for building materials and components used in housing'. In addition to an introduction containing a wide range of background information, the guide covers the main construction elements; external walls, roofing, ground floors, intermediate floors and internal walls. Kitchens, insulation (newbuild and refurbishment) and landscaping are also addressed, with information contained in the appendices on life-cycle assessment and environmental issue categories.

Options under each category are given a summary rating from A to C, A being the recommended, most environmentally friendly option and C being not

---

Green Guide to Housing Specification

external walls

roofing

ground floors

intermediate floors

internal walls

kitchens

insulation

landscaping

---

recommended. Specific issues, also rated A to C for each option, include climate change, fossil fuel depletion, ozone depletion, freight transport, toxicity to humans, waste disposal, water extraction, acid deposition, eco-toxicity, eutrophication (water pollution from algal blooms), summer smog and minerals extraction. Ratings are also applied to: recycled input; recyclability: whether currently recycled; and energy saved by recycling. Indicative comparative costs of options are also given, together with the typical lifespan/replacement period. The *Green Guide to Housing Specification* is available, for about £25, from the BRE (*see* 'Useful Contacts', section 1).

EMBODIED ENERGY AND LIFE CYCLE ASSESSMENT

Embodied Energy

'Embodied energy' is the term given to the energy required to convert a material or product from its most basic constituent raw materials into its final useful form – the energy embodied in the material or product. This might include the energy required for the extraction and processing of raw materials and the manufacture and transportation of products, for example.

Most of us, quite understandably, will be more interested in the energy consumption of the material or product in use as this will have a direct financial impact upon us. Also, it is easier to understand the concept of reducing energy consumption by the use of a certain material or product. The concept of embodied energy is a more abstract one and certainly much more difficult to picture clearly. However, if saving energy means something to us in terms of environmental protection and reducing resource depletion, then it makes sense at least to have an idea of the wider energy implications of the materials and products we choose.

The definition of embodied energy may differ according to exactly which processes are included in the calculation. Figures for embodied energy will vary likewise. The table below shows some indicative relative values for different building materials. Bear in mind that the figures shown are in terms of mass of material. Therefore, less dense products may appear to have a higher embodied energy than denser alternatives.

Embodied Energy and Density of Some Building Materials

	Embodied Energy (kWh/kg)	Density (kg/m³)
brick	0.83	1,700
dense block	0.50	2,300
medium block	0.42	~1,500
AAC block	1.00	600
plaster	0.81	600–1,300
plasterboard	1.22	950
render	0.50	1,200
glass-fibre insulation	1.36	12
timber stud	1.39	~ 500
glass	3.53	2,500
mild steel	9.44	7,800
aluminium	47.2	2,702
copper	27.8	1,350
PVC	22.2	550–650
MDF	3.14	300

As you can see, the more processed a product, the higher the embodied energy. Plasterboard has a higher figure than plaster, and AAC block has a higher figure than medium or dense block. However, AAC block is much less dense and the equivalent mass, compared with dense or medium blocks, would be much lower. Timber stud should come out fairly well, although appears to be getting on for twice as energy-intensive in production as brick. However, as the density figures show, brick is around three times denser than timber. Also, you would use a greater volume of brick to construct a load-bearing wall compared with timber in a timber frame construction.

This approach can also be applied (somewhat laboriously) to whole constructions, such as walls and roofs, to compare alternatives. It is not necessarily recommended that you should go down this road unless you are really interested. However, some awareness of embodied energy is a logical extension of a concern for energy in use.

Incidentally, you may have heard people speculate that it takes more energy to produce certain insulation products than they actually save when in use. I have seen the figures and I can tell you that this is not the case. A basic 'law' of economics would probably confirm this. You would not buy insulation (except that you have to by law) unless it saved you money (it does). For the manufacturers to make a profit, they must make it for less than you buy it for (they do). The energy taken to manufacture the product is only one (possibly fairly small) component of the total production cost. Therefore (even allowing for the fact that manufacturers may be paying less for their energy than we are, due to economies of scale), it is highly unlikely to take more energy to produce the product than it saves. This argument can also be applied to the constituent feedstocks and so on down to the raw materials.

Life-Cycle Assessment

A further extension of the embodied energy approach is life-cycle assessment – taking into account not only the embodied energy but also the transport energy in getting the products to site, the energy used in the construction process, the energy used by the building in its lifetime and that required for the demolition of the building and the disposal of materials, or, conversely, that which can be recouped by recycling. Recycling is not always the most energy-efficient option. Sometimes the energy involved in separating and sorting the constituent materials outweighs that of processing the raw materials, although there is always the resource depletion aspect to consider. However, materials such as steel and aluminium are highly recyclable, which helps to offset their high embodied energy figures. By this time you are really getting down to a level of detail that even the experts argue about, and you can see why. Again, you may feel it is sufficient just to have an awareness of the issues and an understanding that, in general, the more natural a product, the fewer processes it has gone through and the more local the source of its materials, the lower the embodied energy will be (recyclability also being a factor in a life-cycle approach).

THE LEGAL FRAMEWORK

The Building Regulations

The legal framework for advising on and enforcing energy standards (among other things) in buildings takes the form of the Building Regulations (in England, Wales and Northern Ireland and in the Republic of Ireland) or the Building Standards Regulations (in Scotland).

The main energy-relevant parts are those covering the conservation of fuel and power, and ventilation. A different lettering system is used in Northern Ireland and Scotland from that in England and Wales and in the Republic of Ireland, although there has been talk of bringing all areas of the United Kingdom into line. There are also some subtle distinctions in terms of legal entities, although again in time these may be standardized, perhaps along the model of the English and Welsh regulations. At the time of going to press, the following details were correct. Information on changes will be found on each region's website (see 'Useful Contact', section 6).

The essential purpose of the regulations in each region is the same: to ensure the health and safety of people in and around buildings, to promote energy efficiency in buildings and to contribute to the needs of disabled people. The Building Regulations apply

Building Regulations in the United Kingdom and Ireland: Main Parts Affecting Energy Efficiency	
Building Regulations (England and Wales)	
Conservation of Fuel and Power in Dwellings	Part L1
Ventilation	Part F
Building Regulations (Northern Ireland)	
Conservation of Fuel and Power	Part F
Ventilation	Part K
Building Standards Regulations (Scotland)	
Conservation of Fuel and Power	Part 6
Ventilation	Part 3
Building Regulations (Republic of Ireland)	
Conservation of Fuel and Energy in Dwellings	Part L
Ventilation	Part F

to all new buildings and extensions (as in the past retrofit conservatories are exempt up to 30m²) and to existing ones whenever there is a change of use or a material change to the building. A 'material change' covers the following 'building work' as defined in the Regulations:

- erection or extension of a building or loft conversion
- underpinning of foundations
- insertion of insulation into a cavity wall
- washing and sanitary fittings
- hot water cylinders
- foul and rainwater drainage
- replacement windows
- fuel-burning appliances

If you are in doubt regarding the applicability of the Regulations to a proposed action or programme of work, contact your local Building Control office for advice. They will also be able to advise you on good and safe practices, after all, the regulations are there for a purpose, not just to make life difficult. Not only will 'doing it right' mean that you can be confident in the work done, but it will also be beneficial if you ever come to sell the property. Your local Building Control officer is likely to take quite an interest in

you, as a self-builder, so it is much better to be on the safe side and to form a good working relationship with him or her.

Key Areas of Compliance

Thermal Performance

All the Regulations in regions of the United Kingdom and Ireland are heading toward the same approach regarding thermal requirements, that is, a whole-building approach. The basic method of compliance in the past has been the 'elemental method', that is, you do not exceed the maximum allowable U-value for each individual building element – wall, roof, floor or window. This method is straightforward, but does not allow much flexibility in design. Therefore, a trade-off method has also been available whereby you can reduce the performance in one aspect of the design so long as you make up for it in another and satisfy an overall target U-value. For example, you could increase the area of glazing if you wished, while increasing the insulation in the roof to a corresponding extent in energy terms.

The 'whole building' approach, which has been introduced now for all areas of the United Kingdom, is based on a total carbon dioxide emissions rating of the dwelling. This takes into account such factors as dwelling dimensions, building element areas and thermal performance, ventilation characteristics and heating system/fuel type. Allowances are also made for specific energy efficient and low carbon measures, such as renewable energy technologies and low energy lighting.

Ventilation

The key purpose of the ventilation section is to ensure adequate ventilation for occupant health and to avoid any risk of damage to the building fabric from condensation. Aspects covered include background ventilation levels and the areas of openings required to provide such, increased ventilation rates in parts such as kitchens and bathrooms and the means of achieving this by mechanical extract or passive stack ventilation, and rules for ventilating through adjoining spaces.

Again, if in doubt, consult your local Building Control office which should be able to help. If you make it clear to them that you are aiming to make your house more energy-efficient than the minimum requirements demand, they will, one would hope, give you every assistance and maybe (you never know) allow you a little slack in other areas should you need it.

Planning Requirements

Planning permission is a totally separate issue from the Building Regulations. There are some aspects that are subject to the one and not to the other. For example, replacing a boiler will be an issue under Building Regulations but is unlikely to concern the planners. On the other hand, the appearance of your dwelling is of no consequence to Building Control but will certainly be a planning issue. Again, you should check with your local Planning Office regarding the applicability of planning regulations to your proposed works (*see* 'Useful Contacts', section 8).

Some energy-related measures may need planning permission, for example, installing a wind turbine, though if far enough away from other dwellings and not in a sensitive area, it should not present a problem. If you make it clear to the planners that you are aiming for an energy-efficient dwelling they will, again one would hope, appreciate the wider benefits of this approach and give you what assistance they can.

Neighbour Notification

Your local Planning Office may issue neighbour notification notices to owners of the adjacent and facing properties, or of those at the rear if they are likely to be affected. However, it would be sensible for you to make your neighbours aware beforehand of the works you are proposing – it would be regrettable to get on the wrong side of them either during the works or after their completion. Check also if your proposed work is likely to be subject to any other legislation, such as that governing party walls.

Ongoing Legal Developments

In Northern Ireland, a Secretary of State announcement has decreed that all new buildings must include some 'low or zero carbon (LZC) technologies' from April 2008. Similar requirements are being discussed for England and Wales. In parts of the Republic of Ireland, as well as in England, local councils are already moving ahead of current and forthcoming standards by implementing their own requirements regarding low carbon buildings (check with your own local council for more details).

In the UK the bar has been set now following Chancellor Gordon Brown's pre-budget announcement requiring all new housing to be 'zero carbon' by 2017. This presents a considerable challenge. We can build to a zero-heating standard in UK and Ireland right now using super insulation (see Chapter 3), and can certainly achieve zero carbon heating and hot water via combinations of insulation, biomass boilers and solar water heating. However, meeting the residual energy loads of lighting, cooking and electrical power will require the use of renewable 'microgeneration' technologies such as wind and PV, as well as more efficient lighting and appliances.

For the construction industry in general, if we are to meet this exacting standard in ten years' time, we really need to start making some serious moves right now. As individual self builders and/or home-owners, we should bear in mind also that, when the new requirements come in, houses which today are innovative and ground-breaking will suddenly appear hopelessly out of date!

CHAPTER 12

Wider Environmental Issues

WATER ECONOMY

This is not principally an energy-efficiency issue at the householder level, although the reduced usage of hot water will yield energy savings. However, where water is metered there are certainly savings to be made from water economy. Furthermore, energy savings will result at the regional and the national level due to the lower volumes of water needing to be pumped round the distribution system and decontaminated at water treatment plants. In addition, you can save on capital costs as well as standing losses by clustering your hot water services, where possible. For example, place your bathroom above your kitchen and have both close to the boiler. Place any en-suite bathrooms as close as possible (vertically or horizontally) to the main bathroom. If you think that you may want an extra bathroom in the future, locate a suitably-sized, multi-use room adjacent to the existing bathroom – this will greatly facilitate the supply of hot and cold water to the new bathroom.

I have divided water economy measures into two types: appliances that use less water and systems that provide an alternative to metered water.

Water Economy Appliances

Spray Taps
Spray taps reduce the water volume, either by reducing the droplet size or by aeration (entraining air into the water flow). Smaller droplets are formed by small holes which also increase the pressure and thus the velocity, compensating for a lower water volume. The same principle can be applied to showers – *see below.*

Water Brake Taps
These single lever taps contain a mechanism which 'brakes' the lever at about 40 per cent of full throw by providing a mechanical resistance. If you then need to increase the flow you simply push harder against the resistance. The idea is that you reduce your water usage by not opening the tap fully each time.

Low-Flow Showers
Today, the last word in bathrooms seems to be the 'power shower'. I heard of one man who installed such a device in his house and found that he emptied his hot water tank in a single shower. That is the last word I shall say on them …

Low-flow showers and those with aerating heads can provide just as effective a stream of water as higher flow types, but with a much lower usage of water, thus reducing not only the cost of water (where metered) but also that of the energy to heat it.

Low-Flush Toilets
It is a shocking waste of a valuable commodity that so much water is treated to drinking-quality levels only to be flushed down the toilet, along (where metered) with your money. Lower volume cisterns, for instance, 6ltr instead of the conventional 9, can significantly reduce your annual water consumption and are becoming commonplace.

Dual-Flush Toilets
These have not one but two flushing mechanisms, linked to different release buttons and dispensing different volumes of water depending on need; if we call these buttons 'Number 1' and 'Number 2' you

will get the idea. Some systems have volumes as low as 2 and 4ltr for the Number 1 and the Number 2 button, respectively. It should be noted that these mechanisms are more complex than standard cisterns and thus may be more prone to failure. For this reason I would recommend higher quality makes and careful operation. Also, it is essential, as with all non-standard or non-conventional appliances, to make sure that you (or your plumber) are aware of the differences when compared with a standard appliance. If you are using a plumber this is especially important as they may be less likely to read the instructions and, instead, simply do things the way they always have. In the interests of even-handedness, I should add that this observation does not apply only to plumbers. Many people, understandably, feel happier with what they know and are wary of new ideas and so it is important, therefore, to get them on your side. Once they see that the energy-efficient alternative works, they will spread the news to others.

Water-Efficient White Goods

Water-efficient washing machines use faster spin rates than conventional ones. Faster spin rates may require higher-rated motors, although they will run for shorter periods. Water-efficient dishwashers programme wash cycles for reduced water volume. Look for information on cycle efficiency on the EU Energy Label of a new appliance. Also look for the EcoLabel 'Daisy' logo (*see* Chapter 10).

Waterless Appliances

Composting or chemical toilets use no flush water at all, while the end product (I am reliably informed) makes good garden fertilizer. These do require proper maintenance but, so operated, can work well for many years. This type of device would be most appropriate in, say, a rural area off the mains sewage system, where the alternatives would be a septic tank or a mini water treatment plant.

Alternative Water Supply Systems

Uses

Watering the Garden and Washing the Car No treatment is required for the garden, a simple water butt sufficing. The butt could also provide water for car-washing/rinsing, provided that any grit is allowed to settle out at the bottom of the butt.

WC Flushing and Washing Machines I have already mentioned the dreadful waste of potable water which is flushed down toilets. Enough rain falls on the average house in the British Isles to provide one person's entire water needs, or, alternatively, the WC flushing requirement for a family of four (using low-volume cisterns). A dedicated rainwater system for WC-flushing would not require high levels of filtering before use, but simply additional piping, storage tanks and a pump. Alternatively, a rainwater harvesting system, such as described below, can serve WCs as well as appliances such as washing machines.

Other Uses The use of rainwater for potable supplies is perfectly possible, although obviously it requires much greater levels of filtration and treatment. In more remote areas, where mains or reliable good quality spring water is not available or would be costly to provide, this type of system (including 'Grey Water Reuse' – *see* page 146) may be worth considering.

Rainwater Butts

The simplest way to make use of rainwater is to install a water butt to one of your downspouts. The butt should have a well-fitting lid, an overflow to drain and a draw-off tap near the bottom. Such water can be used for the garden – plants will probably prefer it, after all, it is what they are used to. Make sure, however, that the downspout is not joined by the outflow from a sink or bath since the soapy residue will not be appreciated.

I did hear of one ridiculous case where a privatized water company in England threatened to sue a man who installed a water butt to his downspout, for interrupting *their* supply. I trust that, if the case ever got to court, the judge threw it out and made the company pay the full costs.

Rainwater Harvesting Systems

It was good enough for our ancestors and (most of the time) it is good enough for us. This is the most obvious way to reduce significantly a reliance on mains water and thus reduce costs (where the supply

Schematic of the GRAF Herkules Garden and House central rainwater collection system, distributed in the United Kingdom and Ireland by Hibernia ETH Ltd.

is metered), as well as the environmental impact of water treatment. Any pitched roof provides a suitable rainwater catchment area and standard rainwater goods (gutters, hoppers and downspouts) form the first stage of a collection system. Additional storage/ settling tanks will be required and also filtration, the extent of which will depend on the intended use for the water.

Adequate storage will be required in order to bridge dry periods, the precise volume depending on your estimated water consumption, the average rainfall and the likely maximum period without rain. Storage tanks can therefore be quite large and you may need two or three, to allow for the settling of particles, with filtration between each. Alternatively, commercial systems are available which incorporate the storage, settling and filtration functions within a single unit. The size and weight of the tank(s) mean that location in the roof space is not practicable. Instead, they are usually located on or below ground, requiring pumps to supply water to appliances. While this incurs an electricity load, thus offsetting the environmental benefits of the system, the pump need not be high-rated. Moreover, the pump would require only intermittent operation, for example, controlled by the pressure in the distribution system or the water level in a roof space header tank.

The illustration above shows a fairly simple rainwater harvesting system, for the purpose of demonstrating the principle. More recent developments from the same manufacturer include improved filters which divert any unwanted matter straight to the drain and central control systems located within the house showing the tank water level, system status and so on. Automatic switchover to mains (when the tank runs dry) from the control centre, rather than via the tank (as shown in the illustration) is another improvement since this leaves a greater capacity in the tank to receive the next rainfall. Systems can serve the house or the garden alone or both.

Rainwater goods may also receive waste water from baths and basins. This water (termed 'Grey Water Reuse' – *see below*) is also usable for WC flushing but may need higher levels of filtration. If this grey water is not to be reused it will be necessary to provide separate rainwater and grey-water pipework.

Grey Water Reuse

'Grey water' is a term used to describe waste water from baths, showers, wash hand basins and dishwashers (by analogy, 'black water' is effluent from toilets). Grey water, with the appropriate treatment, can be reused for purposes in the home such as toilet flushing, car-washing and possibly watering the garden, where water quality is not important. Black water is generally not treatable on a domestic scale for reuse. The exception would be the use of reed bed water treatment – *see* page 147 – although this takes up much space and requires a sizeable plot of land.

Reed-Bed Systems

This is a specialist operation and should not be attempted by the self-builder except under expert direction. The principle exploits the properties of certain wetland reeds to clean water by extracting from it impurities which act as nutrients for the plant. The reeds are planted in a sand and gravel bed, which provides filtration. A certain area of land is required, a reed bed serving a typical family house occupying around 25m². Also, depending on the planning authority, the bed may be required to be up to 25m from the dwelling. More expensive types, typically comprising at least three chambers, can produce an outflow which can be discharged direct into a watercourse, subject to approval from the appropriate authority. Note that locations with a high water table may not be suitable for these systems.

RECYCLING

Recycling is thought of primarily as an environmental issue rather than an energy one as such. From a resource-depletion angle, recycling is almost always worthwhile, as it is from the aspect of waste disposal. In energy terms the situation is not always so clear. Sometimes it may take more energy to collect, separate and reprocess a material than it would to use a new raw material. However, in most cases the wider energy and environmental benefits prevail. For this reason – and because it is becoming a socially accepted norm – recycling is included here.

It was not always thus. If you have seen John Waters's satirical black comedy *Serial Mom* you will recall the turning point in the film which is set in a courtroom. The main character, played superbly by Kathleen Turner, is an ordinary, everyday mother who turns serial killer to relieve the monotony of everyday life. Events take their course and Serial Mom lands up in court. A key witness for the prosecution is her elderly next-door neighbour who has witnessed some strange goings-on. Serial Mom decides to dismiss her legal team and fight the case herself. She embarks on a character-assassination of her neighbour which culminates in the accusatory question, *Do you recycle?!* Knowing full well the answer (since she has been through her neighbour's bins) Serial Mom watches as the poor old lady

crumbles, mumbling something to effect of, 'Well … I … I always meant to … but … somehow I never got round to it…' There is an audible gasp from the public gallery – Serial Mom's work is done and the prosecution case collapses. That was over ten years ago and is it yet socially unacceptable not to recycle? If not, it is becoming so, and so it should.

Many local authorities now provide a doorstep recycling service or collection points for recyclable materials. In some areas voluntary or charitable bodies provide a 'green box' service for the collection of recyclable materials. Typical materials separated are glass, paper, plastics, tins and cardboard. There is also an increasing concern regarding biodegradable waste (from gardens and compostable food) and also putrescible waste (meat products). More authorities are starting to collect garden waste, which bulks out landfill if disposed of with the rest of household waste. The authorities can make use of the waste to produce mulch for municipal gardens. Uncooked, non-meat food waste can be composted in your own garden. No longer the sprawling, stinking, open heaps of the past, composting bins these days are now little bigger than an old-style dustbin and allow the clean and neat recycling of food waste, providing an excellent fertilizer. Composting is infinitely preferable to a sink-mounted waste disposal unit, which simply chews up wastes and spits them out into the waste-water system – using energy in the process.

Batteries are another area of concern. Although those used in the home are small, they often contain highly toxic substances which can leach out of landfill and pollute water courses. Batteries need to be disposed of in an environmentally friendly way and that can be done only in special facilities. In France they have had battery collection points in supermarkets for around twenty years – so why not here? Rechargeable batteries are available in most sizes now (except the small, disk-shaped watch-type ones) and obviously reduce the problem of disposal. While costing around twice the price of ordinary disposable batteries, the rechargeable ones are most cost-effective since you will get many charges out of them during their lifetime. Someone is bound to point out that it takes electricity and thus energy to recharge the batteries. However, as mentioned elsewhere, if it saves you money (which it does) it will probably be overall energy-saving too. As an illustration, a typical battery charger will be rated at, say, 5.5W. Four AA sized 1.2V batteries will take 16hr to charge, costing just over a penny at a unit price of 12p.

Alternatively, why not opt for battery-free devices such as a solar-powered radio or a wind-up torch? The radio, if placed beside a window, will never run out of power. If you move it away from the window it can still be charged up with a wind-up mechanism. As for the torch, you know the scenario: you go to look for the torch which you have not used for months and … the battery is flat. So the next time you go to the shops you buy a new battery and put it into the torch. Several months later, when you go to use the torch again … the new battery is flat, it has discharged despite its not having been used. Go for a wind-up torch instead – altogether much less of a wind-up.

And, of course, it goes without saying that you should always include your car trips to recycling centres on journeys you would have been making anyway, otherwise you will be undoing some of the environmental benefits of your recycling. (Does your local authority provide all the recycling opportunities you would like? If not, why not contact them to see what provisions are in the pipeline?)

TRANSPORT

Another logical extension of addressing energy efficiency in your home is to look at the implications of your transport usage. In the United Kingdom and Ireland we have a lower rate of car ownership than in many other European countries, but a higher level of usage – those of us who have cars use them more. There may be understandable reasons for this – poorer public transport infrastructure, lack of alternative options in rural areas, people having to work far from home and children not going to school near where they live, for instance. There may be other reasons outside our control, such as the trend for retail outlets to be sited in out-of-town malls (following the American model and not necessarily a good idea). There will always be things we can do nothing about. However, there may be some things we can influence, if we think far enough ahead.

The Location of Your House

If you are planning to build a new house and have not yet settled on a site, why not use its proximity to facilities and public transport nodes as one of your criteria. EcoHomes (see Chapter 11) awards credits for proximity to amenities such as shops, post office, pub and chemist, and also for proximity to public transport nodes having a particular frequency of service during certain periods. If you can find a site that is within walking distance of schools and within cycling distance of, or has public transport access to, your workplace, you will obviously cut down greatly on the number of car trips you need to make.

Use of Public Transport

If you already have your site, or house, which is in a residential area and you do not have a bus stop within, say, 500m, why not contact the local bus company and ask them to consider putting a new stop in? If enough people from one area make such a request they may listen.

If you have a bus stop or train station nearby you may find that, with a little organization and a knowledge of the timetables, you can make significant use of it. For a regular journey (to work, for example) where you are simply travelling between your house and a single location, there is no need to take the car if there is a public transport option. For trips with children you will find that a bus or train ride adds to the excitement.

Sometimes it may be necessary to make connections between different routes or different forms of transport. This can be time-consuming if the connections are not available when you want them, and tedious if delays cause you to miss them. In this case, again, it may be worth bringing these issues to the attention of the transport providers.

Optimizing the Use of the Car

There will always be occasions when you need to use a car – for going on holiday, for visits to remote areas, for multiple trips which would be impracticable with public transport, and for carrying heavy or large objects. However, we should try to be more like our continental counterparts and use our cars less. If the car is unavoidable, try to cluster your trip ends, that is, try to arrange your journeys such that you are not criss-crossing town on a given day or even week. Also, try to make trips multi-purpose – visit the recycling centre on the way to the shops and call in to visit friends on the way back.

At other times you may be able to avoid using the car altogether, by using public transport or by cycling. There are more and more cycle paths (and bus lanes) appearing now which make cycling safer. Contact Sustrans, the cycle network organization, for up-to-date information on cycle networks in your area (*see* 'Useful Contacts', section 3). If your workplace does not have facilities for cyclists, why not suggest that they should introduce them? It is not hard – a secure place to lock the cycle, a place to change, a shower and a locker are all you really need. Some enlightened organizations even give cyclists a mileage allowance to encourage a move away from cars.

Vehicle Energy Rating

Another way of reducing the energy impact of your private transport usage is to opt for a more fuel-efficient car. Already we have seen a reduction in Vehicle Excise Duty (the road tax) for smaller cars and there are moves afoot (which should be in place by the time you read this) to introduce an energy-rating system for cars (*see* the illustration opposite) similar to that used for white goods.

Each make of car will in future bear a fuel economy label, showing a colour-coded letter rating, from A to F, representing an increasing level of carbon dioxide emissions in g/km. In common with the white goods rating scheme, additional information will be provided, such as the estimated annual fuel cost per 12,000 miles, Vehicle Excise Duty, engine capacity, fuel type and fuel consumption in miles/gal as well as ltr/100km on urban, extra-urban (outside urban areas) and combined-drive cycles. While the colour of the car is still likely to be much more of a factor than the colour of the sticker, at least the system will allow an at-a-glance comparison of different makes and types of car.

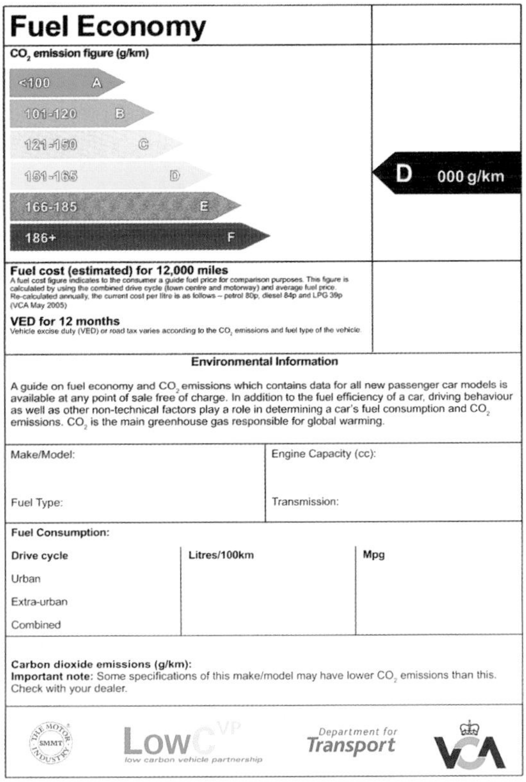

CALCULATING YOUR 'CARBON BUBBLE'

Why not now go the whole hog and estimate your 'carbon bubble'? This is a term coined to represent

Any colour you like as long as it's green! The proposed vehicle energy rating label will give car buyers more information with which to compare the fuel consumption and emissions of different makes and models. (DfT)

the carbon (or carbon dioxide) emissions resulting from your own personal energy consumption throughout the year. It is not practicable to include absolutely everything (the source of all food, for example), so home energy consumption and car type/mileage would be a good start. As an aside, on the subject of food, it makes much sense to buy locally-produced food since not only is it likely to have lower embodied energy but you will also be supporting your local community.

Fortunately, there are carbon calculators available that will do this for you. Two may be found on the Climate Care website (*see* 'Useful Contacts', section 3). The first covers the home and the car and the

149

second covers flights. You may be surprised to find that the carbon impact of a family of four flying to the USA and back can be around half the annual carbon impact of a house and two cars. Aviation is a huge energy user and carbon producer (and aviation fuel is not taxed to anything like the levels of vehicle fuel). Even the British Airports Authority is now on record as saying that the aviation industry is going to have to do something to address the issue.

Climate Care also offers you a way to assuage your guilt: you can make a donation to them at a level proportional to your carbon production to help fund environmentally friendly activities. If you do this, Climate Care will send you a certificate confirming your contribution to creating a more sustainable climate. And, of course, you could also take steps, as discussed previously, to reduce your car miles and domestic energy consumption.

SUMMARY

If you have read this far, you will hardly need a summary, you will already appreciate the benefits of an energy-efficient design and lifestyle. However, here is a round-up of the main themes of the book.

Energy and Running Cost Savings

Taking an energy-efficient approach can yield significant savings in energy consumption and thus costs over conventional housing built to Building Regulations minimum levels. That said, as the legal minimal requirements have been raised steadily over the years, it is becoming harder to better them cost-effectively. However, remember that the minimal requirements are still just that and not a blueprint for energy-efficient design.

Thermal and Visual Comfort

Higher standards of insulation can help to provide comfortable temperatures in winter with lower fuel consumption, while passive solar design can offset conventional energy sources, especially in spring and autumn. The careful design of windows can provide a balance between allowing solar heat and daylighting gains and maintaining a well-insulated envelope.

Amenity Value

Conservatories and sunrooms, as well as other configurations of glazing, can allow us to appreciate the sunshine at times of the year when it would not be comfortable outside. This can add considerable amenity value to dwellings. Beware, however, of heated conservatories which can end up being huge gas-guzzlers. Instead, use an unheated conservatory as a semi-outdoor space to extend either end of the summer.

Total Environmental Profile

Buildings that use less energy are less polluting to the environment. Increasingly (and with the added incentive of rising energy prices) this is likely to have a bearing on the market value of properties. If you also select natural materials this will have an additional benefit in terms of total environmental impact and can also provide a more healthy internal environment. Some finance houses and insurance companies, acknowledging the links between environmental emissions and the risks due to climate change, are starting to reduce mortgage rates and insurance premiums for more energy-efficient and environmentally-friendly buildings.

Potential for Innovation

If you are going through the agonies of self-build there is no point in ending up with a house that looks just like everyone else's, a volume builder could have done that in much less time (although probably at a higher cost by the time they have factored in their profit). Instead you will want to make a statement, you will want your building to say something about who you are. If you are committed to energy efficiency and the environment, there are many ways of expressing this, some high profile (such as renewable energy technologies) and others more subtle (such as higher insulation levels, advanced glazing systems and a greater use of passive solar design). Energy efficiency does not necessarily mean 'whacky'… but it can do. Use energy efficiency as part of your design concept and see where it takes you.

Glossary

AAC autoclaved aerated concrete, lightweight and thermally improved type of concrete block, an alternative to conventional medium or dense block.

Absorber plate part of solar water heater which absorbs solar radiation to be transferred to water direct or via heat transfer fluid.

Acid Rain rainfall that contains significant proportions of sulphuric and nitric acids, formed in the atmosphere by the combination of water with sulphur and nitrogen oxides emitted from fossil-fuel burning.

Aerated taps/showers ones that entrain air with the water flow, thus reducing the amount of water used.

Air changes per hour (ach) expression of ventilation or infiltration levels, the number of times in one hour that the total volume of air in a room or dwelling is replaced with incoming fresh air.

Air-tightness degree to which a building fabric avoids infiltration; in other words, absence of 'leaks'.

Architrave moulding usually timber, surrounding a door or window opening.

Array number of photovoltaic cells contained within a modular panel.

Backdraught damper damper preventing draughts from entering a building through an extract fan while the latter is not in use.

Batt rigid form of mineral fibre insulation.

Biomass general term covering any plant matter used for fuel.

Black water effluent from WCs, not normally treatable for reuse on a domestic scale except via reed beds.

Boiler interlock full control of a boiler whereby it does not fire unless a roomstat is calling for space heating or a cylinder stat for hot water.

BRE Building Research Establishment, former government agency now privatized; leading organization for building R&D and testing in the United Kingdom.

Breathable membrane thin layer of material allowing limited air and water vapour transfer, yet resistant to water penetration, essential element of timber frame and roof construction.

BRECSU Building Research Energy Conservation Support Unit, part of BRE (q.v.), concerned with energy conservation in buildings.

BREDEM Building Research Establishment Domestic Energy Model, underlying methodology of SAP, used to estimate heating and hot water energy consumption, etc.

Brick skin outer brick layer, for example, in a timber frame construction, where the brick is not a structural component of the building.

British Board of Agrément testing procedure for building materials (see BRE).

British Wind Energy Association subscription organization providing information on wind energy in the United Kingdom.

Buffer zone term used in passive solar design either to describe areas such as storerooms and stairways, which may be located to the north of a plan, or the effect of an unheated conservatory on adjacent conditioned spaces.

Building Control body which oversees implementation of Building Regulations in the United Kingdom and to which application must be made for certain proposed measures in a programme of work.

Building element a constituent part of the building, wall, floor, roof, window, etc.

Building fabric materials comprising any part of the building, walls, floors, roof, etc.

Building Regulations legal requirements in England and Wales and in Northern Ireland (called Building Standards Regulations in Scotland), also in the Republic of Ireland, governing minimum standards of performance in various areas, including energy.

Building services engineer may also be known as a mechanical and/or electrical engineer, responsible for designing building services; heating, lighting, ventilation, etc.; not always involved in single dwellings, but should be considered for larger or more complex houses or where unconventional measures are proposed.

Carbon bubble term used to describe the total carbon emissions resulting from an individual's (or household's) energy usage, can include home, car, air-travel, etc.

Carbon dioxide (CO₂) compound of carbon and oxygen produced on combustion of fossil fuels which has been linked to the accelerated greenhouse effect (q.v.).

Carbon index expression of energy efficiency/environmental impact of a dwelling, scale of 0–10, where higher value indicates better energy efficiency.

Carbon monoxide (CO) compound of carbon and oxygen produced by incomplete combustion of fossil fuels, dangerous when allowed to build up inside a house.

CFL *see* Compact fluorescent lamp.

Chartered Institution of Building Services Engineers (CIBSE) professional body representing building services engineers; produces guides and other publications.

Chasing the act of making a recess or channel into masonry to accommodate services (pipework, cables, electrical boxes, etc.), usually done with a hammer drill although special pick required for AAC blocks (q.v.).

Chimney effect term used in passive ventilation to describe the action of air passing over the top of a duct to draw in air at the bottom (much like a chimney to a fireplace).

CHP combined heat and power, process of generating electricity via a generator run off a gas, diesel or biomass gasification engine while simultaneously recovering heat from the engine cooling system and flue to use for space heating and/or domestic hot water.

Clerestorey window high-level window which can be used to allow solar heating or daylighting gains, especially into the north zones of a building.

Cold bridge (or thermal bridge) continuous element of fabric spanning external and internal surfaces, which acts as a route for conductive heat loss.

Colour rendering accuracy with which a light source shows the true tone of a colour or range of colours.

Colour temperature term describing quality of light; whiter light has a higher colour temperature and yellower light a lower one.

Combi boiler boiler providing hot water for space heating and also DHW (q.v.), direct-fired, avoiding the need for an HWC (q.v.) and associated standing losses.

Comfort temperature that temperature which provides comfortable internal conditions (will vary according to time of year, nature of space and activity taking place therein and, most significantly, individual preference).

Compact fluorescent lamp (CFL) low-energy, long-life lamp, formed by coiling a thin fluorescent tube into a compact form.

Compostable waste that which can be broken down by composting, for example, uncooked, non-meat, food waste.

Conditioned space one provided with heating or cooling, although latter should not be necessary in housing in the UK and Ireland.

Condensing boiler one incorporating a condenser to extract heat from the flue gases, thereby making better use of the fuel and increasing the overall boiler efficiency.

Conduction transfer of heat through a material.

Conservatory technically an extension having not less than 75 per cent glazed roof and not less than 50 per cent glazed walls; retrofits exempt from

Building Regulations up to 30m^2.

Convection transfer of heat by air movement.

CoP coefficient of performance (of a heat pump) – ratio of useful heat produced to electrical energy used.

CORGI Council of Registered Gas Installers, organization licensing approved gas appliance installers.

CWS (cold water storage) tank usually located in the roof space, feeds the HWC (q.v.), WC cisterns and wash hand basins in a non-pressurized system.

Cylinder stat short for cylinder thermostat, temperature-sensing device on HWC, part of a well-controlled boiler/DHW (q.v.) system.

Dabs 'blobs' of plaster, for example, used to fix plaster board (or plasterboard/insulation laminate) direct to the internal surface of a masonry wall.

Damp-proof course (DPC) waterproof layer laid between two courses of masonry below ground-floor level to prevent damp rising.

Damp-proof membrane (DPM) a plastic membrane used, say, beneath a cast concrete floor, to prevent damp rising.

Daylight factor percentage of daylight entering a room compared with that provided by an unobstructed, uniformly overcast sky.

Dew point temperature at which water vapour in the air condenses.

DHW domestic hot water, that serving taps and showers, usually produced by the same boiler as serves the heating system but can also be provided by solar water heaters.

Diffuse solar radiation radiation diffused through clouds or reflected off other surfaces.

Direct solar radiation just what it sounds like: when you can see the sun in the sky.

Direct system solar water heater or warm air system where the end product is heated direct via the heater/burner.

Dormer cheeks side walls of a dormer window construction.

Down-draught effect air movement (apparent draught) caused by the rapid cooling of large volumes of air (for instance, by a large area of single glazing).

Draught lobby formed by creating a space (should be at least 2m^2) between two sets of outside doors; the idea is that only one door needs to be open at any one time, thus reducing the volume of heated air lost when leaving or entering the building.

Draught-proofing/sealing any act of reducing air infiltration and draughts, includes draught-stripping as well as blocking air leakage routes in building fabric, for example.

Draught-stripping using strips of foam, for example, around doors and windows to reduce air infiltration and draughts.

Dry-lining technique for finishing internal surfaces, comprising plasterboard fixed to a timber stud, providing the opportunity to incorporate insulation within stud, or using laminated plasterboard with insulation backing laid on plaster dabs.

Driving rain index indication of wind-driven rain, product of annual average wind-speed and annual average rainfall.

Dual aspect used of rooms or flats to describe having windows on more than one side.

Dual flush WC one having a mechanism which can dispense a higher or a lower volume of water, depending on need.

Ecolabel environmental labelling scheme for domestic appliances.

Eco-Homes scheme means of applying an overall environmental rating to a proposed house design, devised and operated by BRE (q.v.) and delivered via licensed assessors.

Electrochromic glazing term describing glazing system which can change its colour (in practice, its opacity) in response to an electric current, used mainly for privacy but could also have shading applications.

Element (of a building) a wall, roof or floor, or glazing.

Elemental method method of compliance with Building Regulations thermal requirements, by not exceeding the maximum allowable U-value for a given element; now superseded in the United Kingdom by a whole-building approach.

Embodied energy that energy bound up in a material as a result of factors such as extraction, processing and manufacture.

Energy label means of rating, for instance, an appliance or window system for energy efficiency.

Envelope the external surfaces and fabric elements of a house; 'insulated envelope' refers to those elements where insulation is placed, that is, not including the roof where insulation is laid in the plane of the ceiling.

Evacuated glazing double glazing with a vacuum between panes instead of air; the glazing gap can be very small, requires tiny metal spacers to prevent panes touching and gives improved thermal performance for a much thinner element.

Evacuated tube solar collector solar water heater comprising finned absorber pipes containing a heat transfer fluid, located under vacuum in glass tubes, connected to a manifold which transfers heat to water to be circulated to a HWC (q.v.).

Exclusive approach (to energy efficient design) excluding the outside environment, and preventing heat from leaving the building (*see* also Super-insulation) to reduce energy use.

Extract air air removed from a building or room.

Fabric *see* Building fabric.

Facing brick brick with a smooth face suitable for use as the outer leaf in a masonry construction.

Fair-faced block concrete block with a smoother than normal face which can be exposed internally or externally if required.

Five-times rule rule applied to timber frame construction to reduce risk of interstitial condensation, whereby the vapour resistance of layers on the warm side of the insulation must be at least five times that of layers on the cold side.

Fixed light term describing window which cannot be opened.

Flashing waterproof barrier (usually of lead) at the junction of two elements, for example, between a roof and a wall, chimney stack or dormer.

Flat-plate solar collector solar water heater comprising a transparent cover and flat absorber plate which transfers heat to water direct or via a heat transfer fluid to be circulated to a HWC (q.v.).

Flow piping piping connecting the boiler and appliances (radiators, HWC) in which water flows away from the boiler.

Focal-point fire a fire, installed as much for a visual cue as for a heating device; can be gas-fired or electric; not recommended since not part of a controlled heating system.

Formwork support (usually timber), for instance, for cast concrete or dry screed, may be temporary (also termed shuttering) or part of structure.

Fossil fuels natural gas, crude oil and coal and their derivatives, carbon-based fuels generated over geological time periods (and therefore of finite reserves) which release carbon dioxide (among other pollutants) on combustion.

Gasification partial combustion, for instance, of biomass fuel, under carefully controlled oxygen conditions, producing a combustible gas for feeding into an engine, for example, for CHP (q.v.).

Glazing ratio ratio of window area to total wall area for a given façade or for the whole building, usually expressed as percentage.

Global warming increase in the earth's average temperature, due in part to carbon dioxide and other emissions generated by humans accelerating the greenhouse effect (q.v.).

GLS general lighting service tungsten-filament lamp, a 'light-bulb' to most people, cheap to buy but expensive to run.

Goings the horizontal parts of a stair on which the foot is placed, also called 'treads'.

Green roof roof with grass or sedum top covering, incorporating tanking and drainage layers over a concrete substructure; may be used to soften visual impact of building or to give some biodiversity back to the site.

Green tariff electricity tariff based on renewables-generated electricity, available from most electricity supply companies, although not all use new renewables capacity.

Greenhouse effect the means by which the earth's atmosphere insulates us from the cold of space, essential for life on earth; current concern is about the rate at which the effect is increasing: the accelerated greenhouse effect.

Greenhouse gases those gases, primarily carbon dioxide, but also methane and others, which contribute to the accelerated greenhouse effect.

Grey water outflow from sinks, hand basins, baths and showers which, with treatment, may be reused in the house and garden.

Grid-linked renewable (or other) electricity-generating system connected to the main electricity distribution network.

Halogen lamp tungsten-filament lamp with halogen gas inside the envelope, which allows a higher operating temperature and thus brighter light for the size of lamp; not very energy efficient, costly, short lifetime and generates much heat.

Heat capacity measure of the ability of a material to store heat (units J/kg°C).

Heat gains term used to describe heating gained from sources other than a heating system, for example, solar gains, occupant gains and lighting gains.

Heat recovery ventilation system providing supply and extraction ventilation, with a heat exchanger to recover heat from the extracted air and transfer it to the incoming air.

Heating season period (usually about October-April) during which the heating needs to be on; better-insulated and/or passive solar houses can shorten the heating season, reducing energy consumption and costs.

High-performance glazing for example low E-coated, inert gas-filled, triple glazing, or any combination of them.

HWC hot water cylinder.

Humidistat humidity sensor, used, for example, to control bathroom ventilation.

Indirect system solar water heater or warm air system in which the end product is heated indirectly via a heat exchanger connected to the heater/burner or collector.

Induction lamp type of lamp used mainly in commercial applications, very long life and thus useful in inaccessible locations; high purchase cost.

Infiltration air entering the house accidentally due to 'leaks' in the fabric.

Inner leaf inner masonry layer in cavity construction.

Inert gas filled higher thermal performance, multiple-glazing unit with argon, krypton or xenon (in order of improved performance) in between panes, instead of air.

Inverter device which converts DC (direct current, such as produced by, for instance, renewable energy technologies) to AC (alternating current, used by normal electrical mains).

Joists horizontal timbers supporting a floor or ceiling.

Joule (J) unit of energy (1kWh = 3,600,000J = 3.6MJ).

k-value (W/mK) also known as λ (lamda), thermal conductance; physical property of a material expressing its ability to conduct heat.

kilowatt unit of power (symbol kW), used to rate output of boilers, for instance.

kilowatt hour (kWh) standard unit of energy consumption, equivalent to using 1kW (1,000 watts) of energy for one hour.

Kelvin (K) unit of temperature; in terms of temperature interval 1K = 1°C.

l length in metres, used in calculation of r-value and hence U-values.

Lamp used in a technical sense to describe what most of us call a 'light-bulb', or a fluorescent tube; anything which is a source of artificial light.

Lap-board exterior-grade timber board used as external cladding, arranged horizontally such that each board is overlapped by the one above, providing weather-proofing.

Leeward the opposite side (of a house) from which the wind is blowing.

Legionella the name of the bacterium causing legionnaire's disease which can be fatal especially in elderly or infirm people; can result from storage of water at too low a temperature (below about 57.5°C).

Life-cycle assessment taking into account not only the energy in use, but energy in the production and demolition/disposal of buildings/materials.

Lightweight blocks concrete blocks with improved thermal and handling properties, also known as AAC blocks.

Low emissivity (low-E) glazing glazing incorporating a very thin, metallic coating which reflects back some of the heat otherwise lost through the glazing, improving U-value and energy efficiency; may be hard- or soft-coated (the latter is higher performing).

Low-flow shower with an aerating head, can be just as effective as a 'power shower' while using much less water and thus less energy to heat it.

155

Low voltage lamp/lighting lighting running at lower than mains voltage (typically 12V) via use of transformers; low voltage is not low energy as the current increases to compensate, however, can be useful in bathrooms for safety reasons.

LPG (liquefied petroleum gas) oil-derivative used in some boilers, but more commonly in portable heaters or for cooking.

Masonry cavity construction wall composed of two layers of masonry (at least one of which is structural) with a cavity between.

Mathematical tiles form of vertically-hung tiling used as an outer skin for walls, which gives the appearance of brick construction.

MDF (medium density fibreboard) board comprising waste wood fibres compressed into an adhesive matrix.

Micro-CHP domestic-scale combined heat and power, simultaneous production of heat and electricity; replaces domestic boiler and produces small electrical output.

Microclimate climatic conditions, sunshine levels, wind-speed and direction, for instance, in the immediate vicinity of a house.

Microporous paint one with microscopic holes which allow it to breathe, as opposed to most paints (especially gloss) which form impermeable layers; good for use on timber.

Monopitch roof, the whole of which slopes in one direction only.

Mullions vertical glazing bars on a window.

MVHR mechanical ventilation with heat recovery, whole-house ventilation system incorporating extract and supply ducts and a heat exchanger to transfer heat from the former to the latter.

Natural buoyancy tendency of warm air to rise.

Natural ventilation for instance, via open windows or vents, that which does not require specific components such as fans or ducts.

Net-metering approach taken in certain European countries whereby independent electricity generators can receive the same rate for exported electricity as they pay for that taken from the grid, greatly enhances the economic viability of renewable self-generation.

Newton unit of force (symbol N).

Nitrogen oxides (collectively NO$_x$) compounds of nitrogen and oxygen produced on combustion of fossil fuels, symptomatic of inefficient combustion and contributors to acid rain and localized poor air quality.

No-sky line point in a room where the sky is no longer visible from the working plane (taken as 0.85m above floor level), determined by window head height and position/height of external obstructions such as adjacent buildings.

Non self-ballasted describes low energy lamps (CFLs) without in-built control gear, where the latter is incorporated into the fitting.

OFTEC (Oil-Firing Technical Association) organization representing manufacturers and suppliers of oil-firing appliances.

Oil for home heating, the oil used is known as 28sec (a measure of viscosity).

Opening any window, rooflight or door, in some cases can describe purpose-built ventilators too.

Opening light term describing part of a window which can be opened.

Outer leaf outer masonry layer in cavity construction.

Overall heat loss method method of compliance with Irish Building Regulations thermal requirements, by not exceeding the maximum allowable overall U-value for all elements.

Parasitic load for instance, in a solar water heater, the load for the pump, which offsets some of the energy saved by the system.

Particulates tiny particles of soot from the combustion of fossil fuels which contribute to poor air quality, soiling of buildings and can be carried across mucus membranes thus posing a health risk.

Pascal unit of pressure (symbol Pa), equal to 1 Newton per square metre (N/m^2).

Passive solar design using orientation, layout, window area and position, fabric thermal mass (qv), for example, to optimize heating (and daylighting) of internal spaces by solar gains.

Passive stack ventilation (PSV) ventilation which uses natural buoyancy (heat rising) and chimney effect (air passing over the top of a duct) without need for fans.

Patio heater (or 'global warmer') avoid these if you have any intentions of being energy efficient and environmentally friendly.

Payback period   period elapsing before the capital cost (or over-cost compared with cheaper alternative options) of an item of energy-saving equipment or other measure is equalled by the energy saved; generally a simple payback is used which does not take into account the future value of money.

Photovoltaic (PV) cells   convert sunlight direct into electricity.

PIR (passive infra-red)   a type of movement detector used in automated lighting control systems.

Plan form   how a dwelling is laid out, location and orientation of zones, for example.

Potable water   water of drinking quality (not required for WC flushing).

Pressure test   method of establishing air-tightness of a building, uses a door-fan to blow air into a house and measures the air volume delivery rate required to maintain a given pressure.

Prevailing wind   the direction from which the wind most frequently blows, generally south-west in the British Isles, although cold winds of high speed can often come from the north or north-east.

Programmer/timer   electronic device that allows on/off periods to be set by the user, for optimum control of heating and hot water systems.

Purlins   large horizontal structural roof timbers supporting rafters.

Putrescible waste   for instance, meat food waste, which is not compostable.

PV   *see* Photovoltaic cells.

PVC   *see* uPVC.

PV tiles/shingles   PV panels designed to look like traditional roof coverings.

r-value (m^2K/W)   resistance of an individual material layer.

R-value   thermal resistance (m^2K/W) of a building element, reciprocal of the U-value, used in North America instead of latter.

Radiation   transfer of heat through air (or other gas or vacuum) direct from one surface to another.

Radon   gas occurring naturally in certain rock types which increases background radiation levels and may be required by Building Control to be addressed via a radon barrier and/or ventilation.

Radon barrier   membrane which prevents seepage of radon from certain rock types into a building; contact local Building Control to determine whether it is an issue for you.

Rainwater goods   gutters, hoppers and downspouts.

Rainwater harvesting   collection, filtration and storage of rainwater for use in the home (typically for WC flushing or other non-potable uses).

Rafters   sloping members of a timber roof.

Reed bed filtration system   natural water-treatment system which can clean 'black' water.

Reflectance   degree to which a surface reflects light, expressed as a percentage.

Response time   time taken between turning on a heating system and comfort conditions being reached; depends on type of heating system and construction.

Return   external area, typically in a terraced or semi-detached house, bounded on two sides by the main body of a house and an extension (which may be original or added later).

Return piping   piping connecting the boiler and appliances (radiators, HWC) in which water flows back towards the boiler.

Reveal   distance by which a window is set back from a wall surface.

Risers   the vertical parts of a stair, between the treads.

Roomstat   short for room thermostat, temperature-sensing device, part of a good boiler and heating system control.

Run-back timer   timer set to allow appliance (such as an extractor fan) to run for a specified time after being switched off.

SAP Energy Rating   Standard Assessment Procedure for Energy Rating of Dwellings, official method in the United Kingdom for assessing the energy efficiency of a dwelling for Building Regulations purposes.

Sarking felt   bitumenized roofing felt used to provide a waterproof layer beneath the outer roof covering.

Sash   sub-division of a window, an opening sash is a part which can be opened and a sliding sash opens via a sliding action, for example.

Secondary glazing   additional glazing layer and frame fixed to an existing frame, for example, as an alternative to replacing single glazing with double-glazed units.

SEDBUK (Seasonal Efficiency of Domestic Boilers in the United Kingdom) online database containing performance data on over 3,000 boilers (www.sedbuk.com).

Selective approach (to energy efficient design) allowing natural solar heating, lighting and natural ventilation into your house, to reduce energy usage from fuels and electricity.

Self-ballasted describes low energy lamps (CFLs) with in-built control gear.

Services heating, hot water, lighting, ventilation, power, for example.

Setting out (of floor slab) laying of slab; for timber frame requires as smooth and level a surface as possible with all angles true.

Sill element below a window both internal and external.

Single aspect of a room or dwelling; this indicates that the windows face in one direction only.

SIPS (structural insulated panel systems) composite panels comprising a sandwich of timber board structural element and insulation.

Sky angle the angle to the vertical that the mid-point of a window makes with any nearby obstructions.

Smoke pen used to identify points and paths of air-leakage, consists of a clear plastic tube with a rubber bulb on one end: a harmless white 'smoke' is released from the tube when the bulb is squeezed.

SNIPEF (Scottish and Northern Ireland Plumbing Employers Federation) represents plumbers and installers especially of oil-fired equipment.

Solar aperture the area (for example, of a window or solar collector) 'seen' by direct solar radiation, a function of solar altitude angle and surface inclination; radiation at right angles to the surface gives maximum solar aperture.

Solar gains heat from the sun that contributes to raising temperatures inside the house (useful gains are those that contribute to achieving comfort temperatures, excess gains are those leading to overheating and excess temperatures).

Space heating simply, the action of heating the spaces in a house.

Spray taps taps that use less water by reducing droplet size or by aeration of the water flow, increased pressure and velocity compensate for reduced volume flow rate.

Stack effect uses natural buoyancy (warm air rising), accentuated in a restricted space such as a duct.

Stand-alone when applied to renewable electricity generating equipment this indicates no connection to the grid, thus battery storage is usually required.

Standing losses heat losses from a HWC (q.v.) and associated piping or any piping containing hot water; incurred even when the system is not in use.

Steady state heat loss heat loss under design temperature conditions used to size heating systems.

Sulphur dioxide (SO$_2$) compound of sulphur and oxygen produced on combustion of sulphur-bearing fossil fuels (oil and coal and derivatives, to varying degrees depending on source), key cause of acid rain and localized poor air quality.

Sun-path diagram chart showing orientation and altitude angle of the sun at different times of the day and year for a given latitude.

Sun-room usually describes a single-storey ground floor extension with higher than normal glazing ratio but conventional roof; distinction from rest of dwelling removed in new UK-wide Building Regulations.

Super-insulation term describing much higher than normal levels of thermal performance in building fabric (and, usually, glazing).

Supply air air (usually 100 per cent fresh air in dwellings) supplied to a building.

Target U-value method (also called calculated trade-off) previous method of compliance with UK Building Regulations thermal requirements, by not exceeding maximum allowable overall U-value for all elements; now superseded by whole-building approach.

Tempered air air which has been heated (or cooled), usually artificially, although could apply to solar-heated air.

Thermal bridge (or cold bridge) continuous element of fabric spanning external and internal surfaces which acts as a route for conductive heat loss.

Thermal mass dense material, for example, masonry, with exposed internal surface, which can absorb, store and release heat; can be used to absorb excess solar or internal heat gains and release later when internal temperatures start to fall.

Thermal performance   simply, the extent to which a material or building element reduces heat loss; high thermal performance means low U-value.

Thermostat   electronic device that senses temperature and, via linkage to the heating system, maintains room temperature at a set point determined by the user.

Thermostatic radiator valve (TRV)   valve fitted to radiator to allow ready control of heat output and thus temperature in a room.

Timber frame construction   wall using timber as the structural element.

Transfer grille   grille, located in a door or wall, to allow movement of air into or from an adjacent space, may be part of ventilation system or warm air heating system.

Transmittance (of glazing)   proportion (expressed as a decimal fraction) of sunlight transmitted through glazing as opposed to that reflected or absorbed.

Transmittance (thermal)   another term for U-value, rate at which a building element transmits heat (units: W/m^2K).

Transoms   horizontal glazing bars on a window.

Transparent insulation material (TIM)   material that acts as insulation while also allowing diffused daylight to pass through.

Treads   the horizontal parts of a stair on which the foot is placed, also called 'goings'.

Trickle vent   part of designed-in ventilation, small opening for controlled ventilation usually located in window frames, may be controllable via adjustable damper.

Tungsten filament lamp   conventional incandescent 'light bulb', cheap to buy but expensive to run.

Tungsten halogen lamp   lamp with tungsten filament which combines with halogen in operation to produce very bright light.

uPVC   unplasticized polyvinylchloride, used extensively in the construction industry due to cost-competitiveness and easy handling; however, concern exists regarding its environmental profile.

U-value   thermal transmittance (W/m^2K), rate at which heat is passed through a building element.

U-value calculator   computer program (for example, from BRE) allowing ready calculation of U-values of building elements.

Underfloor heating   heating usually provided via plastic tubing laid in a concrete screed, carrying water heated via a boiler; electrical resistance type also available although not recommended, slow response system, requires hard floor covering (masonry or timber) laid direct on screed.

Vapour-control membrane   membrane used to prevent water penetration but allow air and water vapour movement (see 'Breathable membrane' qv.)

Ventilation   used here to describe deliberate, designed-in air changes.

Ventilation tray   purpose-designed device to prevent insulation laid in the ceiling plane from blocking ventilation to the cold side of rafters.

VOC   volatile organic compound, found in, for instance, synthetic carpets, furnishings and computer casings, contributor to poor internal air quality.

Volumetric timber frame system   one using prefabricated 'pods' thus providing whole volumes rather than individual elements.

Wall plate   the tops of walls, on which the roof timbers are set.

Warm air heating system   one which uses air to transfer heat around the building, generally comprises a burner, fan, supply ducting and grilles, and return transfer grilles.

Warm roof   pitched roof with pitch followed internally (for example, in loft conversion) and insulation incorporated above as well as between the rafters to keep the top side of the latter warm.

Water-hammer   loud 'knocking' sound resulting from pulsations being set up in water pipes, such as can result from air in the pipe or a TRV (thermostatic radiator valve) installed the wrong way round.

Water-hardness   measure of dissolved mineral content in water supply, can be confirmed by your local water authority, may have a bearing on scaling of water appliances.

Wet heating system   one that uses water as the heat transfer medium, as opposed to warm air heating systems, electric or gas radiant systems, for instance, most commonly comprising radiators or underfloor heating (not electric type).

White goods refrigerators, freezers, washing machines, dishwashers and tumble dryers.

Whole-building method new method of demonstrating compliance with Building Regulations in England and Wales, and in Scotland and in Northern Ireland, replacing elemental method and target U-value method.

Whole house ventilation (with heat recovery) system providing supply and extract ventilation for whole house (with recovery of heat from the extract air and transfer to the incoming air).

Wind resource average wind speed and direction at a range of heights on a site, required to determine viability of a wind turbine.

Wind-speed average speed in miles or kilometres per hour of wind at a given site usually expressed as maximum or average over the year.

Winders the part of a staircase which turns a corner, having trapezoidal treads.

Window head height height of the top of a window, usually expressed in terms of floor level or level of the working plane (usually taken as 0.85m).

Windward the same side (of a house) as that from which the wind is blowing.

Wood-burning stove cast-iron stove used to burn timber for space heating (some types can also produce DHW [q.v.]), must be flued; doors prevent ventilative heat loss when not in use.

Wood chips slivers of wood, usually forest residue or timber processing plant waste, used as fuel in general wood-burning boilers.

Wood pellets processed wood product of high density and low water content, suitable for use in spark ignition, automated, wood-burning boilers.

Working plane the height in a room at which most functions are carried out, usually taken as 0.85m above floor level.

Zone may be an individual room or a number of rooms, having in common their location in the plan form or similar usage, or equal comfort temperatures, for instance.

Useful Contacts, Publications and Additional Information

Contact details are given alphabetically and in the form: organization name; address; telephone number; email; website. For ease of use, this section is divided into the following parts:

1. Companies/Organizations with Featured Products
2. Other Sources Credited
3. Energy/Environment-Related Organizations
4. Energy Regulators
5. Energy Agencies
6. Building Regulations
7. Building Control
8. Planning
9. Architectural Organizations
10. SAP Software and Training Companies
11. U-Value Calculators
12. Condensation Risk Analysis Programs
13. BRE/EST Publications
14. Other Publications
15. British Standards
16. Self-Build Organizations
17. Self-Build Publications and Websites
18. Self-Build Shows
19. Community Self-Build Case Studies
20. Other Information Sources

1. COMPANIES/ ORGANIZATIONS WITH FEATURED PRODUCTS

Amvic Inc., 501 McNicoll Avenue, Toronto, ON, Canada M2H 2E2, +1 416 410 5674
www.amvicsystem.com

Amvic United Kingdom Agents, Springvale EPS, 75 Springvale Road, Doagh, Ballyclare BT39 0SS, 028 9334 0203
www.springvale.com

BPD Building Product Design Ltd, 2 Brooklands Road, Sale, Cheshire M33 3SS, 0161 962 7113
info@buildingproductdesign.com
www.buildingproductdesign.com

Building Research Establishment (BRE), Bucknalls Lane, Garston, Watford WD25 9BA, 01923 664000
www.bre.co.uk

Centre for Sustainable Technologies, University of Ulster, Newtownabbey BT37 0QB, 028 9036 6329
cst@ulster.ac.uk
www.engj.ulst.ac.uk/CST

Department for Transport (DfT), Cleaner Fuels and Vehicles Division, 76 Marsham Street, London SW1P 4DR, 020 7944 4899
www.dft.gov.uk

EcoHomes, BRE, Bucknalls Lane, Garston, Watford WD25 9XX, 01923 664462
www.ecohomes.org

Energy Saving Trust (EST), 21 Dartmouth Street, London SW1H 9BP, 020 7222 0101
www.est.org.uk

Energy Saving Trust (EST) Northern Ireland, Enterprise House, 55/59 Adelaide Street, Belfast BT2 8FE, 028 9072 6006
www.est.org.uk

Evergreen Doors, c/o David Jameson Group,
149 Thomas Street, Portadown BT62 3BE,
028 38333340
enquiries@davidjamesongroup.co.uk
www.davidjamesongroup.co.uk
Excel Industries Ltd, Maerdy Industrial Estate
(South), Rhymney, Gwent NP22 5PY,
01685 845200
sales@excelfibre.com
www.excelfibre.com
Glidevale Ltd, 2 Brooklands Road, Sale, Cheshire
M33 3SS, 0161 962 7113
sales@glidevale.com
www.glidevale.com
Green Building Store, 11 Huddersfield Road,
Meltham, Holmfirth, West Yorkshire HD9 4NJ,
01484 854898
info@greenbuildingstore.co.uk
www.greenbuildingstore.co.uk
Hibernia ETH Ltd, Unit 530 Stanstead
Distribution Centre, Start Hill,
Bishop's Stortford CM22 7DG,
028 9024 9954
rain@hiberniaeth.com
www.hiberniaeth.com
Hibernia ETH Ltd, Knocknagin House,
Balbriggan, Co. Dublin
rain@hiberniaeth.com
www.hiberniaeth.com
Kingspan UK, Kingspan Insulation Ltd,
Pembridge, Leominster, Herefordshire
HR6 9LA, 01544 387 210
info.uk@tek.kingspan.com
www.tek.kingspan.com
Kingspan Ireland, Kingspan Insulation Ltd,
Castleblayney, Co. Monaghan,
042 97 95000
info.ie@tek.kingspan.com
www.tek.kingspan.com
Lakeview Developments
martingraham@hotmail.com
www.lakeviewdevelopments.net
Northern Ireland Housing Executive,
Housing Centre, 2 Adelaide Street,
Belfast BT2 8PB,
028 9024 0588
www.nihe.gov.uk

Nu-Heat United Kingdom Ltd, Heathpark House,
Devonshire Road, Heathpark Industrial Estate,
Honiton, Devon EX14 1SD, 01404 549770
info@nu-heat.co.uk
www.nu-heat.co.uk
Passivent Ltd, 2 Brooklands Road, Sale, Cheshire
M33 3SS, 0161 962 7113
sales@passivent.com
www.passivent.com
Quinn Manufacturing Ltd, Derrylin, Co. Fermanagh
BT92 9AU, 028 6774 8866
info@quinn-group.com
www.quinn-group.com
Richmond Building Products Ltd, 2 Brooklands Road,
Sale, Cheshire M33 3SS, 0161 962 7113
sales@richmondbp.com
www.richmondbp.com
Richmond Building Products Ltd, Belfast, 56/58
Dargan Crescent, Duncrue Road, Belfast BT3 9JP,
028 9077 0021
sales@richmondbp.com
www.richmondbp.com
Richmond Building Products Ltd, Dublin,
Block 520, Greenogue Business Park, Rathcoole,
Co. Dublin, 01412 4600
sales@richmondbp.com
www.richmondbp.com
Richmond Building Products Ltd, Cork, Churchtown
Industrial Park, Churchtown North, Midleton,
Co. Cork, 021 463 5454
sales@richmondbp.com
www.richmondbp.com
Second Nature United Kingdom Ltd, Soulands Gate,
Dacre, Penrith, Cumbria CA11 0JF
017684 86285
www.secondnatureuk.com
Solarcentury, 91–94 Lower Marsh, Waterloo,
London SE1 7AB, 020 7803 0100
www.solarcentury.co.uk
Solartwin Ltd, FREEPOST NWW7888A,
Chester CH1 2ZZ, 01244 403407
hi@solartwin.com
www.solartwin.com
Springvale EPS Ltd, 75 Springvale Road,
Doagh, Ballyclare BT39 0SS,
028 9334 0203
www.springvale.com

Swedish Window Company Ltd, Old Maltings House, Hall Street, Long Melford, Suffolk CO10 9JB, 01787 467297
info@swedishwindows.com
www.swedishconstructionproducts.co.uk
Thermomax Ltd, 7 Balloo Crescent, Balloo Industrial Estate, Bangor, Northern Ireland BT19 7UP, 028 91270411
info@thermomax-group.com
solar@thermomax-group.com,
www.thermomax-group.com
Xtratherm Ltd, Kells Road, Co. Meath, Ireland
info@xtratherm.com
www.xtratherm.com

2. OTHER SOURCES CREDITED

European Passive Solar Handbook (eds Achard and Gicquel), Commission of the European Communities; Publication No. EUR 10 683
Green Architecture (Brenda and Robert Vale, published by Thames & Hudson), ISBN 0-500-27883-0
Green Design – Sustainable Building for Ireland (eds McNicholl and Lewis), Energy Research Group, University College Dublin, ISBN 0-7076-2392-8
R-2000 Programme (Canadian Federal Department of Energy, Mines and Resources and the Canadian Home Builders' Association)

3. ENERGY/ENVIRONMENT-RELATED ORGANIZATIONS

ACTAC – The Technical Aid Network, 64 Mount Pleasant, Liverpool L3 5SD, 0151 708 7607
www.liv.ac.uk/abe/actac
AECB (Association for Environment-Conscious Building)
www.aecb.net
Architectural Association School of Architecture, 36 Bedford Square, London WC1B 3ES,
www.aaschool.ac.uk
BRE Bookshop, Bucknalls Lane, Garston, Watford WD25 9XX, 01923 664262,
brebookshop@emap.com
www.brebookshop.com

British Board of Agrément (BBA), PO Box 195, Bucknalls Lane, Garston, Watford WD25 9BA, 01923 665300
www.bbacerts.co.uk
British Earth Sheltering Association (BESA), Caer Llan Berm House, Lydart, Monmouth NP25 4JS, 01600 860359
peter@caerllan.co.uk
www.besa.uk.org
British Fenestration Rating Council
www.bfrc.org
British Standards Institution, 389 Chiswick High Road, London W4 4AL, 020 8996 9000
www.bsi-global.com
British Strawbale Building Association (BSBA), 5 Chataway Road, Crumpsall Manchester M8 5UU, 0161 202 3566
straw@globalnet.co.uk.
www.users.globalnet.co.uk/~straw/
British Wind Energy Association, Renewable Energy House, 1 Aztec Row, Berners Road, London N1 0PW, 020 7689 1960
info@bwea.com, www.bwea.com
www.embracewind.com
Building Research Establishment (BRE), Bucknalls Lane, Garston, Watford WD25 9BA, 01923 664000
www.bre.co.uk
Cavity Insulation Guarantee Agency (CIGA), 3 Vimy Court, Vimy Road, Leighton Buzzard, Bedfordshire LU7 1FG, 01525 853300
www.ciga.co.uk
CAT (Centre for Alternative Technology), Machynlleth, Powys SY20 9AZ, 01654 702782
www.cat.org.uk
Chartered Institution of Building Services Engineers (CIBSE), 222 Balham High Road, Balham, London SW12 9BS, 020 8675 5211
www.cibse.org
Clear Skies
www.clear-skies.org
(funding for renewable energy technologies)
Climate Care
www.climatecare.org
Construction Resources, 16 Great Guildford Street, London SE1 0HS, 020 7450 2211
sales@ecoconstruct.com,
www.constructionresources.com

EcoHomes, BRE, Bucknalls Lane, Garston, Watford WD25 9XX, 01923 664462
www.ecohomes.org
Energy Saving Trust (EST), 21 Dartmouth Street, London SW1H 9BP, 020 7222 0101
www.est.org.uk
Energy Saving Trust (EST) Northern Ireland, Enterprise House, 55/59 Adelaide Street, Belfast BT2 8FE, 028 9072 6006
www.est.org.uk
Energy Saving Trust (EST) Scotland, 112/2 Commercial Street, Leith, Edinburgh EH6 6NF, 0131 555 7900
www.est.org.uk
Energy Saving Trust (EST) Wales, Wales Albion House, Oxford Street, Nantgarw, Cardiff CF15 7TR, 01443 845930
www.est.org.uk
ENFO (The Environmental Information Service), 17 St Andrew Street, Dublin 2, 01 888 3910
info@enfo.ie, www.enfo.ie
FENSA (Fenestration Self-Assessment Scheme)
www.fensa.org.uk
Forest Stewardship Council (FSC), 01686 413916
www.fsc-uk.info
Glass and Glazing Federation
www.ggf.org.uk
Greenpeace, Canonbury Villas, London N1 2PN, 020 7865 8100
info@uk.greenpeace.org,
www.greenpeace.org.uk
Hockerton Housing Project, The Watershed, Gables Drive, Hockerton, Southwell, Nottinghamshire NG25 0QU, 01636 816902
hhp@hockerton.demon.co.uk
www.hockerton.demon.co.uk
HPA (Health Protection Agency, incorporating the National Radiological Protection Board), Centre for Radiation, Chemical and Environmental Hazards, Radiation Protection Division, Chilton, Didcot, Oxfordshire OX11 0RQ, 01235 831600
rpd@hpa-rp.org.uk
www.hpa.org.uk/radiation

HVCA (Heating and Ventilating Contractors' Association), Esca House, 34 Palace Court, London W2 4JG, 020 7313 4900
contact@hvca.org.uk
www.hvca.org.uk
Irish Agrément Board (NSAI), Glasnevin, Dublin 9, 01-8073800
www.nsai.ie
NHBC (National House-Building Council), Buildmark House, Chiltern Avenue, Amersham, Buckinghamshire HP6 5AP, 01494 735363/735369
www.nhbc.co.uk
Natural Building Technologies Ltd, The Hangar, Worminghall Road, Oakley, Buckinghamshire HP18 9UL, 01844 338338
info@natural-building.co.uk
naturalbuildingproductscouk.ntitemp.com
Radiological Protection Institute of Ireland (RPII), 3 Clonskeagh Square, Clonskeagh Road, Dublin 14, Ireland, 01 269 77 66
rpii@rpii.ie
www.rpii.ie
SEDBUK (Seasonal Efficiency of Domestic Boilers in United Kingdom), Database
www.boilers.org.uk
SEI Renewable Energy Information Office, Shinagh House, Bandon, Co. Cork, 023 29145
www.sei.ie
Sustainable Energy Ireland (SEI), Glasnevin, Dublin 9, 01 836 9080
www.sei.ie, info@sei.ie
Sustrans (National Cycle Network Centre), 2 Cathedral Square, College Green, Bristol BS1 5DD, 0117 926 8893
www.sustrans.org.uk
The Green Building Press
www.newbuilder.co.uk
The Green Shop, Cheltenham Road, Bisley, Stroud, Gloucestershire GL6 7BX, 01452 770629
enquiries@greenshop.co.uk
www.greenshop.co.uk
The Institute of Plumbing
www.plumbers.org.uk
The Stationery Office, London (for UK Building Regulations documents), 0870 600 5522
www.tso.co.uk

TRADA (Timber Research and Development Association), Chiltern House, Stocking Lane, Hughenden Valley, High Wycombe, Buckinghamshire HP14 4ND, 01494 569750
www.trada.co.uk
Windsave Ltd, 27 Woodside Place, Glasgow G3 7QL, 0141 353 6841
info@windsave.com
www.windsave.com
Windsave Ltd, c/o Renewables Ireland Ltd, Unit 21, Mill Road, Avondale Industrial Estate, Ballyclare BT39 9AU, 028 9334 4488
sales@renewablesireland.com
www.renewablesireland.com

4. ENERGY REGULATORS

CER (Commission for Energy Regulation, Republic of Ireland), Plaza House, Belgard Street, Tallaght, Dublin 24, 01 400 0800
www.cer.ie
OFGEM (Office of Gas and Electricity Markets in England, Wales and Scotland), 9 Millbank, London SW1P 3GE, 020 7901 7000
www.ofgem.gov.uk
OFGEM (Office of Gas and Electricity Markets in England, Wales and Scotland), 2nd Floor, Regent Court, 70 West Regent Street, Glasgow G2 2QZ, 0141 331 2678
www.ofgem.gov.uk
OFREG (Office of the Regulator for Electricity and Gas Northern Ireland), Brookmount Buildings, 42 Fountain Street, Belfast BT1 5EE, 028 9031 1575
www.ofreg.nics.gov.uk

5. ENERGY AGENCIES

England

Creative Environmental Networks (Croydon), 8th Floor, Ambassador House, Brigstock Road, Thornton Heath, Surrey CR7 7JG, 020 8683 6600
enquiries@cen.org.uk
www.cen.org.uk

Energy Solutions (North West London) (formerly Brent Energy Network), Ground Floor, Lanmor House, 370–386 High Road, Wembley, Middlesex HA9 6AX, 020 8903 9369
roger@energysolutions.org.uk
Furness Energy Partnership, Town Hall, Duke Street, Barrow-in-Furness LA14 2LD, 01229 894567
energyadvice@barrowbc.gov.uk
www.furnessenergy.co.uk
Greater London Energy Efficiency Network (GLEEN), Skyline House, 200 Union Street, London SE1 0LX, 020 7633 9625
info@gleen.org.uk
Kirklees Energy Agency, Byrom Buildings, Station Street, Huddersfield, West Yorkshire HD1 1LS, 01484 351 550
ashley@energy-help.org.uk
www.energy-help.org.uk
Leicester Energy Agency, Energy Advice Centre, 2–4 Market Place South, Leicester LE1 5HB, 0116 2995132
don.lack@energyagency.co.uk
www.energy-advice.co.uk
Marches Energy Agency, 23 Swan Hill, Shrewsbury, Shropshire SY1 1NN, 01743 246007
info@mea.org.uk
www.mea.org.uk
Milton Keynes Energy Agency, The National Energy Centre, Davy Avenue, Knowlhill, Milton Keynes MK5 8NG, 01908 665566
mkenergy@mkea.org.uk
www.mkea.org.uk
Newark & Sherwood Energy Agency, The Salvin Wing, Kelham Hall, Newark-upon-Trent, Nottinghamshire NG23 5QX, 01636 655 598
e-mail: david.pickles@nsdc.info
Severn Wye Energy Agency (formerly Forest of Dean Energy Agency), Unit 6/15, The Mews, Brook Street, Mitcheldean, Gloucestershire GL17 0SL, 01594 545360
catrin@swea.co.uk
www.swea.co.uk

Sustainable Energy Action (formerly Southwark Energy Agency), 42 Braganza Street, London SE17 3RJ, 0207 582 9191
chrisd@sustainable-energy.org.uk
www.sustainable-energy.org.uk
TV ENERGY: Thames Valley Energy Agency, Liberty House, The Enterprise Centre, New Greenham Park, Newbury RG19 6HW, 01635 817420
info@tvenergy.org
www.tvenergy.org
Wansbeck Energy Agency, c/o Council Offices, Front Street, Bedlington, Northumberland NE22 5TU, 01670 530033
r.gee@wansbeck.gov.uk
Watford & Three Rivers Energy Agency, 22 Tolpits Lane, Watford WD18 6NR, 01923 209404
davidha@watford.gov.uk

Scotland

Argyll, Lomond and the Islands Energy Agency, Kilbowie House, Gallanach Road, Oban, Argyll PA34 4PF, 01631 565183
enquiries@alienergy.org.uk
www.alienergy.org.uk
Northern & Western Isles Energy Agency, Orkney Energy Agency, 26 Bridge Street, Kirkwall, Orkney KW15 1HR, 01856 870534
ken@orkleac.demon.co.uk
South West Scotland Energy Agency (formerly South Ayrshire Energy Agency), 9 High Street, Ayr KA7 1LU, 01292 280109
liz.marquis@south-ayrshire.gov.uk
Western Isles Energy Agency, 16 South Beach Street, Stornoway, Isle of Lewis HS1 2BE, 01851 704300
linda@tighean.co.uk

Wales

Asiantaeth Ynni Sir Gâr (*Carmarthenshire Energy Agency*), Unit 10, St Clears Business Park, Tenby Road, St Clears, Carmarthenshire SA33 4JW, 01994 230009
office@ynnisirgar.org
www.ynnisirgar.org.uk

Conwy Energy Agency/Asiantaeth Ynni Conwy, Junction Way, Llandudno Junction LL31 9XX, 01492 574580
huw@ayc.org.uk
Mid Wales Energy Agency, The Cambria, Marine Terrace, Abersytwyth, Ceredigion SY23 2AZ, 0845 458 5973
info@mwea.org.uk
www.mwea.org.uk
Pembrokeshire Energy Agency, Unit 1, The Old School Business Centre, Lower St Mary Street, Newport, Pembrokeshire SA42 0TS, 01239 820078
gordon@pembs-energy.org.uk
www.pembs-energy.org.uk

Northern Ireland

Belfast Energy Agency, 1–11 May Street, Belfast BT1 4NA, 028 9024 0664,
orla@belfast-energy.demon.co.uk
www.belfast-energy.demon.co.uk
Foyle Regional Energy Agency, 3–5 London Street, 1st Floor Offices, Derry BT48 6RQ, 02871 373430
frea@derrycity.gov.uk
Western Regional Energy Agency & Network, 1 Nugents Entry, Off Townhall Street, Enniskillen, Co. Fermanagh BT74 7DF, 02866 328269
nigel@wrean.co.uk

Republic of Ireland

Association of Irish Energy Agencies
c/o Tipperary Energy Agency (*see* below)
052 43090
www.aiea.ie
info@aiea.ie
Carlow/Kilkenny Energy Agency, Castle Hill (Old Boot Factory), Carlow
059 9143871
ckenergy@eircom.net
CODEMA, Unit 32, Guinness Enterprise Centre, Taylors Lane, Dublin 8, 01 4100659
www.codema.ie
Cork City Energy Agency, The Lord Mayor's Pavilion, Fitzgeralds Park, Cork, 021 425 1104
micheal_lyons@corkcity.ie
Cork County Energy Agency, Spa House, Mallow, Co. Cork, 022 43610
mallowre@indigo.ie

Donegal Energy Action Team, Station Island, Lifford, Co. Donegal, 074 917 2497
radair@donegalcoco.ie
Galway Energy Agency Ltd, City Hall, College Road, Galway, 091 566954
peter.keavney@galwaycity.ie
Kerry Energy Agency, Aras an Chontae, Rathass, Tralee, Co. Kerry,
066 718 3576
wmoynihan@kerrycoco.ie
Limerick/Clare Energy Agency
Foundation Building, University of Limerick, Limerick, 061 234296
www.lcea.ie
info@lcea.ie
Mayo Energy Agency, Arran Place, Ballina, Co. Mayo,
096 76113/76114
www.mayoenergy.ie
mayonrg@eircom.net
Meath Energy Management Agency,
2A (Ground Floor) Cannon Row, Navan, Co. Meath, 046 906 0537
cusackgeraldine@hotmail.com
Tipperary Energy Agency Ltd, Education Centre, Church Street, Cahir, Co. Tipperary,
052 43090
www.tea.ie
tippenergy@eircom.net
Waterford Energy Agency, Civic Offices, Tankfield, Tramore, Co.Waterford,
051 395531
lfleming@waterfordcoco.ie
Wexford Energy Agency Management Ltd,
WORD, Johnstown Castle, Co. Wexford,
053 47400
wexenergy@eircom.net

6. BUILDING REGULATIONS

England and Wales
Office of the Deputy Prime Minister (ODPM),
www.odpm.gov.uk/stellent/groups/odpm_buildreg/
documents/sectionhomepage/
odpm_buildreg_page.hcsp
or navigate from
www.odpm.gov.uk

Scotland
Scottish Executive
www.scotland.gov.uk/library3/development/
bsqa-00.asp
or navigate from
www.scotland.gov.uk

Northern Ireland
Department of Finance and Personnel
www.dfpni.gov.uk/buildingregulations

Republic of Ireland
Department of Environment, Heritage and Local Government
www.environ.ie/DOEI/DOEIPol.nsf/wvNavView/
wwdConstruction?OpenDocument&Lang=en
or navigate from
www.environ.ie

7. BUILDING CONTROL

United Kingdom
www.buildingcontrolpages.co.uk

Republic of Ireland
contact your County Council

8. PLANNING

England and Wales
www.odpm.gov.uk/stellent/groups/odpm_planning/
documents/page/odpm_plan_606151.hcsp
or navigate from
www.odpm.gov.uk

Scotland
www.scotland.gov.uk/Topics/Planning-Building/
Planning

Northern Ireland
http://www.doeni.gov.uk/planning

Republic of Ireland
www.environ.ie/DOEI/DOEIPol.nsf/wvNavView/
Planning?OpenDocument&Lang=, or navigate from
www.environ.ie

9. ARCHITECTURAL ORGANIZATIONS

Royal Institute of British Architects (RIBA), 66 Portland Place, London W1B 1AD, 020 7580 5533
info@inst.riba.org
www.riba.org
Royal Incorporation of Architects in Scotland (RIAS), 15 Rutland Square, Edinburgh EH1 2BE, 0131 229 7545
info@rias.org.uk
Royal Society of Ulster Architects (RSUA), 2 Mount Charles, Belfast BT7 1NZ, 028 9032 3760
www.rsua.org.uk
Royal Institute of the Architects of Ireland (RIAI), 8 Merrion Square, Dublin 2, Ireland, 01 676 1703
info@riai.ie,
www.riai.ie

10. SAP SOFTWARE AND TRAINING COMPANIES

Elmhurst Energy Systems Ltd, Elmhurst Farm, Withybrook, Coventry CV7 9LQ, 01788 833386
www.elmhurstenergy.co.uk
MVM Starpoint Ltd, MVM House, 2 Oakfield Road, Clifton, Bristol BS8 2AL, 0117 974 4477
www.mvm.co.uk
National Energy Services Ltd, The National Energy Centre, Davy Avenue, Knowlhill, Milton Keynes MK5 8NG, 01908 672787
www.natenergy.org.uk

11. U-VALUE CALCULATORS

BRE Bookshop, Bucknalls Lane, Garston, Watford WD25 9XX, 01923 664262
brebookshop@emap.com
www.brebookshop.com
Elmhurst Energy Systems Ltd, Elmhurst Farm, Withybrook, Coventry CV7 9LQ, 01788 833386
www.elmhurstenergy.co.uk
BuildDesk Ltd, Pencoed, Bridgend CF35 6NY, 01656 868230
www.builddesk.co.uk/enbuild/
u_value_calculator.asp

12. CONDENSATION RISK ANALYSIS PROGRAMS

JPL TL, 10 Portland Terrace, Newcastle upon Tyne NE2 1QQ, 0191 281 8393
www.techlit.co.uk/programs.htm
BuildDesk Ltd, Pencoed, Bridgend CF35 6NY, 01656 868230
www.builddesk.co.uk/sw50865.asp

13. BRE/EST PUBLICATIONS

See above for contact details. The following is not a definitive list; some publications may be withdrawn at certain times while new ones are introduced periodically.

Insulation and Building Fabric
Newbuild and Refurbishment
Benefits of Best Practice: glazing (CE14)
Effective Use of Insulation in Dwellings (CE23)
Thermal Insulation: avoiding risks (BR262)

Newbuild
Post-Construction Testing: a professional's guide to testing housing for energy efficiency (GIR64)

Refurbishment
Cavity Wall Insulation: unlocking the potential in existing dwellings (GIL23)
Cavity Wall Insulation in Existing Housing (CE16)
Energy Efficient Refurbishment of Existing Housing (GPG155)
Energy Efficient Refurbishment of Existing Housing: case studies (GPCS418)
External Insulation Systems for Wall of Dwellings (GPG293)
Improving Air Tightness in Existing Homes (GPG224)
Internal Wall Insulation in Existing Housing: a guide for specifiers and contractors (GPG138) (CE17)
Minimizing Thermal Bridging when Upgrading Existing Housing: a detailed guide for architects and building designers (GPG183)
Refurbishment Site Guidance for Solid-Walled Houses: walls (GPG297)

Refurbishment Site Guidance for Solid-Walled Houses: ground floors (GPG294)

Refurbishment Site Guidance for Solid-Walled Houses: roofs (GPG296)

Refurbishment Site Guidance for Solid-Walled Houses: windows and doors (GPG295)

Heating, Lighting and Ventilation

Central Heating System Specifications CHeSS (GIL 59) (CE51)

Controls for Domestic Central Heating and Hot Water: guidance for installers and specifiers (CE50)

Domestic Central Heating and Hot Water: systems with gas- and oil-fired boilers – guidance for installers and specifiers (CE48)

Domestic Condensing Boilers: the benefits and the myths (CE52)

Domestic Heating and Hot Water: choice of fuel and system type (CE49)

Domestic Ground Source Heat Pumps (GPG339)

Domestic Lighting Innovations (ADH001)

Energy Efficient Lighting: a guide for installers (CE61)

Energy Efficient Lighting for Housing: exemplars for builders, installers, owners and managers (GPCS361)

Energy Efficient Ventilation in Housing: a guide for specifiers on the requirements and options for ventilation (GPG268)

Heat Pumps in the United Kingdom: a monitoring report (GIR72)

Humidistat-Controlled Extract Fans: performance in dwellings (IP5/99)

Low Energy Domestic Lighting (GIL20)

Low Energy Domestic Lighting: looking good for less (GPCS441)

Passive Stack Ventilation Systems: design and installation (IP13/94)

Solar Hot Water Systems in New Housing: a monitoring report (GIR88)

General

Newbuild and Refurbishment
Domestic Energy Efficiency Primer (GPG171)

Energy Efficiency Standards for New and Existing Dwellings (GIL72)

Summary Specification of Whole House Refurbishment: cavity walled housing (CE57)

Summary Specification of Whole House Refurbishment: solid walled housing (CE58)

Summary Specification of Whole House Refurbishment: timber framed housing (CE59)

BRE Housing Design Handbook (BR253, ISBN 0-85125-601-5)

Newbuild
Energy Efficiency in New Housing: a guide to achieving best practice (CE12)

Energy Efficiency in New Housing: summary of specifications for England, Wales and Scotland (CE12)

Energy Efficiency in New Housing: summary of specifications for Northern Ireland (CE24)

Solar Hot Water Systems in New Housing: a monitoring report (GIR72)

The Green Guide to Housing Specification (BR390)

14. OTHER PUBLICATIONS

See above for contact details.

Building for a Future (The Green Building Press)

Building the Future – a guide to building without pvc (Greenpeace)

Energy Efficient Housing: A Timber Frame Approach (TRADA)

Glass and Glazing Federation Technical Manual (GGF)

Green Building Digest (ACTAC)

Green Building Handbook (ISBN 0-203-47740-5)

Green Design – sustainable building for Ireland (ISBN 0 7076 2392 8)

NETWORK (Newsletter of AECB)

SAP (The Government's Standard Assessment Procedure for Energy Rating of Dwellings) (The Stationery Office)

Solar Energy and Housing Design (Architectural Association, 2 vols, ISBN 1 870890 45 0)

Testing Buildings for Air Leakage (CIBSE, CIBSE TM23)

The Green Building Bible (The Green Building Press)

15. BRITISH STANDARDS

BS1566:2002, Copper Indirect Cylinders for Domestic Purposes

BS5449:1990, Specification for Forced Circulation of Hot Water Central Heating Systems for Domestic Purposes

BS5617:1985, Specification for Urea-Formaldehyde (UF) Foam Systems Suitable for Insulation of Cavity Walls with Masonry or Concrete Liner and Outer Leaves

BS5618:1985, Code of Practice for Thermal Insulation of Cavity Walls (with Masonry or Concrete Liner and Outer Leaves) by Filling with Urea-Formaldehyde (UF) Foam Systems

BS5713:1979, Specification for Hermetically Sealed Flat Double Glazing Units

BS6262:1982, Code of Practice for Glazing of Buildings

BS7206:1990, Specification for Unvented Hot Water Storage Units and Packages

BS7386:1997, Specification for Draughtstrips for the Draught Control of Existing Doors and Windows in Housing (Including Test Methods)

BS7412:2002, Specification for Plastic Windows made from Unplasticized Polyvinyl Chloride (PVC-u) Extruded Hollow Profiles

BS7880:1997, Code of Practice for Draught Control of Existing Doors and Windows in Housing using Draughtstrips

BS8206:1992, Part 2. Code of Practice for Daylighting

BS8208:1998, Guide to Assessment of Suitability of External Cavity Walls for Filling with Thermal Insulants. Existing Traditional Cavity Construction

BSEN1264:1998, Parts 1–3 (1998), Part 4 (2001) Floor Heating

BS EN 13141/7/8, Component/Products for Residential Ventilation

16. SELF-BUILD ORGANIZATIONS

Associated Self-Build Architects (ASBA), Champness Hall, Drake Street, Rochdale, Lancashire OL16 1PB,
0800 387310
asba@asba-architects.org
www.asba-architects.org

Association of Self-Builders, ASB Membership Secretary, 13 Laburnum Drive, Porthcawl, South Wales CF36 5UA,
0704 1544126
sapsted@which.net
www.self-builder.org.uk

Buildstore, Kingsthorne Park, Nettlehill Road, Houstoun Industrial Estate, Livingston EH54 5DB,
0870 870 9991
www.buildstore.co.uk

Community Self-Build Agency, 40 Bowling Green Lane, London EC1R 0NE, 020 7415 7092
info@communityselfbuildagency.org.uk
www.communityselfbuildagency.org.uk

Community Self-Build Scotland,
19 Blairtummock Road, Glasgow G33 4AN,
0141 766 1999
www.selfbuild-scotland.org.uk

Corry Homebuilding Ltd, 96 Lisburn Road, Saintfield, Co. Down BT24 7BP,
028 9751 0570
info@selfbuild.ie
www.selfbuild.ie

Developing Skills Ltd, 1 The Granary, Brook Farm, Ellington, Cambridgeshire PE28 0AE,
01480 893833
info@selfbuildcourses.co.uk
www.selfbuildcourses.co.uk

Ecology Building Society (ecological self-build mortgages), 7 Belton Road, Silsden, Keighley, West Yorkshire BD20 0EE, 0845 674 5566
info@ecology.co.uk
www.ecology.co.uk

Irish Association of Self Builders
www.iaosb.com
selfbuildit.co.uk

Walter Segal Self Build Trust, Northern UK, 15 High Street, Belford, Northumberland, NE70 7NG, 01668 213544
info@segalselfbuild.co.uk

Walter Segal Self Build Trust, Midlands & South-West UK, 01905 749665
geoff@segalselfbuild.co.uk

Walter Segal Self Build Trust, South & Eastern UK, 01892 614300
robin@segalselfbuild.co.uk

17. SELF-BUILD PUBLICATIONS AND WEBSITES

Build It, Inside Communications Ltd,
19th Floor, 1 Canada Square, Canary Wharf,
London E14 5AP, 020 7772 8300
www.self-build.co.uk
Building Your Own Home, ovolopublishing
www.ovolopublishing.co.uk
Homebuilding and Renovating
www.homebuilding.co.uk
Selfbuild & Design
www.selfbuildanddesign.com
Self Build Extend and Renovate, Corry
Homebuilding Ltd, 96 Lisburn Road,
Saintfield, Co. Down BT24 7BP,
028 9751 0570
info@selfbuild.ie
www.selfbuild.ie
Self Build Guide, Logicworks Ltd, Unit 3,
The Covert, Gravesend, Kent DA13 0SY
www.self-build-guide.co.uk
The Housebuilder's Bible, ovolopublishing
www.ovolopublishing.co.uk
www.selfbuild123.co.uk
www.selfbuildabc.co.uk
www.selfbuilder.com
www.selfbuildit.co.uk

18. SELF-BUILD SHOWS

National Homebuilding and Renovation Show
(several locations yearly in England and Scotland)
www.homebuildingshow.co.uk
Self-Build, Extend and Renovate Show
(several locations yearly in Northern Ireland
and the Republic of Ireland)

19. COMMUNITY SELF-BUILD CASE STUDIES

info@selfbuild.ie
www.selfbuild.ie
Hockerton Housing Project, The Watershed,
Gables Drive, Hockerton, Southwell,
Nottinghamshire NG25 0QU, 01636 816902
hhp@hockerton.demon.co.uk
www.hockerton.demon.co.uk
Ashley Vale Action Group, 228 Mina Road,
St. Werburghs, Bristol BS2 9YP,
selfbuild@ashleyvale.org.uk
avag@ashleyvale.org.uk
www.ashleyvale.org.uk

20. OTHER INFORMATION SOURCES

Boiler efficiency database:
www.boilers.org.uk
Information on PV:
www.est.org.uk/solar

Index